The Heart Chambers of Europe: Franco-German Impulses for the EU's Security Order

Sandra Weeser
Editor

The Heart Chambers of Europe: Franco-German Impulses for the EU's Security Order

Springer

Editor
Sandra Weeser
Betzdorf, Germany

ISBN 978-3-658-51095-4 ISBN 978-3-658-51096-1 (eBook)
https://doi.org/10.1007/978-3-658-51096-1

Translation from the German language edition: "Die Herzkammern Europas: Deutsch-französische Impulse für die Sicherheitsordnung der EU" by Sandra Weeser, © Der/die Herausgeber bzw. der/die Autor(en), exklusiv lizenziert an Springer Fachmedien Wiesbaden GmbH, ein Teil von Springer Nature 2026. Published by Springer Fachmedien Wiesbaden. All Rights Reserved.

This book is a translation of the original German edition "Die Herzkammern Europas: Deutsch-französische Impulse für die Sicherheitsordnung der EU" by Sandra Weeser, published by Springer Fachmedien Wiesbaden GmbH in 2026. The translation was done with the help of an artificial intelligence machine translation tool. A subsequent human revision was done primarily in terms of content, so that the book will read stylistically differently from a conventional translation. Springer Nature works continuously to further the development of tools for the production of books and on the related technologies to support the authors.

This Springer imprint is published by the registered company Springer Fachmedien Wiesbaden GmbH, part of Springer Nature.
The registered company address is: Abraham-Lincoln-Str. 46, 65189 Wiesbaden, Germany

Foreword by His Excellency François Delattre, Ambassador of the French Republic to Germany.

The warning once issued by former Israeli Prime Minister Golda Meir to her country applies to Europe today: In the world as it is emerging, Europe can be anything it wants to be, but it must not be weak.

At a time when the tectonic plates of power are literally shifting beneath our feet and the new geopolitical, demographic, economic, and technological balances of power are not necessarily working in favor of Europeans, one of the great challenges for our generation is to ensure a European awakening and to build its strategic sovereignty. This is the prerequisite for us Europeans to remain masters of our own destiny and not leave it to others to decide on our behalf—or, worse still, to become a pawn in the hands of foreign powers.

Together with Sandra Weeser, I firmly believe that France and Germany, as founding members and driving forces of the European Union, share a special joint responsibility to lead the way on this challenging path. To be clear: there will be no wake-up call for Europe if no impetus comes from the Franco-German engine. This impetus is by no means exclusive; it includes all partners. The current strong momentum of the Weimar Triangle, which connects our two countries and Poland, is a very positive factor in this regard.

Contrary to what has been claimed in numerous commentaries, much has been done in recent years to deepen Franco-German relations in the field of defense and security for the benefit of Europe and the European pillar of NATO. Progress in joint structuring armaments programs such as the Main Ground Combat System (MGCS) or the Future Combat Air System (FCAS) are good examples of this. Another form of cooperation is the Hercules air transport squadron in Évreux, where France and Germany have fully pooled their resources.

Many had predicted that the Russian war of aggression against Ukraine would lead to the collapse of Europe. But the opposite has occurred: today, taking all areas together, Europe is the largest supporter of Ukraine, and our two countries play a leading role within the European Union in this regard. Moreover, the German-French corporation KNDS has established a subsidiary in Ukraine to produce armaments locally.

France and Germany have also played a significant role in the adoption of the European "Strategic Compass" in March 2022, in which the EU member states summarized the main security policy challenges to be addressed jointly, as well as in the decision on the EU's multiannual financial framework for 2021–2027.

Following the highly successful state visit of President Macron to Germany, the Franco-German Ministerial Council and the Franco-German Defense and Security Council in Meseberg on May 28, 2024, enabled the adoption of a joint roadmap. This roadmap, in addition to operationalizing the Franco-German Brigade—particularly to secure the eastern flank of the Atlantic Alliance—also provides for joint work on deep strike capabilities and air defense, as well as on the development of the technological and industrial base of European defense.

In this Franco-German roadmap, which we now need to implement, the final point is of crucial importance. The case of Ukraine has shown us: without an independent industrial policy, a credible defense policy is unthinkable. It is only because Ukraine retained numerous defense industry companies within the country that it is now able, with Western support, to effectively defend itself against the Russian aggressor. For the European Union, one of the lessons from this war is therefore not to rely entirely on other countries for the production of our weapons systems and the development of innovations that will determine the outcome of tomorrow's battles.

As demonstrated by the Draghi Report published in September 2024, it is now urgently necessary for us to go much further in increasing our investments in the defense sector and in giving concrete form to the principle of "European preference" in the service of our collective industrial competitiveness, standardization, and interoperability. This is a central issue in the forthcoming White Paper on the Future of European Defense. The aim is to strengthen our joint ability to protect Europe against the full spectrum of threats, from high-intensity conflict to hybrid warfare, by continuing our efforts in areas such as strategic enablers—particularly in the space sector, integrated European air defense, strategic and tactical air transport, as well as deep precision strikes, drones and counter-drone technologies, missiles and munitions, and artificial intelligence in defense.

France and Germany must take a leading role in all of this.

In France, the military planning law for the period 2024–2030 provides for major investments with a budget of €400 billion. In Germany, the "Zeitenwende" announced in February 2022 has led to a significant increase in defense spending. It is essential to harmonize these measures taken on both sides of the Rhine and, together, to examine the further financing options mentioned by Mario Draghi in order to strengthen European defense resilience and build a more robust European pillar within NATO. This is in our fundamental interest as Europeans, and it is also what our American partners expect from us:

A stronger Europe and a stronger Atlantic Alliance are two sides of the same coin.

In view of the enormous challenges facing Europe, France and Germany, naturally together with their partners, bear a special joint responsibility to set the course. For the unique relationship that binds our two countries is not only a driving force for Europe, but also, as we must never forget, a matter close to our hearts.

In this context, the trust, interpersonal relationships, and numerous friendships that we have built between our two countries over more than 60 years are our most valuable asset. I have experienced these close ties firsthand, when, as a young diplomat in Germany, I had the privilege of witnessing the reunification of this country, which is so dear to my heart, together with my German friends. Sandra Weeser expresses these close bonds better than anyone else, both in her personal life and through her professional commitment. I would like to take this opportunity to express my heartfelt gratitude to her for her exemplary dedication in the service of Franco-German friendship, which this work once again illustrates in a very beautiful way.

François Delattre and Sandra Weeser

Preface by the Editor

A few years ago, I would hardly have expected that I would one day publish a book on German-French defense and security policy. And yet, considering my personal and professional development, it ultimately seems a logical step.

Long before I acquired French citizenship and formally established my close connection to France with all the associated rights and obligations, there existed a deep bond and affinity with the "nation on the other side of the Rhine." This connection was shaped as early as my childhood: through my mother's years of professional work in Normandy, through joint trips to France, and through regular student exchanges with our partner city Decize in Burgundy.

After completing my studies, my path led me to Toulouse, where I worked for several years at a supplier to the Airbus Group. It was there that I met my French husband, with whom I still live in Germany today. France has always remained a significant point of reference in my professional life as well—whether through export activities in my own company or later as the person responsible for the French market at my American employer.

The founding of the Franco-German Parliamentary Assembly (DFPV) in 2019 was, for me, not only a political initiative of great significance but also a personal motivation: As a committed European and a bridge-builder between the two countries, I immediately applied for membership. Since 2021, I have been a member of the Assembly's executive board. In the past legislative period (2021–2025), I had the special task of co-chairing the working group on foreign and security policy together with my French colleague Sabine Thillaye.

This working group became a central forum for bilateral dialogue on security and defense policy challenges—with the aim of formulating concrete initiatives for closer cooperation between France and Germany. Due to the early elections in both countries, our work could not culminate in a joint final report for the working group and a resolution proposal for the parliaments. However, from this unfinished project emerged the idea for this collection of essays: as documentation, further development, and an important source of impetus for the broad expertise found in academia, business, politics, diplomacy, and the armed forces.

The contributions collected here make a substantial and diverse addition to the security policy debate in Europe—well-founded, varied, and united by the shared goal of strengthening the German-French core as the strategic center of an independent European security architecture.

Berlin, Germany Sandra Weeser

Acknowledgements —Merci beaucoup

My special thanks go to my team leader Christine Baur, who, with her foresight, encouragement, and persuasiveness, first inspired me to initiate this book project. I am equally grateful to Nora Zerelli and Niklas Gemm, my two research associates, who have competently and enthusiastically supported my work in the Franco-German Parliamentary Assembly throughout the entire period. In this volume, they also provide an important insight into the work of our Foreign and Security Policy working group.

A heartfelt thank you also goes to the French co-chair of the Working Group on Foreign and Security Policy, Sabine Thillaye, as well as to all the participating members of parliament from France and Germany, with whom the exchange was always open, trusting, and constructive. Our thanks also go to the experts who enriched the work of the working group through their hearings and contributions, as well as to the staff of the parliamentary groups and administrations, whose support was indispensable for the implementation of our meetings and recommendations.

For the professional and reliable support during the creation of this book, I would like to thank Dr. Hanser from Springer Gabler Verlag, who managed the project with great calm and prudence.

Last but not least, I would like to thank all the authors who have made a valuable contribution to this volume with their essays and perspectives. Their texts demonstrate how important, challenging, and at the same time shapeable a deepened security policy cooperation in Europe is—and how central the Franco-German heart chambers are in this process.

Sandra Weeser

Contents

Part I

Introductory Remarks & Genesis of the Franco-German Parliamentary Assembly (DFPV)

Introduction: The Relevance of the Franco-German Engine for European Security and Defense Policy

Sandra Weeser

> ***"We must be clear-eyed about the fact that our Europe, today, is mortal. It can die. It can die, and that depends solely on our choices. But these choices must be made now."*** (***Macron,*** 2024)

This excerpt from President Macron's Sorbonne Speech 2.0 on April 25, 2024, is emblematic of the complex debates about the future of Europe and the stalled progress of the common European security and defense policy, which have gained significant momentum since Russia's renewed aggression against Ukraine on February 24, 2022. With similar emphasis, former Chancellor Scholz already outlined the realignment of German security and defense policy in his Zeitenwende speech shortly after the start of the Russian invasion. If one tries to summarize the opaque conglomerate of ideas and proposals from politics, academia, and society regarding the future of European security and defense policy in a few striking words, it would probably be: "Europeans, finally wake up and act before it is too late!" But where does this urgency come from? Russia has launched a brutal war of conquest against a sovereign state in Europe. We in Europe thus face historic challenges, underpinned by many further geopolitical shifts and raising questions about Europe's future role in the global security architecture. The risk of hostilities and the involvement of European interests through direct or indirect effects on energy security, migration, and counterterrorism has increased significantly. All these upheavals are less the cause and more the symptom of a continuous development in

S. Weeser (✉)
Betzdorf, Deutschland
e-mail: buchprojekt@weeser.com

S. Weeser (ed.), *The Heart Chambers of Europe: Franco-German Impulses for the EU's Security Order*, https://doi.org/10.1007/978-3-658-51096-1_1

which authoritarian actors in an increasingly multipolar world are gradually challenging rules-based multilateralism and the territorial integrity of states. What does this mean for us Europeans? The hotspots and conflicts around us are increasing and becoming more internationalized, military narratives are moving to the center of European politics, and our closest ally across the Atlantic could reduce its security guarantees, which would shake the peace order we have taken for granted. This is all the more true since the clear political shift in the United States under President Trump after his re-election in November 2024. The renewed rhetoric of "America First" and statements about conditioning or even suspending NATO's mutual defense commitment in the event of insufficient European defense spending have once again made it clear: Europe can no longer take the USA for granted. The conclusion for us is: We Europeans must— to use the words of former Chancellor Angela Merkel— "take our destiny more into our own hands [...] if we want to survive as a community" (Merkel 2018). For this, we must above all think and act more strategically autonomously. This narrative by no means implies a departure from the transatlantic security community. Rather, it describes the sustainable consolidation of a European pillar within the transatlantic alliance, so that Europe can act effectively with its partners from a political-strategic, defense-industrial, and operational perspective, but is also capable of acting independently if necessary (Council of the European Union 2016, p. 2). How can Europe be enabled to act in terms of security and defense policy? Fundamentally, it requires an adequate level of financial, material, and human resources so that EU states can ensure better equipment, training, and organization and grow into a strong defense community. To achieve this, resources within the European framework must be efficiently coordinated and pooled to avoid duplication and national parochialism. Initiatives within the EU, such as the European Defence Fund (EDF) or initial instruments for joint procurement, contribute to greater interoperability and are steps in the right direction, but repeatedly reach their limits due to member states' sovereignty reservations and remain modest in scope. All the more, a common understanding of long-term strategic goals, mutual trust, and, as a basis, the political will and conviction to act better with partners rather than alone are needed (Grevi 2019, p. 10). How can the EU member states be moved to act together as Europeans?

It requires appropriate pioneers and spokespersons among the member states who have proven in bi- or multilateral frameworks that joint action is always more worthwhile than purely national action. Here, the Franco-German tandem plays a special role. The former "hereditary enemies" underwent an unprecedented reconciliation after the Second World War, which was both the foundation and catalyst for the European integration process and culminated in the Franco-German Friendship Treaty, better known as the Élysée Treaty, in 1963. Bilateral cooperation in the field of security and defense is rooted in this period and has since developed dynamically with cooperation formats such as the Franco-German Brigade established in 1989 or major defense industrial projects such as the Main Ground Combat System (MGCS). Germany and France thus repeatedly give voice to the call for stronger European cooperation in the field of security and defense and, through their cooperation— which other EU member states have already partially joined— also promote further European defense integration. The close coordination between Berlin and Paris was and remains a necessary— though nowadays no longer sufficient— condition for European compromises.

1 There is no alternative to the Franco-German partnership

The cooperation of two countries that, despite many shared positions, have different strategic cultures, threat assessments, and political conventions, is a challenging process in which misunderstandings must repeatedly be cleared up and common ground explored. This was demonstrated, for example, by the public disagreement between former German Defense Minister Annegret Kramp-Karrenbauer and President Emmanuel Macron on the question of Europe's strategic autonomy. While Kramp-Karrenbauer complained in 2020 that illusions about strategic autonomy must come to an end and that Europe could never replace the USA as the decisive security guarantor, Macron interpreted this as a "misinterpretation of history" (Macron 2020) and, despite the close partnership with the USA, emphasized the goal of autonomous EU capability to act. Even if this controversy is not emblematic of Franco-German coordination processes, it does show that even the closest partners do not always agree on fundamental security and defense policy issues.

It is entirely normal for two countries with different backgrounds to occasionally have disagreements. However, it quickly becomes a problem when the controversies between the two largest economies in the EU are structural in nature and make compromises at the European level more difficult. Without the close cooperation of Germany and France as historical drivers of European integration, these cannot be realized. Thus, despite the ongoing war in Ukraine, the two countries have yet to find a fundamentally common line, which is repeatedly evident through daring statements by the French president or, from the French perspective, the "too transatlantic" Zeitenwende of the Federal Republic (Major and Arnold 2024, pp. 6 f.). Accordingly, there is currently a certain discrepancy between the high expectations of the Franco-German tandem and its diverse political, operational, and industrial cooperation structures and its actual driving force in the current situation.

Recently, there has been increasing speculation about a shift in the balance of power within the EU to create possible alternatives to the Franco-German engine and its European policy plans (Ross and Téterchen 2024, p. 1; Bonse 2023, p. 2). Central and Eastern European countries such as Poland or the Baltic states play a decisive role in this, as they have pursued a more stringent line from the outset in supporting Ukraine and rightly criticize German and French Russia policy in recent years. It is very welcome that the countries of the 2004 EU enlargement are in some cases massively increasing their defense spending and have been given significantly more consideration in the recent appointments to EU institutions. This will not only increase the visibility and acceptance of the European Union in these countries in the medium term, but also enrich Brussels politics with additional perspectives. However, it is a fallacy to believe that the EU, under Polish or Baltic leadership alone, would be able to stand on its own in security and defense policy if necessary. For many of these EU states, their policies are still too focused on US security guarantees, and they still give too little space to a "European solution" to European security problems within the transatlantic alliance. This perspective is particularly one-dimensional in light of Trump's re-election and the feared partial disengagement of the USA from Europe.

This is now evident in the limited security policy support provided by the USA to Europe, for example in response to the recent Israeli-Iranian exchange of strikes. Washington's hesitant involvement of European partners in strategic decisions has led within the EU to a new reflection on dependencies, channels of influence, and the necessity of autonomous European strategies in crisis management.

For several years now, Emmanuel Macron has repeatedly called for a stronger, genuinely European security and defense policy in numerous passionate appeals, and has promoted concepts such as strategic autonomy or European sovereignty, which now shape the relevant debates in Brussels. The initiatives he launched, such as the European Political Community (EPC) or the European Intervention Initiative (EI2), are examples of this direction. We must always keep in mind that the window of opportunity to put such forward-looking initiatives into practice is limited. The Bundestag election in Germany in 2025 and the presidential elections in 2027 are no guarantee of a consolidation of this course, and it is already clear that Emmanuel Macron will no longer be in office after the next presidential election, which in some eyes makes him a "lame duck" in foreign policy. The status quo of two decidedly pro-European governments could thus change abruptly. All the more, Germany must, despite some dissonances and coordination difficulties, seize the president's outstretched hand as quickly as possible. Together with France, we must act in the spirit of the Treaty of Aachen, which is intended to prepare the Franco-German tandem for the changed challenges in Europe and the world and to strengthen cooperation in European policy (Koepf and Koopmann 2024, pp. 8 f.). We must not lose any more time and must finally bring concrete ideas to life, such as the establishment of a European Military Academy, the expansion of joint European defense research programs and procurement mechanisms, the massive strengthening of the European defense industry, or, in the long term, the creation of a defense union under European leadership.

Franco-German initiatives must always be part of a broader, integrative approach that also takes seriously the needs and perspectives of other member states. Especially in an EU with 27 member states, each with its own "historical memory," culture, and way of life, this is not easy, but it is necessary. Particularly in view of Russia's revisionist-aggressive policy, the security instability in North Africa and the Middle East, the "pivot to Asia" (Clinton 2011), and the future reduction of US security guarantees for Europe as well as China's hegemonic-authoritarian foreign policy, we as Europe must learn to stand on our own feet. The traditional US-dominated, rules-based world order is increasingly being questioned or even undermined by non-Western actors. In this emerging new multipolar world order, we Europeans must position ourselves and must not make the mistake of hiding behind the USA in a kind of bandwagoning policy (Sanahuja 2020, p. 403). Europe must find its place in this multipolar world order and— in close partnership with the USA— also become capable of acting on its own. Germany and France, through their historically grown partnership, their central position in the EU, and the numerous positive examples of joint cooperation, are predestined to give this urgently needed path new momentum and, in close cooperation with Poland, Italy, Sweden, and the other member states, to prepare Europe for the future.

2 New momentum for Franco-German cooperation formats

The Franco-German partnership is based on a close network of historically evolved cooperation structures that always radiate onto the European level. The mutual signing of the Treaty of Aachen in 2019 or the joint commitment to the EU Strategic Compass in 2022, for example, have given voice to the call for stronger European cooperation in the field of security and defense. New operational formats such as the Franco-German air transport squadron created in 2022 or joint major defense industrial projects such as the Future Combat Air System (FCAS) or the Main Ground Combat System (MGCS) are also promoting further European defense integration and strengthening joint defense capabilities. Another flagship format is the Franco-German Parliamentary Assembly (DFPV), created in 2019, a globally unique binational parliament that serves as an arena for Franco-German and European debate. Here, 100 members of parliament from both countries come together to provide joint impetus for forward-looking European policy, for example by accompanying the implementation of the Élysée and Aachen Treaties or setting important milestones for the promotion of each other's partner language (Heimbach 2024, pp. 2 f.). Finally, older formats such as the Franco-German Brigade established in 1989 or the Franco-German Defense and Security Council introduced in 1998 are also regaining relevance due to the shock to the European security architecture on February 24, 2022.

At the same time, it is obvious that the current governments in Paris and Berlin are facing enormous domestic and foreign policy challenges, which have repeatedly led to coordination difficulties, unilateral reflexes, or problems understanding the perceptions and positions of the other side. The cooperation formats have proven to be efficient and cushion any negative effects for the most part. However, the question remains whether the historically evolved structures also have enough innovative power to meet the current demands for increased European defense integration, or whether they need to be subjected to a reality check and revitalized.

Here, we must think progressively and consider how Franco-German formats can have an even stronger, more integrative impact on the European level in the context of new geopolitical upheavals. In particular, the change of government in Poland offers a window of opportunity with three liberal, decidedly pro-European governments in Paris,

Berlin, and Warsaw. This could renew the Franco-German-Polish Weimar Triangle within the EU and expand it into a viable strategic decision-making space that covers a broad discourse and cultural area within the EU (Skóra 2024, p. 82). The traditional Franco-German relations are indispensable, but must definitely be supplemented in order to do justice to the diverse mentalities and cultures in Europe and to reconcile different perspectives. Specifically, trilateral talks in the Weimar Triangle format could be institutionalized and held at regular intervals. This applies to the foreign and European ministers, but also to the heads of government as well as the presidencies and relevant specialist committees of the parliaments. The various permanent structures that enable regular meetings between German and French representatives could serve as a model. It would be helpful to appoint a commissioner for strengthening the Weimar Triangle, who would coordinate and coherently shape cooperation between Paris, Berlin, and Warsaw. Furthermore, it should also be clarified how the DFPV can connect with members of the Polish Sejm and, in the long term, how the DFPV can gradually become a Franco-German-Polish Assembly. The aim here could be to enable networking and exchange at the parliamentary level in the Weimar Triangle format, in order to clear up misunderstandings and explore common ground through direct exchange.

In addition, we must also initiate new considerations on how the EU, with its driving forces Germany, France, and Poland, can enter into even more productive military cooperation within the transatlantic alliance. For example, the originally Franco-German FCAS project is now having a pan-European impact through the accession of Spain and Belgium, and the Franco-German Brigade could also be broadened at the command corps level through the participation of Poland. Furthermore, in view of Donald Trump's election victory and his questioning of the NATO mutual defense clause, we must also discuss a European perspective on nuclear deterrence, which has been repeatedly raised by French presidents. In this regard, an open dialogue should be held in close coordination with NATO partners about the expanded role of the French nuclear arsenal for Europe as well as cooperation opportunities with the United Kingdom, which is indispensable for a future Europe capable of acting autonomously.

The tense situation in the Middle East has once again highlighted the importance of credible strategic deterrence. Not only vis-à-vis Russia, but also in relation to potential threats from regional actors or asymmetric warfare, as could arise from the Israeli-Iranian conflict.

Close cooperation between Germany and France is necessary for progress in security and defense policy at the European level, but is no longer sufficient today. All the more, the two states must institutionally align their various cooperation formats for the future, open them up to other EU and non-EU partners, and always keep the big picture in mind: the completion of the European integration process in the field of security and defense policy and the associated strengthening of the European pillar within NATO.

Especially in a world where alliance loyalty is no longer automatically derived from history, but from concrete strategic interests, European states must learn to stand together for their security.

References

Bonse, E. (2023). Überforderter Motor: Die deutsch-französische Europapolitik aus Brüsseler Sicht (Publikationsreihe Endlich zusammen für Europa? Frankreich und Deutschland nach den Wahlen N° 4). Stiftung Genshagen.

Clinton, H. (2011). America's Pacific Century. Foreign Policy. https://foreignpolicy.com/2011/10/11/americas-pacific-century/. Zugegriffen: 27.06.2025.

Grevi, G. (2019). Strategic autonomy for European choices: The key to Europe's shaping power (EPC Discussion Paper), European Policy Centre.

Heimbach, H. (2024). A Watchdog on the Leash 5 Years of Franco-German Parliamentary Assembly (Policy Brief, 04. September 2024). Hertie School - Jacques Delors Centre.

Koepf, T., & Koopmann, M. (2024). 5 Jahre Aachener Vertrag: Eine Zwischenbilanz. Schlussbericht der Arbeitsgruppe „5 Jahre Aachener Vertrag – Welche Fortschritte in den deutsch-französischen Beziehungen?“ (Genshagener Papiere N° 30). Stiftung Genshagen.

Macron, E. (2020). Die Macron-Doktrin. Ein Gespräch mit dem französischen Staatspräsidenten. Le Grand Continent. https://legrandcontinent.eu/de/2020/11/16/macron/. Zugegriffen: 27.06.2025.

Macron, E. (2024, 25. April). Discours du Président de la Republique sur l'Europe à la Sorbonne. https://www.elysee.fr/emmanuel-macron/2024/04/24/discours-sur-leurope. Zugegriffen: 27.06.2025.

Major, C., & Arnold, S. (2024). Frankreichs disruptive Zeitenwende (SWP-Aktuell 2024/A 23) Stiftung Wissenschaft und Politik.

Merkel, A. (2018, 13. November). Rede von Bundeskanzlerin Merkel vor dem Europäischen Parlament am 13. November 2018 in Straßburg. https://www.bundesregierung.de/breg-de/aktuelles/rede-von-bundeskanzlerin-merkel-vor-dem-europaeischen-parlament-am-13-november-2018-in-strassburg-1549538. Zugegriffen: 27.06.2025.

Rat der Europäischen Union (2016). Council conclusions on implementing the EU Global Strategy in the area of Security and Defence. Dokumentennummer 14149/16, 14.11.2016.

Ross, J., & Téterchen, N. (2024). Für einen europäischen Plan B bleibt die deutsch-französische Kooperation alternativlos (DGAP Memo 22.). Deutsche Gesellschaft für Auswärtige Politik.

Sanahuja, J.A. (2020). The EU Global Strategy. Security narratives, legitimacy, and identity of an actor in crisis. In E. Conde, Z. V. Yaneva & M. Scopelliti (Hrsg.), The Routledge Handbook of European Security Law and Policy (395–414). Routledge.

Skóra, M. (2024). Polen ist zurück – Chancen für ein polnisch-deutsches Engagement in Europa nach den Parlamentswahlen 2023. integration, 47 (1), 76–84.

A Franco-German Parliament? Insights into the Binational Parliamentary Cooperation of the Franco-German Parliamentary Assembly

Christine Baur, Niklas Gemm and Nora Zerelli

1 The Franco-German Parliamentary Assembly—A Novelty

Bilateral or multilateral cooperation between countries has so far—with the exception of a few emblematic examples such as the Baltic Assembly—taken place primarily at the executive level, as is also demonstrated by the usual cooperation formats between Germany and France. Whether it is the Élysée Treaty and the Treaty of Aachen, the famous handshake between François Mitterrand and Helmut Kohl, or the regular meetings of the Councils of Ministers—the central figures in the public eye have always been the heads of state and government as well as the respective cabinet members.

In 2019, the predominantly executive-driven Franco-German relations were expanded by a unique parliamentary component: the Franco-German Parliamentary Assembly (FGPA) was established. Its genesis was mainly due to the sluggish cooperation at the executive level. When Emmanuel Macron became President in May 2017 and delivered his famous Sorbonne speech with ambitious demands for European integration, these initially went unanswered by Germany in the context of a difficult government formation (Demesmay and Seidendorf 2021, pp. 99 f.). In response, Bundestag members Franziska Brantner (Alliance 90/The Greens), Andreas Jung (CDU), and Michael Link (FDP) published a guest article in the Frankfurter Allgemeine Zeitung, proposing a joint initiative at the parliamentary level to address Macron's demands (Brantner et al. 2017). On

C. Baur (✉)
Esslingen, Deutschland

N. Gemm
München, Deutschland

N. Zerelli
Berlin, Deutschland

S. Weeser (ed.), *The Heart Chambers of Europe: Franco-German Impulses for the EU's Security Order*, https://doi.org/10.1007/978-3-658-51096-1_2

this basis, the circle of interested parliamentarians in the Bundestag and the Assemblée Nationale expanded, and the idea of institutionalizing parliamentary cooperation quickly emerged. In the resolution jointly developed by both parliaments in January 2018, which later led to the Treaty of Aachen, a Franco-German parliamentary agreement was also called for (Demesmay and Seidendorf 2021, p. 101). The working group responsible for drafting the parliamentary agreement consisted of 18 members of parliament from both countries. The agreement was signed in March 2019 by the two parliamentary presidents, thereby officially establishing the broadly defined Franco-German Parliamentary Assembly described in Chap. "Introduction: The Relevance of the Franco-German Engine for European Security and Defense Policy".

The FGPA functions to some extent as a binational parliamentary chamber, but with an advisory and coordinating rather than legislative role. The main goal of the assembly is to monitor the implementation of Franco-German treaties, accompany the Franco-German Councils of Ministers, and initiate its own proposals for Franco-German cooperation in Europe (Heimbach 2022, p. 152).

Its 50 members from each country's parliament, selected on a parity basis, meet at least twice a year in the respective neighboring country for a plenary session. In addition to hearings with ministers or other high-ranking politicians, there are also deliberations and votes on proposals and amendments, as well as general debates on current topics (German Bundestag). Furthermore, working groups are established on various policy areas, whose results are presented to the assembly in various forms (including final reports, drafts for joint resolutions) and can lead to proposals for resolutions for both parliaments. In addition to a working group on "Energy Sovereignty" and a working group on "The Future of Europe," there was until recently also a working group on "Foreign and Security Policy."

This type of parliamentary cooperation is unique in the world, but so far often remains in the shadow of the media-staged appearances of leading government members during the FGPA plenary sessions. This dominance of the executive has made public perception of parliamentary work more difficult and significantly limited its visibility—a grievance repeatedly criticized by Sandra Weeser. In contrast stands the very substantive work and debate in the parliamentary sphere, as opposed to, for example, the staged fish sandwich lunch in Hamburg with former Chancellor Olaf Scholz, President Emmanuel Macron, and other government representatives.

It must also be noted here that members of parliament in both countries enjoy different degrees of sovereignty or dependence on their respective governments and are thus politically able to act to varying extents. This automatically leads to a divergent perception of the relevance of the bodies and their work.

Binational Foreign and Security Policy Cooperation at the Parliamentary Level

The working group "Foreign and Security Policy" directly followed a previous working group "Foreign and Defense Policy," which, after six months of work, was only able to agree to present its results orally at the FGPA meeting on June 28, 2021 (Heimbach 2022,

p. 160). The positions were so entrenched that neither the German nor the French side could present a draft resolution or a written report that would at least have deciphered the differing positions. This clearly shows how different the strategic cultures and foreign policy traditions of the two countries are—and above all, it highlights how difficult it is to identify points of overlap in foreign, security, and defense policy despite all commonalities and cooperation mechanisms.

After the foreign and security policy situation in Europe fundamentally changed following Russia's renewed aggression against Ukraine on February 24, 2022, and some members of parliament from both countries advocated for a new attempt at a foreign policy working group despite internal and external resistance, the group was re-established by resolution on May 22, 2023. Unlike its predecessor, whose resolution encompassed very broad demands and goals at the "meta-level," the new working group "Foreign and Security Policy" was closely aligned with the EU's Strategic Compass and set out very concrete goals such as strengthening cyber defense or joint discussions on the future of the Franco-German Brigade (Franco-German Parliamentary Assembly 2023).

The chairs of the working group were the two Franco-German liberal members of parliament Sandra Weeser (FDP) and Sabine Thillaye (Démocrate), who have both advocated for even closer cooperation between the two countries since taking office. Both politicians share a profound knowledge of the foreign and security policy debate in both countries and, due to their own dual citizenship, a deep understanding of the culture of debate in both France and Germany. At the time, both parliamentarians belonged to governing factions and already had long-standing personal and political relationships since the founding of the FGPA in 2019.

The two members of parliament set themselves the ambitious goal of achieving concrete, practically applicable results in order to present a joint resolution to the plenary and subsequently to both parliaments. They set themselves the following three core objectives:

- "Formulation of concrete recommendations with the aim of passing legislation and monitoring and evaluating Franco-German measures in the field of foreign and security policy, particularly according to areas of focus;
- Creating a better understanding of the German and French visions in the field of security and defense policy;
- Supporting the implementation of the European Union's Strategic Compass and strengthening the European pillar of NATO" (Excerpt from the roadmap of the Working Group on Foreign and Security Policy, Franco-German Parliamentary Assembly).

To achieve these goals and avoid repeating the mistakes of the previous working group, the members of parliament, together with their offices, coordinated joint areas of focus and a detailed "roadmap" in an intensive process lasting two months. The latter was intended to serve as the basis and "red thread" to structure the entire working process of the group and gradually contribute to the formulation of concrete policy recommendations. Each meeting was chronologically assigned to one of the four defined areas of focus, which were as follows:

- "1st focus: Joint assessment of our strategic and geopolitical environment;
- 2nd focus: Assessment of the coherence of ongoing measures—creation of an inventory;
- 3rd focus: Identifying new ways to improve our collective capabilities;
- 4th focus: Setting clear goals and milestones to measure progress" (Excerpt from the roadmap of the Working Group on Foreign and Security Policy, Franco-German Parliamentary Assembly).

In addition, all meetings also referred to one of the "baskets" of the EU's Strategic Compass (Secure, Act, Invest, Cooperate with Partners), which served as the group's reference document. Based on these assignments, the two chairs proposed twelve meetings with concrete topics, to be held from July 2023 to summer 2024, so that the results could be presented at the second FGPA meeting at the end of 2024. Each meeting consisted of a detailed expert hearing followed by a Q & A session.

A particularity regarding the financing of armaments expenditures should be noted here: while in France defense expenditures are set within the framework of a multi-year military program (LPM) adopted by parliament, in Germany the defense budget is decided annually by parliamentarians as part of the federal budget, with the possibility of establishing a special fund for the Bundeswehr.

The working group was fundamentally oriented along three dimensions: political, industrial, and operational. Experts from the respective fields were consulted, including EU officials, industry representatives, military officers, academics, and diplomats, and political-strategic questions were discussed with them. For example, the group members exchanged views with high-ranking military representatives from both countries and from Brussels on identifying obstacles to bi- and multilateral operational cooperation and concrete proposals to strengthen Franco-German operational cooperation. Particular attention was also paid to newly emerging threats such as cyberattacks, hybrid dangers, or information warfare. Before an interim assessment could be made with the group members in one of the final meetings and, finally, the defense ministers of both countries were to be heard, the entire work came to a standstill. Due to the early parliamentary elections in Paris in summer 2024 and the collapse of the traffic light coalition in November 2024, followed by new elections in Berlin in February 2025, the work of the group and the entire FGPA was put on hold. It was not until the course of 2025 that work truly resumed. Due to the new composition of the FGPA, it remains unclear for the "Foreign and Security Policy" working group whether previous work can be continued or whether a new start will be necessary. However, since Sandra Weeser and Sabine Thillaye have thoroughly compiled the results from the individual meetings and derived concrete policy recommendations, a continuation would be highly sensible and desirable.

2 Next steps for the Working Group "Foreign and Security Policy"—An Outlook

When the two chairs of the working group began their work, their goal was to formulate policy recommendations coordinated with the group members and capable of achieving consensus in the FGPA plenary, which should be as concrete as possible. Even though the group's work has not yet been continued or brought to a conclusion, positive conclusions can be drawn from its activities. The intensive preparatory work by both parliamentary offices in structuring the group meetings and creating a detailed roadmap paid off. The clearly defined topics and the clear references to the areas of focus and the Strategic Compass contributed to clarity and made it easier to draw clear proposals and recommendations from the results of each individual meeting.

The interim results show that the two group chairs, with their approach, have come closer to the goal of compiling concrete results that could provide real added value for Franco-German cooperation:

- One example is the relevance of "war-gaming scenarios," mentioned in several meetings, which could, for instance, be conducted between the "Centre interarmées de concepts, de doctrines et d'expérimentations" (CICDE) and the "German Institute for Defence and Strategic Studies" (GIDS) in cooperation with the Bundeswehr Command and Staff College. Together with regularly held conferences that create a discussion space for Franco-German experts to reach joint definitions of currently debated concepts and needs, these formats contribute to a more coherent foreign and security policy.
- Another focus of possible policy recommendations for the joint resolution is the revitalization of the Franco-German Brigade. One initiative could be the introduction of a bilateral, single-language "laboratory battalion." This would have a purely tactical laboratory function (including artillery, cavalry, infantry) and could cooperate with the Franco-German Research Institute in Saint-Louis, which would handle the preliminary research work. In this way, in addition to joint equipment, it would also be possible to experiment with equipment from Germany and France, allowing each side to train on the other's artillery.
- Furthermore, the chairs have agreed on initial policy recommendations to strengthen cooperation in the industrial sector. Industry stakeholders should be invited to adopt key principles such as "Best Athlete," clear rules regarding intellectual property, or structuring governance through a 50/50 split in major joint projects like the "Future Combat Air System" (FCAS) or the "Main Ground Combat System" (MGCS). Political actors should be invited to develop a "system of systems" for unified platforms, thereby creating conditions for a land defense Airbus, for example. In addition, they should focus on reducing bureaucracy and accelerating financing and certification issues.

- Finally, the group members also discussed strengthening the Weimar Triangle, which has become increasingly relevant in light of recent geopolitical shifts. Sandra Weeser and Sabine Thillaye have also noted this in their preliminary results and proposed inviting their respective governments to seek and strengthen dialogue with their Polish counterparts on issues such as Russia policy and support for Ukraine. In addition, they wish to initiate a reflection process on how to intensify exchanges between the FGPA and members of the Polish Sejm. The aim is to enable networking and exchange at the parliamentary level in the Weimar Triangle format, to which other formats at the parliamentary level, such as parliamentary and friendship groups, can also make an important contribution.

The relaunch of a working group on foreign and security policy has clearly shown that intensive preparatory work, concrete thematic complexes and goal definitions, as well as structured exchanges between group members and experts, can lead to the formulation of common points and practical policy recommendations despite different foreign policy histories and security cultures. Therefore, it would be highly desirable if, in the future, parliamentary work could build on the concrete interim results of Sandra Weeser and Sabine Thillaye and present them to the parliaments in Paris and Berlin via the FGPA plenary. Furthermore, these very foreign and security policy topics should be further strengthened within the framework of the FGPA, as this unique Franco-German format can generate innovative ideas and proposals that would hardly be heard in everyday government business. This dynamic in particular deserves to be secured and further developed in the long term. In view of growing geopolitical challenges, it could even make sense in the future to more closely integrate German and French intelligence services in a structured format in order to pool joint risk analyses, early warning capabilities, and technological innovations. The FGPA could play an important role here by providing parliamentary impetus for such deepened intelligence cooperation and thus contributing to better democratic embedding.

The parliamentary exchange between Germany and France is of strategic importance for Europe: it creates an exemplary political resonance space in which, despite different security policy traditions, common courses of action can emerge. In this way, not only is European resilience strengthened, but the opportunity is also created to anchor security policy priorities democratically and credibly in the long term.

References

Brantner, F., Jung, A., & Link, M. (2017, 11. November). Macrons Vorschläge aufgreifen. Frankfurter Allgemeine Zeitung.

Demesmay, C., & Seidendorf, S. (2021). Die Deutsch-Französische Parlamentarische Versammlung—ein Schritt zur Europäisierung der Parlamente? Integration, 44(2), 97–114.

Deutscher Bundestag. (o. J.). Deutsch-Französische Parlamentarische Versammlung. https://www.bundestag.de/dfpv. Zugegriffen: 24.05.2025.

Deutsch-Französische Parlamentarische Versammlung. (2023, 22. Mai). Beschluss: Einsetzung einer Arbeitsgruppe „Außen- und Sicherheitspolitik“ im Rahmen der Deutsch-Französischen Parlamentarischen Versammlung (Dokument Nr. 2023/3). Deutscher Bundestag.

Heimbach, H. (2022). Die Deutsch-Französische Parlamentarische Versammlung: Ein Schlüsselakteur für die Annäherung der politischen Positionen zwischen Frankreich und Deutschland. In Deutsch-Französisches Institut (Hrsg.), Frankreich Jahrbuch 2022 (S. 151–164). Nomos.

Christine Baur As team leader and research associate to Member of Parliament Sandra Weeser, she has closely supported committee work in the German Bundestag, particularly with regard to the DFPV, and has prepared and followed up on meetings of the Working Group on Foreign and Security Policy, including the relevant expert hearings, as well as overseeing plenary sessions and publications. She is currently a policy advisor for economic affairs with a focus on foreign trade issues at the Baden-Württemberg Entrepreneurs' Association (UBW) in Stuttgart.

Niklas Gemm As research associate to Member of Parliament Sandra Weeser, he closely supported committee work in the German Bundestag, particularly with regard to the DFPV, and prepared and followed up on meetings of the Working Group on Foreign and Security Policy, including the relevant expert hearings, as well as overseeing plenary sessions and publications. After his time in the German Bundestag, he worked in project management for the Munich Security Conference 2025. Mr. Gemm is currently employed as a consultant at the Munich-based management consultancy RGE & Partner.

Nora Zerelli As research associate to Member of Parliament Sandra Weeser, she closely supported committee work in the German Bundestag, particularly with regard to the DFPV, and prepared and followed up on meetings of the Working Group on Foreign and Security Policy, including the relevant expert hearings, as well as overseeing plenary sessions and publications. After her work at the Cambridge Security Initiative and participation in the NATO Field School 2025, she is currently employed as a consultant at London Politica.

Part II

The Relevance of the Franco-German Engine for European Security and Defense Policy

Towards European Defense Capabilities: Europe between Sovereignty and Dependence

Marie-Agnes Strack-Zimmermann and Sandra Weeser

> *"When Germany and France move forward together, a dynamic is created that will motivate other nations to join. A gradual integration of the armed forces is not only desirable, but necessary."*

Sandra Weeser:

"In this conversation, we do not only want to analyze the current situation, but above all consider long-term perspectives for German-French cooperation and thus European defense capability. German-French cooperation is particularly close to my heart due to my co-coordination of the "Foreign and Security Policy" working group in the Franco-German Parliamentary Assembly.

A first very important aspect is the integration of European armed forces. Do you believe that a truly integrated European army is realistic within the next two decades?"

Dr. Marie-Agnes Strack-Zimmermann:

"I consider the establishment of a European army to be absolutely desirable. Germany and France have already created an example of successful military integration with the Franco-German Brigade—a model that can also serve as an example for close cooperation with other member states. We have also achieved this very consistent and successful cooperation particularly well with the Netherlands. Germany and France have a key role to play here, as the European Union is historically based on this partnership. The cooperation between Charles de Gaulle and Konrad Adenauer was the initial spark for

M.-A. Strack-Zimmermann (✉)
Europaparlament, Brüssel, Belgien

S. Weeser
Betzdorf, Deutschland
e-mail: buchprojekt@weeser.com

S. Weeser (ed.), *The Heart Chambers of Europe: Franco-German Impulses for the EU's Security Order*, https://doi.org/10.1007/978-3-658-51096-1_3

the European Union. Without the courage and vision of both nations, a common European currency would never have become reality. Our nations agreed that when Germany and France, as different as they are, move forward together, a dynamic is created that can motivate other states to join. A gradual integration of the armed forces into a European structure is, in my view, not only desirable but also necessary. It would strengthen Europe's ability to act in all security policy challenges and improve our defense capability in the long term. An integrative European army would therefore be absolutely worthy of support."

Sandra Weeser:

"I share the view that a 'coalition of the willing' should pave the way as the beginning of an integrated army, rather than relying on all EU member states from the outset, otherwise the idea would fail due to the heterogeneity of political actors within the EU."

Dr. Marie-Agnes Strack-Zimmermann:

"I think it is wise if we establish a so-called 'coalition of the willing.' After all, defense still remains the responsibility of individual states. The nations that are willing to join such a coalition can set a good example and build the structures in such a way that other EU states can gradually join. It will be crucial that Germany and France in particular take the lead and drive the process forward consistently. None of this is trivial. But I am optimistic that it can succeed. However, it requires determined and consistent action, the courage to abandon old ways of thinking, and, of course, a long-term political strategy."

Sandra Weeser:

"What institutional hurdles must be overcome to enable deeper military integration within the EU? What are the administrative or cultural obstacles to a joint European army?"

Dr. Marie-Agnes Strack-Zimmermann:

"When we talk about deeper military integration within the EU, we face very practical administrative and cultural challenges. One example is the Franco-German Brigade: Here it becomes clear how different national regulations are, even in closely cooperating armed forces. An example of such a problem is the EU Working Time Directive. In Germany, this European directive is implemented consistently, even though exceptions are permitted, whereas in France it is handled differently in the military. Such bureaucratic requirements may make sense in the civilian sector, but for the operational readiness and efficiency of an army, they actually impede operational readiness, because as a result, the day-to-day operations of both armies are handled differently. This significantly weakens their military efficiency.

Apart from this challenge, there is another major difference between France and Germany. The French presidency provides for far-reaching executive powers in military matters, whereas in Germany, the deployment of the Bundeswehr is subject to parliamentary approval. So if we are aiming for an integrated European army, we must not only focus on strategic issues, but also on very practical aspects of cooperation. Uniform regulations in these areas are a prerequisite for improving the interoperability of both armed forces."

Sandra Weeser:

"The possibility of transferring certain security policy decision-making processes to a European level would certainly be an important step—but that is not currently provided for in the treaties, is it?"

Dr. Marie-Agnes Strack-Zimmermann:

"The current EU treaties do not provide for this at all. Each nation is responsible for its own defense and declares its military capabilities within an alliance, such as NATO. We are only just beginning to cooperate much more closely on defense issues, especially in response to the acute Russian threat. A contractual adjustment within the framework of the EU treaties would be extremely difficult, as all member states would have to agree. There are still major reservations about Brussels in some states, especially when it comes to security policy competences. Many fear that Brussels would then decide on the deployment of national armed forces or channel financial resources into a centralized defense structure. The mistrust runs deep, so it will not be easy to gradually transfer sovereignty rights to the European level. Of course, it would be ideal if the European Parliament were given more powers in this regard. But there is no pan-European government. We are not the United States of Europe. Therefore, a pragmatic approach would make sense, starting with individual willing states in order to expand integration as gradually as possible. If this cooperation were to prove successful, then it would only be logical to command a European army at the European level and to decide on its deployments."

Sandra Weeser:

"What time frame do you have in mind for this?"

Dr. Marie-Agnes Strack-Zimmermann:

"That, of course, depends heavily on geopolitical and, above all, security policy circumstances. We are currently experiencing how rapidly old certainties are dissolving. But life teaches us that the greater the pressure on individual states, the faster changes can be implemented. I would therefore not rule out that we will make faster progress than some could have imagined not long ago. Just two years ago, many of today's security policy developments—especially the extensive financial packages for defense—would have been completely unthinkable. Moreover, in view of the ever-increasing personnel shortages in the armed forces, closer cooperation is not only a strategic necessity, but also a pragmatic way to ensure Europe's defense capability in the long term."

Sandra Weeser:

"Despite the turning point in the German discourse and the new realities since the Russian invasion of Ukraine, does Europe need a change in mentality in security and defense policy in order to be able to compete globally?"

Dr. Marie-Agnes Strack-Zimmermann:

"Strategic sovereignty means that up to now, every country has developed its own strategy—and that is exactly part of the problem. Every country has done its own thing.

We need to understand that NATO has drawn up a precise plan for how Europe is to be defended. Each country has different security policy tasks to fulfill. This refers to all European states, not just those that are members of the EU. The fulfillment of these tasks naturally also has to do with the geographical location of each nation. It makes an enormous difference whether a state shares a border with Russia or—like Germany—is located in the middle of Europe and would therefore have to assume a key role for military mobility. NATO leads the alliance and demands capabilities. Ideally, these are then provided by the countries. The implementation of these plans into the European defense architecture presents all nations with structural challenges that require a completely new way of thinking about security policy. I hope that the younger generation will think more flexibly, question old structures, and develop new concepts accordingly, rather than remaining stuck in established patterns of thought. Ultimately, we must strengthen Europe's strategic autonomy. That would be the ideal state. Europe must be put in a position to ensure its own arms production and defend itself with its own means. The reality is currently different. Building such structures takes time, and in many areas the US defense industry has technological capabilities that do not exist in Europe. This means that for the foreseeable future, Europe will remain dependent on the USA—but our goal must be to invest in European defense structures and build up European production capacities."

Sandra Weeser:

"The security policy cooperation between the USA and Europe that you mention has been the foundation of the transatlantic security architecture for many decades. NATO and close intelligence cooperation have decisively shaped Europe's defense capability. But in view of the changing geopolitical situation—from the USA's increased focus on the Indo-Pacific to new strategic uncertainties in Washington—Europe is increasingly faced with the question: How can we strengthen our own defense autonomy without endangering transatlantic relations?"

Dr. Marie-Agnes Strack-Zimmermann:

"There is a technological dependency. The USA is the global technological leader and, in a sense, offers a full range. They control key components, data access, and maintenance processes. The recent uncertainty over aid to Ukraine, when US President Donald Trump suspended support for Ukraine, shows how quickly such dependencies can be used politically. However, I do not see the danger that the United States will sell us military components and then cause us problems afterwards. US companies are very interested in staying in business with us. The F-35, the most modern fighter jet in the world, we recently purchased because it is certified for nuclear sharing and therefore required. The Tornado is obsolete and a subsequent certification of the Eurofighter would have taken years. The solution, therefore, will and can only be that Europe develops its own defense-capable systems, invests significantly more money in research, and thinks more European.

This is already happening in various programs. This process, and above all this joint EU procurement, must be launched as quickly as possible. We really do not have a minute to lose. Of course, it is illusory to think that we can become independent of the United States overnight. But we can gradually expand European production without jeopardizing existing capabilities."

Sandra Weeser:

"The FCAS jet and the MGCS tank project are prime examples of German-French and thus European defense cooperation. How can it be ensured that such major projects actually proceed in the interest of all of Europe and are complemented by further transnational industrial initiatives? Since the tension between political security interests and industrial constraints was just mentioned: Where do you currently see the greatest (conflict) potential?"

Dr. Marie-Agnes Strack-Zimmermann:

"Every company wants to operate as profitably as possible. Cooperation and interconnection in the defense industry is already international—no country produces autonomously anymore. The blockades often arise in governments and less in industry. France pursues a strongly state-directed defense policy, which is why the French president has a direct interest in keeping contracts in the country—this strengthens the domestic economy and secures jobs. Germany, on the other hand, has a private defense industry, with very few exceptions where the state is involved. This leads to different priorities, which make joint European projects more difficult. That is why politics must set a clear framework: If Europe wants to cooperate more closely in defense, national interests must take a back seat to an overriding strategic goal. The industry will adapt if the political will is consistent and unambiguous. However, this presupposes that not only fine declarations of intent are made, but that joint armaments projects are actually advanced in a binding manner."

Sandra Weeser:

"Yes, I also believe that it is crucial for politics to send a clear signal that it stands behind major defense cooperation projects. I hear this again and again in conversations with defense companies—such as in connection with FCAS or MGCS. They need the assurance that long-term investments are politically supported. Another topic is nuclear sharing. You have already emphasized that we will continue to work with the USA, while Europe should become more independent at the same time. How do you see Germany's role if a European nuclear protection strategy were to develop?"

Dr. Marie-Agnes Strack-Zimmermann:

"I find this debate extremely difficult and do not like to engage in it. Some people believe that you just place a nuclear bomb and then deterrence is guaranteed. We must always keep in mind that nuclear bombs were constructed so that they would never be used. They are and remain an instrument of deterrence. That is why this discussion should not become something 'normal.' Our task is to take care of conventional defense, to strengthen air defense, to manufacture drones, and to have enough ammunition. We must protect cyberspace, keep an eye on underwater infrastructure, and also take care of space, where our satellites are located and accordingly at risk.

I assume that the USA will not abandon its nuclear umbrella for Europe. Nuclear deterrence is a highly complex military strategy that has developed over decades and cannot simply be ended or replaced by an ad hoc alternative. Our contingent also remains a strategically and logistically necessary location for the USA. Yes, there are always proposals—especially from France—that Europe should build its own nuclear protection. French President Emmanuel Macron has offered that France is ready to take a leading role in nuclear deterrence. But if you look at it soberly, France does not have nearly the deterrent potential compared to the USA. Experts say that in a real emergency, France might be able to help defend Germany, but credible deterrence for the Baltics or other European regions would hardly be possible. In addition, nuclear deterrence is extremely expensive. France is therefore understandably looking for potential partners to share the costs. Of course, it makes sense and is important to think through scenarios—such as whether France and the UK could jointly build a European nuclear deterrent. But until such a structure would actually be functional, it would be a very long, extremely complex process."

Sandra Weeser:

"What role does the United Kingdom play in this nuclear deterrence strategy?"

Dr. Marie-Agnes Strack-Zimmermann:

"The British Prime Minister is seeking closer ties with Europe—this is good news for the European security architecture. Of course, we must think strategically beyond the EU framework. Europe's defense does not end at the EU external borders. That is why we must further deepen partnerships with European non-EU states such as the United Kingdom or Norway. However, a central problem remains that we have some blockers within the EU. Hungarian Prime Minister Viktor Orbán repeatedly counteracts security policy decisions. To make Europe more capable of action, we should develop mechanisms that make it possible to take decisions even without the unanimous consent of all EU members. One possible way would be to set up security-relevant treaties between EU and European non-EU states in order not to make strategic projects dependent on individual vetoes."

Sandra Weeser:

"Yes, especially with regard to Viktor Orbán, there have been ideas and catalogues of measures to make Europe more flexible and capable of making decisions—especially in the area of voting modalities. How far along is the implementation?"

Dr. Marie-Agnes Strack-Zimmermann:

"The fundamental problem in Europe is the complexity of decision-making structures. Especially in the field of defense, there is a lack of a common strategy. Now the EU program 'RearmEurope' is starting. That is good, but at the same time we must restore our economic competitiveness. Europe must hold its own in global competition with China, the USA, and other actors in order to secure long-term economic prosperity and thus also security policy stability. Europe stands on two legs—security and economy. Without economy, there is no security; without security, there is no economy. That is why, in view of the current threat situation, Europe must finally cut red tape, reduce regulations, enable private investment, and allow a common internal market for defense goods. Especially in the military sector, we still do not have a functioning internal market. In view of the current security situation, this is a massive deficit that must be urgently addressed."

Sandra Weeser:

"I fully agree with you, including on the capital market. But what risks arise if Europe tries to become more strategically sovereign, especially with regard to long-term security policy?"

Dr. Marie-Agnes Strack-Zimmermann:

"Any change in the security architecture entails risks. There is the well-known principle: 'Never change a running system'—and that does not apply to technical processes, but to strategic deterrence. Our deterrence strategy has ensured stability for the past 75 years. To tamper with it—whether from the American side or through European initiatives—is a risky undertaking because it could potentially make us more vulnerable. Russia is watching how resilient or volatile Europe acts in security policy matters. The same applies to China. China has been observing the free world for years, what we are doing, what we are prepared to invest in the future, and how resilient we really are. Do we only talk about our freedom, about our values, or are we actually prepared to defend this freedom."

Sandra Weeser:

"How can Europe arm itself without getting lost between dependence and isolation?"

Dr. Marie-Agnes Strack-Zimmermann:

"For the time being, we will also have to continue buying from the USA, but immediately build up and promote European alternatives. There are areas in which the Americans are far ahead of us technologically—one example is Starlink. Elon Musk has already created a functioning infrastructure with this system, while Europe, with its own projects, does not expect to establish a complete protection and communication system until 2030. This process is now being accelerated, but the next few years are a critical transition phase. As I said, Europe must expand European defense production, massively promote research in order to become more autonomous in key technologies, and think and buy European. But I see a problem in our own bureaucracy and regulatory mania."

Sandra Weeser:

"Let's move on to another important technology. In addition to classic threats, we are also facing threats in cyberspace. What role must Germany and France play in European cyber defense? Should both specialize in certain areas, or is it more sensible to develop a joint overarching strategy in order to bring other European states along as well?"

Dr. Marie-Agnes Strack-Zimmermann:

"Cyberspace knows no physical borders, and it is necessary for states to work closely together in cyber defense. This applies not only to Europe, but also to transatlantic cooperation with the USA, since we are constantly exchanging security-relevant information. Germany and France should build a structure to which other European states can connect. Such a cyber strategy needs a core alliance—a few countries must lead the process, while others are integrated according to competence and economic potential. Cyberspace differs from other threat areas because it knows no national or continental borders. That is why it is crucial that Europe also looks beyond its own backyard and cooperates with international partners. With New Zealand, Australia, South Korea. What is often underestimated: Most cyberattacks worldwide, in addition to Russian attacks, come predominantly from China. China is an extremely dangerous player on the world stage. Silent but highly aggressive. That is why Europe must keep a close eye on China in terms of security policy. Even though we trade with each other, we are dealing with a systemic rival who poses a huge technological challenge not only in the cyber sector. There will not be a complete withdrawal from China by business, but there are now many companies rediscovering the European market and also producing there. That, too, is part of strategic security."

Sandra Weeser:

"Thank you for the fascinating exchange."

Dr. Marie-Agnes Strack-Zimmermann has been a member of the European Parliament since 2024, where she serves as Chair of the Subcommittee on Security and Defence (SEDE). From 2017 to 2024, she was a member of the German Bundestag and from 2021 to 2024 Chair of the Defence Committee. The holder of a doctorate in journalism has been committed for years to a resilient democracy and a strong European security architecture. She is particularly dedicated to a common European defence policy as the foundation of a sovereign EU.

Part III

Historical Development of German-French Security Cooperation

"Économie de Guerre" on the Left Bank of the Rhine and "Resilience Economy" on the Right – One Goal and Two Concepts

Hans Christoph Atzpodien

> *"In view of geopolitical dangers, there is a need on both sides of the Rhine for an even more determined implementation of the program for an 'Économie de Guerre' on the left and a 'resilience economy' on the right side of the Rhine."*

1 Franco-German Reactions to Russia's Invasion of Ukraine in February 2022

1.1 West of the Rhine

It was at the opening of the "Eurosatory" arms fair in Paris on June 13, 2022, when French President Emmanuel Macron insisted on personally inaugurating the event and, for the first time, called on the industry present to adopt a "war economy." He stated verbatim: "Because Eurosatory is much more than a laboratory for military innovations, … it is a concept of our European sovereignty, and when I stand before you today, it is first and foremost a sign of trust in our armed forces, and I know how much our industry, especially for our army these days and for all our armies, is fully mobilized. … This trust has arisen in a completely new context, and I think we all must, on this occasion and in the time to come, draw the consequences from it, namely the entry into a war economy, in which, in my opinion, we must organize ourselves permanently. This also means an economy in which we must act faster and think differently about rhythms, increased workloads, and margins, in order to be able to restore more quickly what is essential for our armed forces, our allies, or for those we want to help. Basically, an economy in

H. C. Atzpodien (✉)
BDSV, Berlin, Deutschland

S. Weeser (ed.), *The Heart Chambers of Europe: Franco-German Impulses for the EU's Security Order*, https://doi.org/10.1007/978-3-658-51096-1_4

which one can no longer live at the same pace and with the same grammar as a year ago. Everything has changed." (Eurosatory Paris 2022)

This term was also reaffirmed in the new edition of the French "Revue Stratégique" of 2022. In sections 121/122, it states: "Building an economy that contributes to the spirit of defense means mobilizing all the nation's resources to transition to a 'war economy,' i.e., organizing so that French industry can sustainably support war efforts when required for the armed forces or for the benefit of a partner. To maintain a war effort over the long term (high ammunition consumption, attrition, etc.), the best compromise is to manage three main levers: building strategic reserves (complete equipment, but also raw materials and critical components); relocating the most sensitive production chains; and diversifying supply." (Revue Stratégique 2022)

1.2 East of the Rhine

On November 21, 2022, the BILD newspaper headlined "Hard-hitting demand from Wolfgang Ischinger: Germany needs the 'war economy'!" (BILD 2022) The background was an interview with the former head of the Munich Security Conference and former German ambassador, Wolfgang Ischinger, in which he had called for more speed in armaments. In the article, he was quoted as saying: "The defense industry could deliver many things off the shelf if the Ministry of Defense now called for market-available products. But due to the aforementioned bureaucratic obstacles, hardly anything has been called up so far. That will only change if corresponding decisions are made at the highest political level, i.e., in the cabinet." The criticism was not long in coming. Among others, it was even the CSU parliamentary group leader Alexander Dobrindt who warned against calls for a "war economy" in Germany and Europe. The term war economy was "simply too much war rhetoric and sounds very much like economic mobilization" (dpa-AFX 07.02.2023), Dobrindt said in February 2023. His concern: "Too much war rhetoric in Germany" would endanger the still high public support for the delivery of battle tanks to Ukraine and the strengthening of the country's right to self-defense. Other critical voices pointed out that a formal state of defense as defined in Art. 115a of the Basic Law did not exist and that until then, one could not speak of a "war economy," or that a war economy-style planned economy was not compatible with our economic order in peacetime.

On October 30, 2023, it was Federal Minister of Defense Pistorius who, with his call for "war readiness," for the first time introduced another term using the word component "war" into the German public sphere in a ZDF interview. He used the word deliberately, as he said, to "wake up" German society. Germany must prepare itself in order to ultimately be able to effectively prevent war. With regard to this term, the Federal Minister of Defense received little to no public support from the rest of the federal government in the following months. This was not changed by urgent warnings from the Inspector General of the Bundeswehr, General Carsten Breuer, as well as prominent NATO officials or the heads of the three German intelligence services. All of them had repeatedly and vividly pointed out that Russia under President Putin was operating a "war economy," whose output far exceeded the needs of the Ukraine war and which therefore led NATO to conclude that within a few years—at most five from now—we would have to prepare for correspondingly aggressive actions by Russia against NATO as well. Finally, high-ranking NATO representatives repeatedly stated publicly that the military capability requirements for the European member states would have to be significantly increased, which in Germany, for example, would lead to expenditures of 2.5 to 3% of GDP for defense. Despite these urgent warnings, however, this did not lead, over the course of 2024 up to the election of the new US president, to a decision to plan the urgently needed additional defense expenditures for the following years, nor were the aforementioned voices able to trigger a public debate about our general threat situation in the German public. Instead, the newly founded party "Bündnis Sahra Wagenknecht" (BSW for short) received surprisingly strong support in the autumn of 2024 in three state elections in Thuringia, Saxony, and Brandenburg for its populist "peace rhetoric" directed against further armament and further support for Ukraine.

2 French "Économie de guerre" and German "Resilience Economy"

2.1 West of the Rhine: A Clearly Configured Government Program

In France, the call issued by President Macron in the summer of 2022 was promptly and in parallel with the development of the "Revue Stratégique 2022" translated into a program for concrete government action. The focus is on the intention, through the "Économie de guerre," to create a state of tension among the industrial forces crucial for domestic armaments in times of increased pressure. The aim is to further develop the capacities for the production of weapons systems and ammunition as well as to maintain operational readiness, oriented around five so-called "Chantiers" ("worksites"):

[1] Worksite: Planning Security for Industry
So that industry can invest in its production facilities in the long term, planning security over seven years is being created for the defense industry, which is intended to include all actors in the production chain, especially small and medium-sized enterprises, in order to gain strength together.

[2] Worksite: Simplification
Since it is easier to produce what is simple, the goal is to begin simplification already at the stage of defining requirements. The aim of the necessary "value analysis" is to reduce the level of requirements by twenty percent.

[3] Worksite: Securing Supply Chains
Because of the importance of supplier chains for procurement cycles, the goal is to limit the defense industry's dependence on foreign countries, build precautionary reserves especially for raw materials, and replace foreign sources with domestic ones.

[4] Worksite: Recruitment
According to the French Ministry of Defense, the aim is to "bring people behind the machines." A dialogue is to be initiated on this topic with companies, training institutions, and the Ministry of Education.

[5] Worksite: Financing
Since investments only work if companies are able to raise money for investments, securing access to private financing for companies in the defense industry is given a decisive importance.

In the "Revue Stratégique 2022," the priorities of a war economy orientation are addressed in sections 121 to 130, under the following concise headings:

> "An economy that contributes to the spirit of defense: (1) Securing critical supplies and adjusting stockpiles to production capacities, (2) Shortening production and support cycles in the gradual development of a 'war economy,' and (3) Implementing simplifications in standards, regulations, procurement, and support processes within a risk management logic." (Revue Stratégique 2022)

However, if you listen to practitioners west of the Rhine, you may get the impression that while France has made rapid programmatic progress on the "Économie de guerre," the implementation of these good intentions has lagged far behind for a long time.

2.2 East of the Rhine: Long Without a Coherent Policy Framework, but a "Resilience Economy" Proposal from the BDSV

After Russia's invasion of Ukraine, Germany initially focused on energy supply issues, i.e., the "gas shortage" that suddenly arose after the halt of Russian gas deliveries and its legal management in the form of the LNG Acceleration Act. As a kind of conceptual derivative of the LNG Act, the German Bundestag passed a "Bundeswehr Procurement Acceleration Act" in July 2022, which primarily restricted legal protection against procurement decisions and suspended the SME-friendly, lot-wise awarding of contracts for Bundeswehr procurement. Further steps to accelerate procurement were initiated by the Federal Ministry of Defense in April 2023 with the simplification decree by Armaments State Secretary Benedikt Zimmer and the simultaneous directive from Inspector General Carsten Breuer, followed in May 2024 by a new procurement framework called "Project-Based Demand Fulfillment and Utilization" (PBN for short). The aim of the decree and directive from April 2023 was to free Bundeswehr procurement from non-legally mandated internal regulations and at the same time to involve the branches of the armed forces more closely in procurement decisions, but also to hold them responsible. Both initiatives, given their extremely strong "path dependency" within the procurement apparatus, have so far only had limited effect. The new PBN framework has yet to prove its effectiveness, especially in the intended rapid initial determination of a "market-available" product to be procured. As an interim assessment, it can be stated: Good intentions and implementation efforts at the top of the Bundeswehr procurement administration are still opposed by forces of inertia, which pose the risk of the new initiatives "seeping away" in the depths of the procurement apparatus. It also plays a role that all civil servants, quite rightly, see themselves individually bound by law and statute, and that compliance with the Federal Budget Code, monitored by the Federal Audit Office, creates a strong anticipatory constraint.

What was lacking overall on the part of the federal government in 2022 and 2023 was a holistic consideration of the framework conditions for increased armament, as France had undertaken with its "Économie de guerre" program. This was due not least to the fact that the "National Security Strategy" envisaged in the coalition agreement of the traffic light government and intended as an "umbrella document" did not materialize until mid-2023. This, and an ill-conceived linkage of further industrial policy programs with a planned arms export control law, prevented work from beginning for months on a new edition of the "Strategy Paper to Strengthen the Security and Defense Industry" from February 2020. Above all, however, the traffic light parties were unfortunately unable, in their summer 2024 deliberations on the 2025 federal budget and the associated medium-term financial planning, to bring themselves to make the necessary decisions to prospectively increase the Ministry of Defense budget beyond 2026/2027. Since the Bundeswehr special fund decided in 2022 will be exhausted by 2027 at the latest, it was already foreseeable at the time that there would be significant double-digit billion-euro gaps in the budgets for 2026/2027 and beyond. According to the Ministry of Defense, from 2026 onwards, only the sharply rising fixed costs of the Bundeswehr can be covered from the regular defense budget planned until the end of 2024, but not new equipment. Therefore, without a recognizable, binding increase in the Ministry of Defense budget, companies were also unable to reliably design their business cases for new production capacities.

Even though financial planning security is the most important element, other measures must be added—as in France—to enable the security and defense industry to consistently build further capacity. To comprehensively address these German "worksites," the concept of a "resilience economy" is intended to serve, which deliberately uses a different term than "war economy" and is intended to be even broader in scope than the French "Économie de guerre" concept. The overriding goal of a comprehensive "resilience economy" must be to achieve both "war readiness" of the armed forces and overall societal resilience against a potential aggressor. This overall societal "war readiness" is the prerequisite for effective deterrence in advance of a possible state of defense, which will hopefully never occur. This must also include all security and defense policy aspects of a future "Operations Plan Germany." The relevant timeline is determined by the geopolitical situation and, according to NATO and the leadership of the Ministry of Defense, comprises only a few years. The following will address the challenges of a "resilience economy" in Germany in more detail, with some elements appearing equally relevant for achieving internal security as for external defense and alliance capability:

> "Fiscal honesty towards citizens as a prerequisite for comprehensive financial planning security for industry"

Achieving overall societal resilience stands and falls with the willingness of government, parliaments, and the population to make the inevitable financial sacrifices required. Politicians must be frank with citizens about the extremely tense international security situation and clearly address the financial sacrifices that result from it. The Bundeswehr alone needs, in addition to the special fund, at least another €120 billion between 2025 and 2028—possibly even more—to enable further procurements. Creating "war-ready" infrastructure and securing it against possible attacks (primarily from the cyber, air, and sea domains), as well as establishing facilities for comprehensive civil protection, will certainly require significant additional budgetary resources. Anyone who does not take this into account can immediately write off the goal of deterrence capability, with all the consequences that we have so far been unwilling to face.

For industry, not only must there be multi-year planning security in financial terms, but also coordination of the substantive procurement intentions between the Bundeswehr and industry. It must be determined as precisely and as long-term as possible what is expected from each other. A clear priority for national procurements must be defined and implemented through the appropriate handling of § 107 GWB in conjunction with Art. 346 TFEU. The recent decision of the Higher Regional Court of Düsseldorf on the handling of Art. 346 TFEU shows that this is possible. On the industry side, this enables correspondingly long-term, precautionary procurement of materials that could be subject to shortages or export restrictions in a crisis. On the Bundeswehr procurement administration side, such stockpiling requires a willingness to make corresponding advance payments, which should also be possible administratively after the lifting of the advance payment decree.

Other Elements of a Holistic "Resilience Economy" Approach

Security and sustainability are in reality not opposites in socio-political terms. Sustainability presupposes security. Only in the absence of war can we preserve our livelihoods in terms of the environment and human dignity for ourselves and for future generations. This logic must be followed at all levels. For example, it must not be the case that the EU, with its "REACH" regulation (REACH = "Restriction, Evaluation and Assessment of Chemicals"), bans the use of substances without which certain high-tech defense products can no longer be manufactured in the EU. The counterargument that the respective regulations allow exceptions for military applications is only valid to a very limited extent, because manufacturers of these substances cannot survive on military products alone and will therefore generally simply close their production. We must also admit that military equipment powered by climate-neutral fuels or drives generally cannot fulfill its military purpose. Here, too, a simple exception for military products is not enough. Rather, the entire stockpiling and logistics chains for the military must be maintained, and not only for our own armed forces, but for all those who, in an emergency, must be transported to the respective theater of operations via the German hub and supplied there.

Another requirement is to design environmental standards for the approval of new infrastructure, facilities, and manufacturing sites important for our resilience—including for armaments—in such a way that no security risks arise from them. While emission control and other environmental protection aspects must not be overlooked in the construction of new arms factories, the public disclosure of construction documents and operating descriptions is just as incompatible with a resilience economy as the public handling of objections with subsequent possibility of legal action with suspensive provisional legal protection. It is therefore primarily aspects of confidentiality and acceleration that must be reconsidered and regulated for construction projects—such as for arms production—from a resilience perspective. With regard to the crucial factor of time, resilience requires a whole bundle of special legal regulations, comparable to those created in the shortest possible time under the impression of the impending gas shortage in 2022 by the LNG Acceleration Act.

In this respect, it would only be consistent for the federal government to also stop the EU initiative for a "Corporate Sustainability Due Diligence Directive" (CSDDD). Despite the FDP's last-minute efforts, however, this could not stop the EU legislative machinery. Now it is only a matter of how we in Germany deal with the requirements of the CSDDD directive when transposing it into German law, and how we can avoid cost-increasing and bureaucratic excesses, also in relation to the already applicable German Supply Chain Due Diligence Act. Above all, especially in the defense industry, care must be taken that the possibility for NGOs to bring legal action does not provide adversarial forces with an instrument to hinder and damage security and defense industry actors and projects. It is astonishing how little this aspect has so far been considered by other European governments.

Questions of recruiting qualified personnel for the capacity ramp-up of the security and defense industry are also an issue in Germany, even if no particularly serious bottlenecks are known so far. All the more reason why, as part of a forward-looking resilience economy, a concerted approach should be practiced between the reduction of jobs in other similarly qualified sectors (see the example of the automotive industry) and the ramp-up in the security and defense industry. The opportunity for this is more favorable now than ever. This requires, among other things, accelerated repurposing of facilities, but also the rapid granting of security clearances for employees transferring to the defense sector. In general, there is currently a critical bottleneck in the slow issuance of such security and classified information clearances.

We should also follow the French example when it comes to government measures to reduce dependencies on critical raw materials and semi-finished products for the defense industry. This will only work if the federal government is prepared to build a bridge for suppliers with additional financial resources and sufficiently flexible technical requirements, in order to achieve appropriate resilience for standard products over a reasonable period of time. This also includes coordination on how to deal with potential conflicts with the Supply Chain Due Diligence Act when diversifying sources of supply.

Resilience Only by Strengthening All Identified Weak Points

Given a threat situation that, in the so-called "worst case," would be characterized not only by a military attack on NATO territory but by the full range of hybrid attack scenarios, the weakest vulnerable link in the security chain determines the overall resilience of the system. The goal must therefore be to strengthen the resilience of all identified weak points, because otherwise strengthening all other areas would be pointless. Here, the planned "Operations Plan Germany" is particularly important. In any case, it is advisable to communicate with the population about corresponding scenarios, as is done, for example, in Sweden and Finland, in order to ensure the most orderly behavior possible in the event of an emergency. This, too, is part of deterrence capability.

3 West and East of the Rhine—An Outlook

In the meantime, the federal government has been able to coordinate key points in the development of a "National Security and Defense Industry Strategy" derived from the "National Security Strategy." However, as of 2024, these have essentially remained at the level of a qualified collection of topics. In view of the geopolitical dangers described, both sides of the Rhine need an even more determined implementation of the program for an "Économie de Guerre" to the west and a "resilience economy" to the east of the Rhine. The success of both concepts ultimately depends above all on the extent to which the national goals of comprehensive societal resilience are made transparent and comprehensible by the state on the one hand, and on the other hand, can be implemented by the companies concerned in the form of economically viable entrepreneurial decisions. In this respect, Germany always looks a little enviously at France, even though the widespread admiration in Germany for the French national security strategy must also be measured by what actual gains in resilience are ultimately achieved.

References

Eurosatory. (2022, 13. Juni). *Eröffnungsrede des französischen Präsidenten Emmanuel Macron.* https://www.defensenews.com/digital-show-dailies/eurosatory/2022/06/13/macron-petitions-europe-to-support-its-own-defense-industry-amid-new-war-economy/

Secrétariat général de la défense et de la sécurité nationale (SGDSN). (2022). *Revue nationale stratégique 2022.* https://www.sgdsn.gouv.fr/files/files/rns-de-20221202.pdf 01.04.2025

BILD-Zeitung. (2022, 21. November). https://www.bild.de/politik/inland/politik-inland/knallhart-forderung-von-wolfang-ischinger-deutschland-braucht-die-kriegswirtscha-82012636.bild.html

Dr. Hans Christoph Atzpodien is Chief Executive Officer of the Federation of German Security and Defence Industries (BDSV), Berlin. Previously, he held senior positions in the German defense industry, including as Chairman of the Executive Board of Thyssen-Krupp Industrial Solutions AG. The holder of a doctorate in law has many years of experience in the defense sector and in Germany's security policy cooperation with international partners. His particular interest lies in strengthening the European defense industry as well as security and defense policy cooperation between Germany and France.

Long-Term Thinking for Europe's Future: What Adenauer and de Gaulle Still Mean Today

Armin Laschet

1 From the Franco-German Hereditary Enmity to the Treaty of Aachen

On January 18, 1871, the Süddeutsche Telegraf reports: "... the unexpectedly tremendous effect of the bombardment of Paris is supposed to finally open the eyes of the French and bring about a final concession in the near future."

Today, relations between France and Germany are close and friendly. That was not always the case. Anyone wishing to grasp the historical dimension of the transformation in Franco-German relations should compare two newspaper articles side by side.

The first article was published on January 18, 1871, during the Franco-Prussian War of 1870/1871 in the Süddeutsche Telegraph. Reporting from Berlin, it stated that the city was "today filled with rumors of peace, based on private rumors from Versailles that have reached some financiers. Chanzy's (Antoine Chanzy, a French general in the Franco-Prussian War) defeats and the unexpectedly tremendous effect of the bombardment of Paris are supposed to finally open the eyes of the French and bring about a final concession in the near future. It is also said that Paris will fall by the end of next week, thus reaching a stage of the war that will make the end foreseeable." (Süddeutscher Telegraf, January 18, 1871, p. 1)

In the same issue, the newspaper reported on the situation in Versailles on January 12, 1871:

> "Yesterday was the first day on which a favorable northeasterly wind carried the sound of the thunder of our siege guns in an uninterrupted sequence directly to Versailles. A

A. Laschet (✉)
Deutscher Bundestag, Berlin, Deutschland

S. Weeser (ed.), *The Heart Chambers of Europe: Franco-German Impulses for the EU's Security Order*, https://doi.org/10.1007/978-3-658-51096-1_5

> somewhat trained ear could discern that the cheerful sound of our cannons alone thundered."
> (Süddeutscher Telegraph, January 18, 1871, p. 2)

Almost 150 years later, on January 22, 2019, the Treaty of Aachen was signed. It builds on the Élysée Treaty signed between France and Germany in 1963 and sets new priorities for cooperation and friendship between the two countries. The "Frankfurter Allgemeine Zeitung" quoted Chancellor Angela Merkel in its January 21, 2019 edition as saying the agreement "is a response to populism and nationalism," and French President Emmanuel Macron explained that it is about a "shield for our peoples against the new storms of the world." (Aachener Vertrag. Merkel und Macron beschwören Einheit Europas, Tagesspiegel, January 22, 2019)

The change in tone and choice of words from the "cheerful sound of our cannons" to the "shield for our peoples" could not be more striking. For centuries, Germans and French regarded each other as hereditary enemies. The term describes an enmity passed down from one generation to the next. The war of 1870/71 was followed by even worse catastrophes. Germans and French fought bitterly against each other in both the First and Second World Wars. The excessive German nationalism of that era went far beyond the relationship with France. A well-known slogan from the Second World War was: "Every shot a Russian, every thrust a Frenchman, every kick a Brit, every slap a Jap."

The battles not only claimed the lives of the dead and wounded, but their respective outcomes were also manifested in humiliating gestures. To humiliate the French, the Prussian leadership chose the Hall of Mirrors at Versailles on January 18, 1871, for the proclamation of the German Emperor and the founding of the German Empire. When before had a state ever been founded on the territory of another country? There could be no greater humiliation than to choose Versailles, with all the splendor of King Louis XIV, for this purpose.

After the end of the First World War, Germany was forced to sign a peace agreement that assigned war guilt to the Germans and obligated them to extensive reparations payments. At the request of French Prime Minister Georges Clemenceau, the signing of the treaty again took place in the Hall of Mirrors at Versailles. This time, it was the Germans who were to be humiliated. In the very place where they had once founded the German Empire, they had to acknowledge the consequences of their defeat.

The legendary railway carriage of Compiègne was associated with similar symbolism. The armistice signed on November 11, 1918, by Germany, France, and Great Britain ended the fighting of the First World War. The armistice, to which Germany saw itself compelled, was signed in this railway carriage in a forest clearing east of the French city of Compiègne. When France had to capitulate after the German invasion in 1940, Hitler had the old railway carriage brought from a museum in southern France to the same clearing in Compiègne for the signing of the armistice.

2 Learning from History: The Vision of Adenauer and de Gaulle

"I would also like to tell you when the idea became alive in me that, under all circumstances, a good understanding had to be established between France and Germany. That was in the first years after the end of the First World War, in the 1920s. It became absolutely clear to me what madness it is when two neighboring peoples, who are related to each other, who have grown from the same soil, who are so similar in all their views, fight each other." (Konrad Adenauer at a dinner speech on the occasion of the reception for Charles de Gaulle on July 4, 1963*)*

The Second World War, with an estimated 60 million dead and the mass murder of European Jews, demanded a fundamental new beginning. German and French statesmen saw themselves as bearing a special responsibility. Never again should Germans and French wage war against each other. Never again should the catastrophe of the Second World War be repeated. Just a few years after the end of the war, the difference in the new thinking of Germans and French compared to previous decades began to show its first successes.

On May 9, 1950, French Foreign Minister Robert Schuman presented a plan that envisaged the merger of the West German and French coal and steel industries. In a government declaration given before members of the press at the French Foreign Ministry, Schuman stated: "The French government proposes to place the entire French and German coal and steel production under a common High Authority, in an organization open to the participation of the other European countries." (European Union. The Schuman Declaration of May 1950)

The Coal and Steel Community, founded in 1951, was not simply an economic project. Coal and steel were materials with which wars could be waged. Steel could be used to manufacture weapons and tanks, coal could be used to transport weapons and soldiers. The decision to pool the coal and steel industries was primarily intended to consolidate lasting peace in Europe.

The same idea underpinned the Pleven Plan. On October 24, 1950, French Prime Minister René Pleven proposed the creation of a European army under the command of a European defense minister. German battalions were also to be involved, even though the young Federal Republic at that time did not yet have its own army. The Pleven Plan envisaged that the European states would contribute to a European army. Chancellor Konrad Adenauer agreed to the creation of a European army. Adenauer was aware that the Federal Republic had to make a military contribution to a united Europe. After lengthy negotiations, the Pleven Plan led to an agreement on the establishment of a European Defense Community. It was signed on May 27, 1952, by the foreign ministers of Germany, France, Italy, and the Benelux countries (Treaty establishing the European Defense Community, Federal Law Gazette, March 29, 1954).

Nevertheless, the agreement failed on August 30, 1954, due to the vote of the French National Assembly. The reasons for this were manifold. On the one hand, concerns were raised in the French parliament that France could lose sovereignty by participating in the Defense Community. On the other hand, there was concern that the USA might be prompted by a European Defense Community to withdraw its protection of Western Europe from the Soviet Union. The deputies also had reservations about German troops becoming almost equal members of a European army just a few years after the end of the war. Understandably, it took time to overcome these reservations.

This required visionary statesmen such as Charles de Gaulle and Konrad Adenauer. Charles de Gaulle led the French resistance against the German occupation during the Second World War. Despite the conquest of his country by German troops and despite the German crimes on French soil, the later French president was already thinking about a new policy towards Germany as early as 1943. His assessment at the end of the war was: "Germany was defeated, we all lost." (quoted in: Speech by Chancellor Angela Merkel, 11.11.2018).

Konrad Adenauer demonstrated his talent for crisis diplomacy during his time as mayor of Cologne. He had already proven his diplomatic skills in 1923, when the devaluation of money plunged Germany into a crisis that affected broad sections of the population. In the left-bank areas occupied since 1919 and in the Ruhr region, the situation was particularly tense. The invasion of French troops exacerbated the situation, which took on almost civil war-like conditions. Adenauer lobbied the Reich government in Berlin and the French authorities for the creation of a Rhenish federal state to defuse the crisis. In his dinner speech at the signing of the Élysée Treaty in 1963, he emphasized that he had already been concerned with the reconciliation of Germans and French in the 1920s. According to Adenauer, it was "madness … when two neighboring countries, who are related to each other, ---, fight each other." (Adenauer, July 4, 1963) Although Adenauer was unable to implement his ideas in the 1920s, they are representative of the thinking and actions of the first German chancellor after the end of the war. Because, as de Gaulle recognized, everyone loses through war, the realization prevailed that instead of war and hereditary enmity, friendship and reconciliation should be pursued.

The decisive step towards friendship and reconciliation was taken with the signing of the Franco-German Friendship Treaty, also known as the Élysée Treaty, on January 22, 1963. By the time the treaty was signed, the process of European integration had already begun. The Treaties of Rome, which established the European Economic Community and the European Atomic Energy Community, had already been signed in 1957. The Franco-German Friendship Treaty was concluded in the awareness that Germany and Europe would play a special role in the unification of Europe. Adenauer emphasized that "this close friendship, this close bond between France and Germany, acts as a driving force in Europe." (Adenauer, July 4, 1963).

The treaty contained three core agreements. It provided for binding consultation mechanisms between the president and the chancellor, the foreign ministries, and leaders from other ministries. Even then, the necessity was recognized for France and Germany to reach the most unified positions possible on all important issues of foreign, European, and defense policy. Special importance was attached to young people. They were to be convinced of how important Franco-German relations are for Europe and for peace. For this reason, just a few months after the signing of the Élysée Treaty, the Franco-German Youth Office was founded on July 5, 1963.

With the Franco-German Friendship Treaty, the institutionalization of relations between the two countries began on a large scale. Joint bodies, town twinning, training programs, and educational partnerships were intended to create opportunities for encounters between Germans and French. An important step, for example, was the founding of the Franco-German Defense and Security Council on January 22, 1988, 25 years after the signing of the Élysée Treaty. Shortly before the fall of the Berlin Wall, Germany and France established the Franco-German Brigade, a now 6,000-strong binational infantry brigade with its headquarters in Müllheim.

3 Germany and France in a New Europe

In France and in many other European countries, skepticism about German reunification was great in 1990. Helmut Kohl made it clear: "German unity and European integration are two sides of the same coin."

On November 9, 1989, the Berlin Wall fell. Then-Chancellor Helmut Kohl recognized the opportunity to reunite divided Germany. Despite the progress in Franco-German relations, there was still great skepticism in France about a united Germany in the center of Europe. In France, as in other European countries, there was concern that a politically and economically strengthened Germany could once again endanger Europe with hegemonic ambitions (Mitterrand feared "evil" Germans. Fear of reunification, ntv, September 11, 2009).

Helmut Kohl convinced French President François Mitterrand that the new Germany would be a European Germany. The chancellor summed it up with the formula: "German unity and European integration are two sides of the same coin." (European Union. Helmut Kohl and François Mitterrand. Leading figures of reconciliation 2019).

Up to that point, the process of European integration had focused primarily on economic issues such as the European single market. However, the intention to also strengthen united Europe politically had long existed. The European Political Cooperation, agreed from 1970 onwards, was only intended to promote foreign policy cooperation among the member states; unified positions, however, were not coordinated. The end of the East-West conflict and the reunification of Germany offered the opportunity and necessity to advance political integration in Europe as well. With the collapse of the Soviet Union, the Eastern European states broke away from its sphere of influence and the communist ideology imposed on them. The countries wanted to resume their pre-Second World War ties in Europe and become part of the European project.

But the European Community also had to change. It still operated according to the rules of the six founding members. In an expanding community, not all members could or wanted to take all integration steps at the same time. It had to prepare for an enlargement to include more member states and establish procedures that would enable enhanced political cooperation. For this reason, the Maastricht Treaty was signed on February 7, 1992, as the first of a total of four EU treaties. With it, the European Community became the European Union. The Maastricht Treaty defines three pillars in which the EU was to integrate: Common Foreign and Security Policy, Economic and Monetary Policy, and Justice and Home Affairs.

The desire for connection to Western Europe made it necessary to integrate the new eastern partners. Here, too, responsibility lay with Germany and France. On August 28, 1991, the foreign ministers of Poland, Germany, and France, Krzystof Skubiszewski, Hans-Dietrich Genscher, and Roland Dumas, met in Weimar, Thuringia. In an effort to expand cross-border cooperation and jointly assume responsibility for the unification of Europe, the three foreign ministers launched the Weimar Triangle.

The political unification of Europe and the impending enlargement made it clear that not all members and accession candidates of the EU would be able to complete the integration process at the same speed. This led to the concept of differentiated integration, also known as the "Europe of two speeds." In 1994, the then chairman of the CDU/CSU parliamentary group, Wolfgang Schäuble, and the group's foreign policy spokesman, Karl Lamers, published a position paper of the CDU/CSU entitled "Reflections on European Policy." (Schäuble et al. 1994) The paper took into account the different willingness and ability of members and future members of the European Union to integrate. Germany, France, and the Benelux countries were to form a "core Europe" that would take the lead in deepening European unification. The Franco-German friendship predestined both countries to take a pioneering role in this process, for example in the introduction of the euro. Here, the concept of differentiated integration became particularly clear. Anyone wishing to become a member of the euro area had to meet the necessary criteria. This was not possible for all EU states at the same time.

4 Shared Responsibility for New Challenges

The Treaty of Aachen, signed on January 22, 2019, is an expression of the will to place mutual friendship at the service of a strong Europe and to reach common positions on as many issues as possible.

Since then, the geopolitical environment of the European Union has changed significantly. New security risks have become visible. These included, among others, the consequences of the failed Arab Spring, the civil war in Syria, an increasingly aggressive Russian foreign policy, the emergence of the "Islamic State" and numerous associated terrorist attacks, the United Kingdom's exit from the European Union, and the alienation between Europe and the USA under the presidency of Donald Trump. Added to this were new technologies that enabled cyberattacks and new methods of hybrid warfare. The danger of the proliferation of weapons of mass destruction has increased because existing international treaties have either been terminated or even ignored. In June 2017, Chancellor Angela Merkel stated: "The times when we could completely rely on others are to some extent over." (Speech by Chancellor Angela Merkel, Federal Government, May 29, 2017) Franco-German security cooperation became all the closer in many areas.

The suspension of the Association Agreement with the European Union by the Ukrainian government in 2013 triggered the Maidan demonstrations in Kyiv, against which the Ukrainian government responded with brutal force. As part of the Weimar Triangle, the foreign ministers of Poland, France, and Germany, Radoslaw Sikorski, Laurent Fabius, and Frank-Walter Steinmeier, participated in mediations between the demonstrators and the Ukrainian government. After the pro-Moscow incumbent President Viktor Yanukovych left the country on February 21, 2014, and was subsequently deposed by the Ukrainian parliament, Russia, in violation of international law and numerous treaties, annexed the Ukrainian peninsula of Crimea. Subsequently, Russia supported separatist movements in eastern Ukraine, which then proclaimed the self-declared, internationally unrecognized People's Republics of Donetsk and Luhansk.

To contain what was then still a regional war against Ukraine, France and Germany engaged in the so-called "Normandy Format" to find a framework with Russia and Ukraine. The goal was to resolve the conflict by political means. The venue for the corresponding agreement was the Belarusian capital, Minsk. On the second attempt, an agreement was reached that included, among other things, a ceasefire, the exchange of prisoners, and the withdrawal of heavy weapons. The Minsk Agreement was a success of Franco-German diplomacy in bringing the parties to the conflict to the table and reaching an agreement, even if, unfortunately, it did not prove to be permanently viable.

Another example of Franco-German security cooperation followed the terrorist attacks in Paris on November 13, 2015, attributed to the so-called "Islamic State." On the basis of the mutual assistance clause anchored in Article 42, paragraph 7 of the EU Treaty, the French government asked its EU partners for help. The German government then decided on December 1, 2015, to support France in its planned military action against IS. Germany was already involved in the fight against the "Islamic State" by training and equipping Kurdish Peshmerga fighters in northern Iraq. To support France, Germany contributed air-to-air refueling, reconnaissance, and the provision of staff personnel. French President François Hollande described the German support as "a new testimony to the solidarity between France and Germany." (The mutual relations of Germany, France, and Poland since the fall of the "Iron Curtain," with special consideration of the "Weimar Triangle" initiative, German Bundestag, May 16, 2016, p. 7).

Germany also decided to relieve the French armed forces in their military engagement in Africa. On January 28, 2016, the Bundestag approved the expansion of the German contingent in the United Nations Multidimensional Integrated Stabilization Mission in Mali (MINUSMA) by 650 soldiers, thus extending the mission to the north of the country.

At the 18th Franco-German government consultations on April 7, 2016, in Metz, the Franco-German Defense Council emphasized: "France and Germany share a common view on security issues on the European continent. We hope that our cooperation on security issues will continue to play a pioneering role (…) in strengthening the EU in the field of security and defense, particularly within the framework of the Common Security and Defense Policy (CSDP)." (Declaration of the Franco-German Defense Council, April 7, 2016)

Despite this optimistic assessment, Germany and France fell short of the potential of their cooperation. French President Emmanuel Macron recognized that Europe was responding too slowly and too weakly to the challenges of the times. In his speech at the Sorbonne in Paris on September 26, 2017, just a few days after the federal elections in Germany, Macron called for a new foundation for Europe in order to respond to the crises of the times with strength and unity (Speech by President Macron at the Sorbonne. Initiative for Europe, September 26, 2017). Unfortunately, concrete responses from the German side were a long time coming, as a new government did not take office until March 2018 due to the failure of the Jamaica coalition negotiations and the subsequent negotiations with the SPD.

The Treaty of Aachen, signed on January 22, 2019, as a further development of the Élysée Treaty of 1963, was a major step and part of the response to Macron. However, his institutional ideas for the EU did not result in a Franco-German guideline. The Treaty of Aachen defines the priorities of Franco-German relations in many policy areas. Above all, however, it emphasizes the common will to place mutual friendship at the service of a strong Europe and to reach common positions on as many issues as possible. The armed forces of both countries are to cooperate even more closely. Article 5, paragraph 1 of the Treaty of Aachen explicitly emphasizes once again that both countries will provide mutual assistance in the event of an attack on their territory. In his speech at the signing of the Treaty of Aachen, French President Emmanuel Macron emphasized that Europe is a "project that we have agreed upon of our own free will, that we have chosen, and that we reinvent every day; where no one decides for another or for others, but where all members always decide together in their own interest. Our Europe is not a new dream of an empire, but a new democratic project. That is what we are celebrating today." (Speech by President Emmanuel Macron on the occasion of the signing of the Treaty of Aachen, January 22, 2019).

5 What Adenauer and de Gaulle Mean for Europe Today

A "my country first" policy will create neither peace nor prosperity. It is the joint task of Germany and France to implement Emmanuel Macron's call to revitalize the European idea with new visions on the path to European sovereignty.

The foresight shown by the founding fathers of the European Union and the signatories of the Élysée Treaty is more evident today than ever. On February 24, 2022, Russia launched a war of aggression against the whole of Ukraine. The tendency to break international law has increased worldwide. The bipolar world order of the East-West conflict has become a multipolar world order in which many major powers and regional actors vie for influence. In addition to the USA and Russia, these include China, India, Brazil, Saudi Arabia, Iran, and North Korea. Compared to many other regions of the world, people in Europe live with high social standards, legal certainty, and prosperity. This was made possible because Europe is a peace project that Germany and France have played a decisive role in advancing. It is no coincidence that Franco-German friendship is referred to as the "engine of European integration."

The European project remains attractive, even if it faces domestic resistance in many countries. Even today, states in the vicinity of the European Union want to join, including the Western Balkan states and Ukraine. Why is that? It is because these countries recognize that a "my country first" policy cannot create peace or prosperity.

The demand for more responsibility by Europeans for their own security is not new. The pressure on Europe is growing because there is a strong tendency in the USA for Americans to no longer be able or willing to take responsibility for European security to the same extent as before. That is why the European heads of state and government are working hard to ensure that Europe can defend itself.

Germany and France will also assume joint responsibility here. The proposal by French President Emmanuel Macron to also protect Europe with French nuclear weapons should definitely be pursued further. The former ambassador and chairman of the Munich Security Conference, Wolfgang Ischinger, recently called in an opinion piece for "Welt am Sonntag" for Germany to trust France and place its security in the hands of a French nuclear umbrella. (Ischinger, Welt am Sonntag, March 18, 2025). For a joint and successful European defense, Germany must contribute the conventional component with its partners and France – hopefully together with Great Britain – the nuclear component. This is how credible European deterrence can succeed. In addition, the Franco-German Brigade, together with the Eurocorps, provides a good basis for building joint European armed forces.

The idea of a European Defense Community is more relevant than ever. Europe must become capable of global action, and that above all means being able to act. Yes, more could have been done for European defense in the past. But thanks to the groundwork and foresight of Konrad Adenauer, Charles de Gaulle, and other founding fathers of the European Union, we can build on Franco-German friendship and say: If we have the will, we can accomplish this task together. It is up to us, especially Germany and France, to take up Emmanuel Macron's call and revitalize the European idea with new visions on the path to European sovereignty.

References

Aachener Vertrag. Merkel und Macron beschwören Einheit Europas, Tagesspiegel, 22. Januar 2019, https://www.tagesspiegel.de/politik/merkel-und-macron-beschworen-einheit-europas-5000515.html 27. 05.2025

Adenauer, Konrad, Tischrede aus Anlass eines Abendessens zu Ehren des französischen Präsidenten Charles de Gaulle, 4. Juli 1963, Bulletin der Bundesregierung, 117/63, S. 1050, zitiert auf: https://www.konrad-adenauer.de/seite/4-juli-1963/ 27.05.2025

Die wechselseitigen Beziehungen Deutschland, Frankreichs und Polens seit Wegfall des „Eisernen Vorhangs" unter besonderer Berücksichtigung der Initiative „Weimarer Dreieck", WD 2 – 3000 – 075/16, 17. Mai 2016, https://www.bundestag.de/resource/blob/433608/974b65521ade6d93abca67ce5aec98d1/WD-2-075-16-pdf.pdf 27.05.2025

Erklärung des Deutsch-Französischen Verteidigungsrates vom 7. April 2016 in Metz, zitiert in: Deutscher Bundestag, Wissenschaftliche Dienste, Die wechselseitigen Beziehungen Deutschland, Frankreichs und Polens seit Wegfall des „Eisernen Vorhangs" unter besonderer Berücksichtigung der Initiative „Weimarer Dreieck", WD 2 – 3000 – 075/16, 17. Mai 2016, https://www.bundestag.de/resource/blob/433608/974b65521ade6d93abca67ce5aec98d1/WD-2-075-16-pdf.pdf 27.05.2025

Europäische Union. Die Schuman-Erklärung vom Mai 1950, https://european-union.europa.eu/principles-countries-history/history-eu/1945-59/schuman-declaration-may-1950_de 27.05.2025

Europäische Union. Helmut Kohl und François Mitterrand. Leitfiguren der Versöhnung. (2019). https://european-union.europa.eu/principles-countries-history/history-eu/eu-pioneers/helmut-kohl-and-francois-mitterrand_de (zuletzt geöffnet: 27. Mai 2025)

Ischinger, Wolfgang, Warum wir jetzt französische Abschreckung brauchen, Welt am Sonntag, 18. März 2025, zitiert: Münchener Sicherheitskonferenz, 18. März 2025, https://securityconference.org/news/meldung/wolfgang-ischinger-nukleare-abschreckung-welt-am-sonntag/ 27.05.2025

Mitterrand fürchtete „böse" Deutsche. Angst vor der Wiedervereinigung, ntv, 11. September 2009, https://www.n-tv.de/politik/Angst-vor-der-Wiedervereinigung-article499787.html 27.05.2025

Rede von Bundeskanzlerin Angela Merkel, 29. Mai 2017, zitiert in: Bundesregierung, Bulletin 60-2, 30. Mai 2017, https://www.bundesregierung.de/breg-de/service/newsletter-und-abos/bulletin/rede-von-bundeskanzlerin-dr-angela-merkel-797972 27.05.2025)

Rede von Bundeskanzlerin Angela Merkel bei der Eröffnung des „Forum de Paris sur la Paix", 11. November 2018, Bulletin der Bundesregierung Nr. 123-2 vom 13. November 2018, Nr. 123-2 vom 13.11.2018 Bundeskanzlerin beim Friedensforum Paris 27.05.2025

Rede von Staatspräsident Emmanuel Macron anlässlich der Unterzeichnung des Vertrages von Aachen, 22. Januar 2019, Ambassade de France en Allemagne, https://de.ambafrance.org/Rede-von-Staatsprasident-Emmanuel-Macron-anlasslich-der-Unterzeichnung-des 27.05.2025

Rede von Staatspräsident Macron an der Sorbonne. Initiative für Europa, 26. September 2017, Frankreich-Info, Herausgeber: Französische Botschaft, 2017, https://www.diplomatie.gouv.fr/IMG/pdf/macron_sorbonne_europe_integral_cle4e8d46.pdf 27 27.05.2025

Schäuble, Wolfgang / Lamers, Karl/ / Glos, Michael (1994), Überlegungen zur europäischen Politik, Positionspapier der CDU/CSU-Fraktion vom 1. September 1994, in: Blätter für deutsche und internationale Politik, Oktober 1994, https://web.archive.org/web/20110928064140/http://www.cducsu.de/upload/schaeublelamers94.pdf 27.05.2025

Süddeutscher Telegraph, IV. Jahrgang, München, 18. Januar 1871, Nr. 15

Vertrag über die Gründung der Europäischen Sicherheitsgemeinschaft, Bundesgesetzblatt, Teil II, S. 342–379, Bonn, 29. März 1954, https://www.bgbl.de/xaver/bgbl/start.xav?start=%2F%2F*%5B%40attr_id%3D%27bgbl254s0342.pdf%27%5D#/switch/tocPane?_ts=1748341437421 27.05.2025

Armin Laschet was the federal chairman of the CDU of Germany from 2021 to 2022 and, until October 2021, Minister President of the state of North Rhine-Westphalia. The lawyer, former Member of the European Parliament (1999–2005), and current member of the Bundestag has been active for many years in state and federal politics, particularly on European issues. As a board member of the Franco-German Parliamentary Assembly (DFPV) and a committed European, he advocates for close Franco-German cooperation. A particular focus of his work is on strengthening security and defense policy cooperation between Germany and France as the foundation of a sovereign European policy.

Part IV

New Challenges: Cooperations since 2016 and Responses to the War in Ukraine

Franco-German Defense Cooperation: A Balancing Act between Industry and Politics

Armin Papperger

> *"Even though Germany and France have different starting positions, the greatest possible alignment in foreign and defense policy is nevertheless an indispensable prerequisite for the success of future armaments cooperation."*

1 Milestones of Franco-German Defense Cooperation—A Retrospective

Looking back at Franco-German relations after the Second World War, a common thread emerges: it was always the personalities at the helm of our two countries who, with their experience and charisma, shaped and advanced these special neighborly relations. It is well known that French President Charles de Gaulle and Chancellor Konrad Adenauer, based on their personal experiences in the Second World War, laid the foundations for the special Franco-German friendship from the mid-1950s onwards. This friendship reached its first institutional peak with the signing of the Élysée Treaty in January 1963. Even then, a chapter on defense cooperation and a sentence on armaments cooperation were included. This read: *"In the field of armaments, the two governments endeavor to organize joint work from the stage of developing suitable armaments projects and preparing financing plans"* (Deutscher Bundestag 1963). This statement of intent, as general as it is programmatic, contains several elements that remain significant for the armaments cooperation between the two countries to this day: First and foremost, the success of bilateral armaments cooperation depends on the efforts of the two governments, for without their political will, there can be no successful "joint armaments

A. Papperger (✉)
Rheinmetall AG, Düsseldorf, Germany

S. Weeser (ed.), *The Heart Chambers of Europe: Franco-German Impulses for the EU's Security Order*, https://doi.org/10.1007/978-3-658-51096-1_6

work." It is always necessary first to clarify which projects appear suitable for cooperation from a political perspective and how they can be financed in concrete terms. Ultimately, it is the governments—each also involving their national industries—that must organize the "joint work." The insight expressed here, that armaments cooperation can only succeed where there is a certain degree of political alignment between the partner countries, may explain why, in the period that followed, no particularly striking successes in Franco-German armaments cooperation were initially achieved. On July 1, 1966, France withdrew from NATO's military bodies; thereafter, Germany moved closer to the USA in military and armaments policy. In the immediate aftermath, cooperation was mainly civilian, including the signing of the agreement to establish the Franco-German aircraft manufacturer Airbus, which came about largely through the initiative of Ministers Franz-Josef Strauß and Karl Schiller during the Grand Coalition government in Germany in 1969. Nevertheless, the Élysée Treaty—albeit with some delay—did lead to several initiatives for concrete Franco-German armaments cooperation: For example, the companies Aerospatiale and Messerschmidt-Bölkow-Blohm (MBB) established a consortium under the name Euromissile G.I.E. for the development and production of anti-tank and anti-aircraft missiles of the MILAN, HOT, and ROLAND types, which would become one of the forerunners of the European joint armaments company MBDA. The key to this cooperation was the deployment of the respective weapons in both the French and German armed forces, as well as the very pragmatic German approach to exporting these cooperative products. For France, arms exports have always been a defining motive, whereas in Germany, political restrictions have tended to prevail. Against this background, the so-called Schmidt-Debré Agreement of 1972—again due to the collaboration of two influential political figures who were then defense ministers in their respective countries—created a pragmatically manageable basis for coordinating export decisions, with Germany promising to refuse French export decisions only in narrowly defined exceptional cases. In the following decades, Franco-German relations were repeatedly shaped by the interaction of the personalities at the top of the two countries. We recall the duo of Helmut Schmidt and Valéry Giscard d'Estaing, who set milestones particularly in economic and financial policy. Unforgettable is the more than merely symbolic show of unity between President François Mitterand and Chancellor Helmut Kohl, who—much like the relationship between the founding fathers de Gaulle and Adenauer—repeatedly emphasized the deep historical dimension in view of the horrors of the First and Second World Wars. On the 25th anniversary of the Élysée Treaty, President Mitterand and Chancellor Kohl decided in 1987 to establish a Franco-German military unit in the form of the Franco-German Brigade. This was intended to usher in a new phase of military cooperation and to create a basis for greater interoperability between the two armed forces. Kohl also had a close partnership with French President Jacques Chirac. Finally, it is worth recalling the much more sober, yet very deliberate and again close working relationships between Chancellor Merkel and Presidents Nicolas Sarkozy and François Hollande, for example in overcoming the financial crisis of 2008/2009, the subsequent euro crisis, and also in the face of Russian aggression against Ukraine (see

Minsk Agreement). The Franco-German security and defense partnership was expected to receive a significant boost with the inauguration of Emmanuel Macron in 2017. In his famous speech at the Sorbonne University on September 26, 2017, he offered Germany a special partnership and a renewal of the Élysée Treaty. He said verbatim: "We will not agree on all issues, not even at first, but we will talk about everything. To those who say this is an impossible task, I reply: You may be used to giving up; I am not. To those who say it is too difficult, I say: Think of Robert Schuman five years after a war whose blood had barely dried. On all the issues I have addressed, France and Germany can provide decisive, practical impetus." Inspired by this spirit, President Macron and Chancellor Merkel signed the "Aachen Treaty" on January 22, 2019, which in particular provides for a deepening of relations in the field of joint foreign, security, and defense policy. Article 4 (3) of the treaty states: *"Both states undertake to further strengthen cooperation between their armed forces with a view to a common culture and joint operations. They will intensify the development of joint defense programs and their extension to partners. In doing so, they intend to promote the competitiveness and consolidation of the European defense technological and industrial base. They support the closest possible cooperation between their defense industries on the basis of mutual trust. In joint projects, both states will develop a common approach to arms exports"* (Federal Foreign Office 2019).

Shortly thereafter, on February 16, 2019, Chancellor Merkel said in her speech at the 55th Munich Security Conference: "We now want to develop joint weapons systems, and in connection with the Aachen Treaty, which we have now signed with France, the issue of arms exports naturally played a role. If we in Europe do not have a common culture of arms exports, then the development of joint weapons systems is, of course, also at risk. That means you cannot talk about a European army and a common armaments policy or armaments development if you are not also prepared to pursue a common arms export policy" (Federal Government 2018). This subsequently led to the "Supplementary Agreement to the Aachen Treaty," which, apparently functioning well to this day and now including Spain , is intended to harmonize the practical handling of arms export control standards among the participating countries, in the spirit of the Schmidt-Debré agreement. Also at the Munich Security Conference, but at its 56th edition in 2020, President Macron for the first time offered Germany a dialogue on French nuclear weapons protection, an offer he later repeated. However, this idea was never officially taken up by the German side, probably also out of concern that it could erode the partnership in the form of "nuclear sharing" with the USA.

Since Chancellor Scholz took office, the security partnership with France has seemingly cooled again, which from the French side is also associated with Germany's decision to purchase F-35 fighter jets, which Germany saw as indispensable for fulfilling its future obligations under nuclear sharing with the USA. If we look at what has actually resulted from the close Franco-German cooperation over the decades in terms of joint armaments cooperation, the outcome varies significantly between the domains of land, air, and sea. In the land domain, a main battle tank development project begun at the end of the 1970s under the name KAMPFPANZER 90 was already discontinued in 1982, not least due to differing requirements from the armed forces of both countries. The wheeled armored vehicle program BOXER also began in 1988 as a Franco-German project with the further participation of the United Kingdom. However, France withdrew from this in 1999. In 2015, at the instigation of industry, the tank manufacturers Krauss Maffei Wegmann (KMW) from Germany and Nexter from France merged to form "KMW + Nexter Defence Systems" (KNDS for short). However, KNDS initially continued to produce the established KMW and Nexter product lines and did not bring any joint products to market. It was only from 2017 onwards, with the MGCS ("Main Ground Combat System") project, that there has been the prospect of a significant new Franco-German cooperation project in the land domain. Military programs in the air domain have been more successful. A key foundation for this was the decision by Germany, France, and Spain in 2000 to combine most of their activities in civil and military aerospace in the "Aeronautic Defense and Space Company" (EADS for short, now renamed Airbus). However, a further consolidation step attempted by Airbus management in 2012 in the form of a merger with BAE Systems was blocked by the German government under Chancellor Merkel. This would have fundamentally changed the European defense industry landscape in terms of the internationally much-needed scale of European "champions." In terms of applications, there have been a whole series of products in the air domain used by the air forces of both countries, such as the "FOUGA CM 170 Magister" aircraft, the transport aircraft "Nord Aviation NORATLAS 2501," "TRANSALL C-160," and "A 400 M," the helicopters "ALOUETTE II," "NH 90," "TIGER," and "COUGAR AS 532," the light attack aircraft "ALPHA JET," the maritime patrol aircraft "BREGUET 1150 Atlantic," the reconnaissance drone "CL-289," and various types of missiles and munitions. Against this background, it is not surprising that several projects are currently underway in the air domain. The most prominent is the "Future Combat Air System" (FCAS for short), a combat aircraft development project agreed between Germany, France, and Spain in 2017. In addition, there are joint projects in other areas, such as the development of the "MALE RPAS" drone for ground and maritime surveillance. The results of Franco-German armaments projects in the sea domain are comparatively modest, which is certainly also due to the very different missions and operational areas of the two navies. Early cooperation programs were therefore limited to "CREUSOT LOIRE" type guns, "TIGER" class fast attack craft, the "EXCOCET" and "ANS" missiles, while currently only the anti-submarine weapon "UAW 90" can be listed.

2 Challenges and Opportunities of Franco-German Defense Cooperation—A Prospective View

In view of a U.S. administration taking office at the beginning of 2025 that is likely to pay significantly less attention to transatlantic cohesion than President Biden has recently done, and due to attempts by Russia and China to divide Europe, not least in terms of its security policy cohesion, the Franco-German axis in foreign, security, and defense policy is more important than ever. It should not be forgotten in this context that the Aachen Treaty of January 22, 2019, also contains a very explicit mutual assistance and harmonization commitment. Article 4 (1) states: "Both states will deepen their cooperation in matters of foreign policy, defense, external and internal security, and development, while at the same time working to strengthen Europe's ability to act independently. They will consult each other with the aim of establishing common positions on all important decisions affecting their common interests and, whenever possible, act together" (Federal Foreign Office, 2019). However, the implementation of such political programmatic statements always depends on people, combined with the personal commitment of the respective heads of state and government. President Macron's term of office runs until May 2027, although his political room for maneuver is already limited by the parliamentary strength of Marine Le Pen's "Rassemblement National" party. Should Le Pen become the next President of France, this will— as she has already stated— foreseeably lead to a noticeable cooling of Franco-German cooperation. But even Macron himself has expressed disappointment with the state of Franco-German security and armaments partnership in his own statements. Although his speeches in Dresden and Münster during his state visit to Germany in May 2024 still read as very conciliatory, his major speech—again at the Sorbonne University on April 25, 2024 (commonly referred to as "Sorbonne II")—in which he sought to measure himself against his first Sorbonne speech and to formulate a further outlook, provides a clear insight. Both the Aachen Treaty and the armaments projects FCAS and MGCS are mentioned only very briefly here, and in a list alongside corresponding treaties or projects with other European states. The speech no longer breathes the spirit of a particularly close security policy axis with Germany. Rather, Macron says: *"You see: Taking responsibility means deciding for ourselves and taking our European defense measures into our own hands. The creation of a new paradigm. More cohesion and concrete joint initiatives. For this, we already have frameworks, innovative partnerships. The British are close, unwavering allies, and the treaties that bind us, including the Lancaster House Treaty, form a solid foundation. This must be built upon. It must be strengthened. Because Brexit has not affected our relationship. Perhaps this foundation should even be made accessible to other partners? The European Political Community is undoubtedly the right place to build this new security paradigm, this additional cohesion, and to set this common security and defense framework. Ultimately, there is no defense without a defense industry. In this respect, support for Ukraine must urgently be transformed into long-term efforts. This is the so-called war economy, which we are pushing so hard together with the minister. The road there is long, because for decades we have invested too little in our own production, as we must admit. In essence, the peace dividend has led Europeans to produce and invest too little, which has also created a very strong dependence on non-European manufacturers. In view of this, we must therefore produce faster, more, and in Europe—this is fundamental. That is why I am committed to a European preference in the procurement of armaments"* (Présidence de la République française

2024). The emphasis on the security partnership between the two European nuclear powers, France and the UK, is likely as deliberate as the statement elsewhere in this speech that France's nuclear deterrent is the "heart" of French defense strategy, but also an "indispensable element of the defense of the European continent." From this, Macron derives the claim that France is inviting a European defense initiative with the aim of building security guarantees "that all our partners throughout Europe expect." He sees this French defense initiative as being called upon "to build the common security framework that guarantees security for all. And it is this security framework that will enable us, even after the war, to build neighborly relations with Russia." A look at Macron's vision of European armaments harmonization is provided by the following passage from his Sorbonne II speech: *"The goal of a European strategy for the defense industry is to produce faster, more, and in Europe. For us, who have a strong defense industry, this is an extraordinary opportunity, because if we know how to organize ourselves, we can also advance our standards. Incidentally, we have done this in recent years with the Rafale fighter jet. From Croatia to Greece—who would have thought seven years ago that the Rafale would become one of the solutions for European air defense? It is indeed on its way to becoming just that. But this will also lead us to develop common standards at the European level."* (Présidence de la République française 2024). In line with this, it was only in October 2024 that French Defense Minister Sébastian Lecornu announced the further development of the RAFALE 5 by producing an accompanying combat drone by 2033. Furthermore, Macron's explicit mention of the first-ever sale of French submarines to the Netherlands, which he proudly highlights in his Sorbonne II list, cannot be seen in Germany as an encouraging signal, given the local naval shipbuilding strategy and the resulting breakdown of European weapons system harmonization in the underwater sector. It must be repeatedly acknowledged that France acts in these matters from a holistic strategy focused primarily on French national security. The current version of the French "Revue Stratégique" from 2022, in the context of Russia's attack on Ukraine, follows this comprehensive deterrence and resilience approach. With regard to the industrial part, it states in para. 121: *"Building an economy that contributes to the spirit of defense means mobilizing all the nation's resources to move to a 'war economy,' i.e., organizing so that French industry can sustainably support war efforts when required by the armed forces or for the benefit of a partner"* (Secrétariat général de la défense et de la sécurité nationale 2022). The importance of national industrial resilience is reflected in paras. 122/123: "To maintain a war effort over the long term (high ammunition consumption, attrition, etc.), the best compromise is to manage three main levers: building strategic reserves (complete equipment, but also raw materials and critical components); relocating the most sensitive production chains; and diversifying supply. In addition, on the initiative and under the responsibility of industry, joint reserves of components or raw materials could be built up to support industrial activities in the military sector in the event of conflict or in the civilian sector in the event of an economic or health crisis. The development of recycling chains should also lead to a circular economy that reduces supply needs and contributes to sustainable development." And further (para. 126): "Since a stable security situation is a prerequisite for the sustainability of our society, the DTIB (technological and industrial defense base) must be able to benefit from favorable financing instruments, also in connection with the development of sustainable finance. Therefore, future standards for taxonomy or environmental, social, and governance criteria (Environmental Social Governance ESG) must not discourage investment in defense industry companies." Germany can certainly learn a lot from this when formulating its own security and defense industrial strategy. Above all, however, beyond the formulation of nationally sovereignty-defining "key technologies," what is needed is their concrete implementation, not least in the continued pursuit of the Franco-German armaments projects FCAS and MGCS. If, in conclusion, the aim is to formulate policy recommendations for the future based on the history of Franco-German armaments initiatives and the analysis of the current situation, the following three points seem decisive to me:

(1) Even though Germany and France have different starting positions due to their location, history, and security policy capabilities, the greatest possible alignment in foreign and defense policy is nevertheless the indispensable prerequisite for the success of future armaments cooperation. If this is also promoted by a good understanding among the actors at the respective government or state leadership level, the conditions are almost optimal. This must be actively pursued in every possible Franco-German presidential and government constellation, ideally in remembrance of the predecessors who decisively advanced Franco-German friendship through their personal visions.

(2) Concrete and ultimately successful work on individual armaments projects requires the political will to deal with product requirements, procurement, and subsequent marketing to third parties in a mutually harmonized manner. This particularly includes respect for the industrial strengths, interests, and also the intellectual properties of the other side. It should be taken into account that maintaining certain capabilities in each of the participating countries is indispensable in order to have a fallback level of national competence in times of crisis.

(3) An agreement on armaments harmonization or cooperation on individual armaments projects in each of the participating countries touches on issues of national security, which in the foreseeable future should not be overridden by a common European security architecture. Dealing with this requires openness with one another. At the same time, the idea of a "European Defence and Technological Industrial Base" (EDTIB) is strengthened if France and Germany, on the platform of a joint armaments policy "master plan"—possibly expanded to include Spain, Italy, Poland, and also the UK—for the next two or three decades, attempt to shape and steer the European armaments landscape. This approach seems far better than one determined by the European Commission, which ultimately—often motivated by structural policy—leads to greater fragmentation in armaments policy and the strengthening of regional

particular interests. France and Germany, in particular, therefore have a key joint role to play in setting the course for armaments policy and the defense industry in Europe towards a real strengthening of the European industrial base. In the end, the inclusion of the UK on an equal footing will also be crucial.

References

Auswärtiges Amt. (2019, 22. Januar). *Vertrag zwischen der Bundesrepublik Deutschland und der Französischen Republik über die deutsch-französische Zusammenarbeit und Integration* (Aachener Vertrag). https://www.auswaertiges-amt.de/resource/blob/2178596/7b304525053dde3440395ecef44548d3/190118-download-aachenervertrag-data.pdf 06.03.2025

Bundesregierung. (2018, 18. Dezember). *Rede von Bundeskanzlerin Dr. Angela Merkel anlässlich der Generaldebatte im Deutschen Bundestag am 12. Dezember 2018*. https://www.bundesregierung.de/breg-de/service/newsletter-und-abos/bulletin/rede-von-bundeskanzlerin-dr-angela-merkel-1581394 06.03.2025

Deutscher Bundestag. (1963, 22. Januar). Elysée-Vertrag 1963. https://webarchiv.bundestag.de/archive/2008/0912/geschichte/parlhist/dokumente/dok06.html 06.03.2025

Présidence de la République française. (2024, 24. April). *Rede von Präsident Emmanuel Macron zur Zukunft Europas*. https://www.elysee.fr/de/emmanuel-macron/2024/04/24/europa-rede 06.03.2025

Secrétariat général de la défense et de la sécurité nationale (SGDSN). (2022). *Revue nationale stratégique 2022*. https://www.sgdsn.gouv.fr/files/files/rns-de-20221202.pdf 06.03.2025

Armin Papperger has been Chairman of the Executive Board of Rheinmetall AG, Düsseldorf, since 2013. Previously, he held various senior positions within the company. As a mechanical engineer and President of the Federation of German Security and Defence Industries (BDSV), he possesses extensive experience in the defense industry and drives the technological advancement of European security and defense capabilities. A particular focus of his commitment is on strengthening a competitive European defense industry.

New Challenges: Cooperations since 2016 and Responses to the War in Ukraine

Sabine Thillaye

"The war in Ukraine, the re-election of Donald Trump, and the partly contradictory signals from the USA make Franco-German and European cooperation more urgent than ever."

1 Introduction

Russia's violation of international law in its attack on Ukraine marks a profound turning point for all member states of the European Union—especially regarding security policy and the further development of a European defense. This war, characterized by its high intensity and the use of new forms of conflict such as drones and cyber weapons, challenges Europe—and the EU as a political entity—in many ways. Beyond the military aspects, this war compels us to counter numerous destabilizing measures by Russia that directly affect our societies. Examples include the coffins under the Eiffel Tower, the Shoah memorial sprayed with red hands, or the manipulation of refugee movements at the EU's external borders orchestrated by Russia and Belarus (France Info 2024). Added to this are cyber and information attacks, which make it clear that war is no longer confined to land, water, and air, but is opening up new theaters of conflict. The French Chief of Defense Staff, Thierry Burkhard, refers to this as the "l'environnement multi-milieux/multi-champs des opérations" (Burkhard 2021).

The return of high-intensity warfare has led to the realization in all EU member states that defense can no longer be treated as a variable budget item—the era of the "peace dividend" is over. Between 1999 and 2021, China's defense spending increased

S. Thillaye (✉)
Assemblée Nationale, Paris, France

S. Weeser (ed.), *The Heart Chambers of Europe: Franco-German Impulses for the EU's Security Order*, https://doi.org/10.1007/978-3-658-51096-1_7

by 592%, Russia's by 292%, the USA's by 66%, while that of the EU states rose by only 20% (Barotte 2025). France was an exception, with its program legislation adopted as early as 2019, which provided for a significant increase in the defense budget. The determination to invest massively in armaments and personnel—especially in the cyber sector—reflects the adaptation to this new, multidimensional environment. Since World War II, Europe has experienced conflicts of low and medium intensity—such as in the Balkans under direct NATO involvement—but no one would have thought a war of this intensity on European soil possible. Foreign Minister Annalena Baerbock put it at the start of the war: "We woke up in a different world" (Baerbock 2022). President Emmanuel Macron added a few days later: "These events will not only have short-term consequences. They mark a change of era. War in Europe is no longer part of our history or schoolbooks—it is real, before our eyes. Democracy is no longer an undisputed model—it is up for debate, right before our eyes." (Macron 2022)

2 Transatlantic Relations in the Face of New Geopolitical Challenges

Despite a period of political and economic rapprochement between Europe and Russia after the Cold War, several developments—such as the invasion of Georgia in 2008 and the annexation of Crimea in 2014—showed that Russia has not abandoned its Soviet-influenced imperialist and anti-Western mindset. As early as 2007, Vladimir Putin declared at the Munich Security Conference: "It seems obvious to me that NATO enlargement has nothing to do with the modernization of the alliance or with security in Europe. On the contrary, it is a provocation that undermines mutual trust, and one can rightly ask against whom this enlargement is directed" (Marchand 2020, pp. 52–53).

At the same time, the USA, long regarded as the "world's policeman," has suffered several political and military setbacks in recent years—especially in Afghanistan and Iraq. The once dominant role now seems less self-evident. Already under Obama, then even more so under Trump, and most recently under Biden, the role of the USA as a global arbiter has been increasingly questioned—even to the point of calls for withdrawal from the international stage (Kaim & Kempin 2024, p. 13). This reflects a profound shift in mentality within the US population—a change that would likely not be reversed even under a new Trump administration. This urgently raises the question of the United States' role as guarantor of NATO and its position in the European security architecture. Within the EU, there is also no consensus regarding attitudes toward the USA—due to geographic proximity to potential aggressors such as Russia and Belarus, as well as historical experiences. France, for example, attaches great importance to national independence and seeks European strategic autonomy. Economic factors also play a role, as the consequences of a cooling of transatlantic relations are not the same for all EU member states.

The EU must urgently respond to these new geopolitical challenges with enhanced European cooperation. The independence of individual member states is inextricably linked to the sovereignty of the Union as a whole. Had Ukraine been a member of the EU, Article 42.7 of the EU Treaty—analogous to Article 5 of NATO—might have had a deterrent effect and secured the country's territorial integrity.

Despite internal differences, the Franco-German relationship currently serves as an example of constructive partnership. Yet both countries hold different views on transatlantic relations. France traditionally insists on strategic autonomy. Even at the inception of NATO, relations with the USA were tense. The United States rejected the French nuclear weapons program, while President de Gaulle emphasized France's independence and opposed American dominance within the alliance (Vaïsse 2009, p. 863). More recently, one recalls France's refusal to intervene in Iraq in 2003—a decision that left its mark on relations between France and the United States. More recently still, in 2021, the affair over the Australian submarines led to the recall of the French ambassadors to the United States and Australia, when Australia canceled the €56 billion contract (described by France in 2016 as the "contract of the century") originally signed with the French manufacturer Naval Group, in order to sign with an American manufacturer. For France, this decision represented far more than a financial loss: it was perceived as a severe diplomatic crisis. After Paris had repeatedly emphasized the importance of the contract, it felt betrayed by its partners in Washington. In the field of defense, these precedents have only strengthened France's position: it wants to maintain a certain autonomy from the USA while simultaneously emphasizing the importance of NATO, especially in the Indo-Pacific region.

Germany, on the other hand, has been and remains a staunch supporter of NATO and the transatlantic partnership. The Bundeswehr, founded in 1955, was immediately integrated into NATO after the failure of the European Defense Community. While France closed all US bases in 1966, Germany still hosts around forty US bases on its territory today (Tenenbaum & Péria-Peigné 2023, p. 65).

Since the beginning of the war in Ukraine, Berlin has closely coordinated every military or political measure with Washington—whether tank deliveries, financial aid, or diplomatic initiatives. The German message is clear: Germany does not want to stand alone under any circumstances and sees no advantage in emancipating itself from the USA. The often criticized slowness of German decisions is ultimately an expression of the desire for strategic backing. France, by contrast, pursues a more self-confident course: it actively advocates for European strategic autonomy and the strengthening of the European pillar within NATO.

3 The State of Military Cooperation: Between Political Ambition and Practical Implementation

Comparing armed forces and their structures in different countries is fundamentally a sensitive undertaking. Each country has a unique military history that has shaped its organizational and strategic decisions. Germany and France, despite their geographic proximity, are no exception. Nevertheless, an analysis of the current state of both armies and their developments—especially since the start of the war in Ukraine—provides a better understanding of the challenges facing the Franco-German partnership.

The German Bundestag has exceptionally far-reaching powers in almost all policy areas—including foreign and defense policy. While France can deploy its armed forces by decision of the President of the Republic—after consultation with the Defense and Security Council and in compliance with Article 35 of the Constitution, which requires parliamentary consultation after four months—Germany expressly requires the approval of the Bundestag.

This structural arrangement is the result of profound historical ruptures caused by the two world wars and a complete realignment after 1945. The Bundeswehr is—a contrast to the French army—a continental army more focused on internal security within the framework of NATO. The French armed forces, on the other hand, are considered deployment-oriented ("armée d'emploi") and report directly to the President. They are characterized by a modernized structure and organization that reflects continuous adaptation to current requirements. Equipped with nuclear capabilities, the French army has demonstrated its effectiveness in operations—especially in Africa and the Indo-Pacific region. It also enjoys high recognition in French society, which further strengthens its status and legitimacy.

3.1 Rearmament of Both Armies: A Significant Fiscal Policy Shift

For both countries, the return of high-intensity warfare marks a turning point that has triggered profound transformations within their armed forces. Here, clear differences in response to this new situation go well beyond mere nuances.

Despite considerable political instability and ongoing debates about national debt and deficits, the French defense budget remains fully protected by the current program law. Its implementation is reviewed annually. The 2008 White Paper, which imposed severe cuts on the armed forces under austerity constraints, now seems distant and outdated. In today's "broken" world order—a term from a work by Grand Continent under the direction of Giuliano Da Empoli—France recognizes the need to invest massively in armaments and personnel, especially in the areas of space and cyber, where Russia and China have been rearming for years. This realization led to the adoption of a military program law providing for investments of €413 billion between 2024 and 2030. President Emmanuel Macron described this law in his speech on January 20, 2023, at the

Mont-de-Marsan air base as a "transformation law." It follows the so-called "repair law" from 2019 to 2024, which totaled €295 billion and aimed to restore the French armed forces to an appropriate level after years of chronic underfunding.

In Germany, the paradigm shift was more drastic. The end of the "peace dividend" was marked by a historic break: the "Zeitenwende" included the provision of a special fund of €100 billion for the modernization of the Bundeswehr. Financed by debt, this fund is intended exclusively for the procurement of new equipment for the army, air force, and navy, as well as for the digitalization of the armed forces.

Germany, long criticized as a laggard in defense spending, committed itself to achieving the NATO target of 2% of GDP for defense expenditures. Another significant change in Germany is the extent of military support for Ukraine. While Berlin still refuses to supply long-range missiles, it is now among Kyiv's most important military supporters—especially through the delivery of Leopard 2 tanks.

3.2 A Strategic Partnership on Multiple Pillars: Politics, Military, Industry, and Science

For effective cooperation, it is crucial to distinguish between the various levels of interaction: the political level, which sets the strategic guidelines; the industrial level, which aims at joint capability expansion and infrastructure development; the military level, which focuses on operational cooperation and interoperability; and the scientific level, which encompasses research and innovation.

The foundation of Franco-German relations is the Élysée Treaty of 1963 and the Aachen Treaty of 2019. While the first treaty laid the basis for reconciliation between former enemies, the second treaty gave new momentum to the bilateral relationship, 56 years after the original signing. The aim is to take cooperation to a new level and better prepare the two countries for the challenges of the 21st century. The treaty defines 15 concrete priorities, including closer cooperation in the UN Security Council, in space, and within the EU.

In addition, a Franco-German Parliamentary Assembly was established in 2019—consisting of 50 members each from the Bundestag and the Assemblée nationale. This unique institution is intended to bring the political cultures closer together, make decision-making structures more understandable, and better convey the institutional framework—for example, the difference between a centralized state with a strong executive (France) and a federal state with a strong parliament (Germany).

However, health or political crises and the election calendar influence the effectiveness of this format of parliamentary cooperation. For example, a working group on "Foreign and Security Policy" was specifically established within the Franco-German Parliamentary Assembly, co-chaired by MP Sandra Weeser and myself, with precise objectives: to create a better understanding of French and German perspectives on security and defense issues, to support the implementation of the European Union's Strategic

Compass and the strengthening of the European pillar of NATO, to develop concrete recommendations for improving industrial cooperation in the field of defense capabilities, and to ensure better interoperability (Assemblée nationale 2025).

The dissolution of the National Assembly on June 9, 2024, and the early Bundestag elections in Germany following the collapse of the coalition have brought the working groups and all activities of the Franco-German Parliamentary Assembly to a standstill. Since the composition of the Assembly depends on the election results, the members of the Assembly and the composition of its presidium must now be renegotiated.

At the government level, the Franco-German Ministerial Council has existed since 2003, regularly addressing topics ranging from defense and foreign policy to the economy, education, and industry. It played a key role in major projects such as FCAS (Future Combat Air System) and MGCS (Main Ground Combat System). However, the Council suffers from political instability and differing views on the organization of European defense and the role of NATO (Deschaux-Dutard 2024).

Nevertheless, FCAS and MGCS are considered industrial symbols of the shared political ambition to strengthen European strategic autonomy. Both programs aim to have a lasting impact on the European defense architecture and to strengthen the technological and industrial base. This joint initiative, which originated in peacetime—long before Russia's invasion of Ukraine—fits into the long tradition of cooperation between France and Germany. However, the optimism often displayed by both countries was not always shared by the French and German industry representatives involved in the two programs. The goal, therefore, is for them to overcome their rivalries so that the programs can be completed by 2040. In both cases, these rivalries caused delays at the start of the programs, which could prove disadvantageous in a context where arms procurement is increasing. FCAS and MGCS will face foreign competition from the USA, South Korea, and Israel, which will continue their exports throughout the 2030s. At the same time, they must deal with the interests of the industrial companies directly involved in these programs, which are also developing the Rafale F-5, the Leopard 2AX, and the KF51 Panther in parallel—whose market launch is expected much earlier than that of FCAS and MGCS.

The Institute for International and Strategic Relations (IRIS) points to insufficient use of the Franco-German Defense and Security Council (DFSVR), which includes not only the defense ministers but also heads of government, foreign ministers, and chiefs of staff. Greater use of this body—for example, by reviving the "Armaments Cooperation" working group and involving the parliaments through the Parliamentary Assembly—could strengthen strategic coordination (Schnitzler & Arnold, 2024). One of the recommendations is to reactivate the "Armaments Cooperation" working group and to involve the national parliaments more closely in the work of the DFSVR, particularly through the Franco-German Parliamentary Assembly.

At the military level, the Franco-German Brigade, founded in 1989 and based in Müllheim, is an outstanding example of interoperability. It comprises around 5,400 soldiers from both countries. However, General Bertrand-Louis Pflimlin expressed doubts about the operational capability of this unit in "Le Grand Continent," citing, among other things, political reluctance and divergent rules of engagement (Roger-Lacan 2023). Similar challenges exist with the binational C-130J air transport squadron in Évreux, with around 300 soldiers under Franco-German dual command.

The Franco-German Brigade, as well as the Franco-German air transport squadron, contribute to strengthening the interoperability of the two armies—a prerequisite for European defense. Things are moving in the right direction. Recently, the French Minister of Defense and the German Federal Minister of Defense announced that the Franco-German Brigade will be integrated for three years into the multinational corps of the northeastern flank under NATO command. In addition, a fundamental agreement has been reached on the operation of the Franco-German air transport squadron in Évreux. In 2021, the squadron was equipped with its own training center for the training of its crews on the C-130J. This center is certified by the French civil aviation authority (DGAC) as an approved training organization. The companies Thales and Rheinmetall were commissioned, together with Lockheed Martin, the main contractor of the center, to provide the personnel and services necessary for this certification. The qualification of the center was to be completed in the first quarter of 2024, with training activities to begin in the same year (Thales 2021).

To improve interoperability, the "Foreign and Security Policy" working group of the Parliamentary Assembly has developed concrete proposals: reducing bureaucratic hurdles in financing and certification, promoting industrial mergers (keyword "Airbus of defense"), deepening NATO cooperation, and introducing joint war simulations.

In the scientific field, the French-German Research Institute Saint-Louis (ISL) has existed in Alsace since 1958. The institute, founded on the basis of a bilateral agreement, conducts research on electronic warfare, cyber defense, acoustics, and ballistics, among other topics. It works closely with the French DGA and the German BAAINBw, but is also recognized at the EU level—for example, by the European Defence Agency. The ISL is considered a prime example of successful scientific cooperation and should be brought more into the public eye. One problem is the gap between technological research and practical capability development. In addition, English is currently used predominantly as the working language—over the long term, German and French should also be established as equal working languages at the institute to reflect the close bilateral partnership.

4 War in Ukraine and US Elections: A Turning Point for the Franco-German Partnership and European Defense

The war in Ukraine has exposed the limits of European dependence on the US in defense policy. While the conflict has underscored the necessity of transatlantic cooperation and a transformation of NATO (since 2019), it has also reignited the debate on European strategic autonomy.

The Franco-German partnership plays a key role in an EU striving for greater sovereignty in the defense industry and stronger integration of military capabilities. However, this goal is hampered by differing national visions, industrial hurdles, and continued dependence on non-European equipment. Until the recent re-election of Donald Trump, many EU states relied on the transatlantic security guarantee. Germany now faces the challenge of breaking free from decades of US dependence. France, on the other hand, has—since General de Gaulle—always sought a certain degree of independence, following the motto: "être alliée sans être alignée" ("to be allied but not aligned") (Handelsblatt 2001). In this sense, bilateral and multilateral cooperation continues to play a central role.

4.1 A Partnership in Transition

In January 2023, on the 60th anniversary of the Élysée Treaty, France and Germany reaffirmed their defense policy objectives: reducing industrial differences in FCAS and MGCS, strengthening military interoperability through joint exercises of the Franco-German Brigade in Lithuania and Romania, as well as enhanced cooperation in space and cyber domains (Élysée 2023). On April 26, 2024, Defense Ministers Sébastien Lecornu and Boris Pistorius signed the agreement for phase "1A" of the MGCS program. The basis was the High Level Common Operational Requirement adopted in 2023—a joint list of requirements from both countries' general staffs, prioritizing military needs over industrial interests. Finally, after Donald Trump's inauguration on January 23, 2025, Boris Pistorius traveled to Paris for another meeting with Sébastien Lecornu. This resulted in concrete progress for European defense and the strengthening of the Franco-German partnership. As stated in the final declaration: "Their discussions focused on strengthening the strategic defense partnership between France and Germany, in particular through the signing of a ministerial agreement on the operation of the Franco-German squadron in Évreux as well as on the deployment of the Franco-German Brigade for NATO. In the industrial sector, Sébastien Lecornu and Boris Pistorius announced the signing of an agreement between the industrial companies of both countries for the development of the next-generation main battle tank, the MGCS (Main Ground Combat System)."

The statement continues: "Between now and 2035, the MGCS will replace the French Leclerc tanks and the German Leopard 2." (Ministère des Armées 2025).

The signed letter of intent regarding the Franco-German Brigade marks a qualitative leap: for the first time, all 5,000 soldiers are to be trained together and operate as an integrated unit under NATO command on the eastern flank—not as two parallel national contingents. The agreement is valid for three years.

A central issue in any military cooperation is export regulation. Here, too, a bilateral arms export agreement was signed in 2019, which in 2021 was expanded into a trilateral agreement with Spain (in the context of FCAS). It simplifies export processes, harmonizes control procedures, and reduces bureaucratic hurdles. The "de minimis" principle guarantees automatic approval, provided there are no security policy concerns and the economic value is below defined thresholds. A permanent committee also enables rapid dialogue and dispute resolution—a key contribution to strengthening European defense cooperation (République Française 2023).

Dialogue is the engine of the partnership—and stagnation carries risks. For example, in 2022 Chancellor Olaf Scholz alienated France by proposing a European missile defense system based on US and Israeli technology without involving France or Italy—even though they are jointly developing the SAMP/T-MAMBA system. France sharply criticized these unilateral moves, as they prolong Europe's technological dependence (Vincent, 2023). In a constantly changing world, it is more important than ever to coordinate immediate and long-term needs through intensive consultation and to formulate joint strategic responses.

4.2 Bilateral and Multilateral Cooperation

The FCAS and MGCS programs, launched in 2017 shortly after Emmanuel Macron's election, are symbolic of the effort to strengthen the European pillar of NATO. The long-term goal is to reduce Europe's dependence on non-European armaments—especially US weapons, which currently dominate.

In his speech at the Sorbonne on September 26, 2017, Emmanuel Macron declared: "In the field of defense, our goal must be Europe's autonomous capacity for action—as a complement to NATO" (Élysée 2017). According to the Stockholm International Peace Research Institute (SIPRI), around 55% of European states' arms imports between 2019 and 2023 came from the US (SIPRI press release 2024). The war in Ukraine has further reinforced this trend. In its new defense strategy, the European Commission pointed out that by June 2023, about 78% of EU member states' arms acquisitions came from third countries—63% of which from the US alone (Commission européenne 2024). This dependence is problematic—especially given that, according to SIPRI, France is among the world's top three arms exporters, alongside Russia and the US (Gaudiaut 2024). Germany, too, has significantly increased its exports since February 2022, reaching a volume of €13 billion in 2024—ranking sixth worldwide.

Programs such as FCAS, MGCS, or the Eurodrone—a European MALE drone initiative involving, among others, France and Germany and intended to replace the US MQ-9 drones—are forward-looking. Nevertheless, they alone are not sufficient to stabilize the European Defense Technological and Industrial Base (EDTIB) and transition to a war economy. That is why, in 2024, the European Commission, led by Thierry Breton, presented its European Defense Industry Strategy (EDIS). The aim is to reduce dependence on third countries and expand European production capacities. In parallel, the European Defense Industry Programme (EDIP) was launched—with €1.5 billion for 2025–2027—to promote joint investments by EU states. Even though this initiative appears to be a step in the right direction (especially with regard to upcoming programs involving France and Germany), it still has certain weaknesses that could undermine the intended goals. First, the objectives set by EDIS are not binding: for example, the target of producing 50% of defense equipment in Europe by 2030 is purely indicative. Furthermore, EDIP and the €1.5 billion fund remain open to foreign military equipment, as defense journalist Nicolas Cuoco explains. He points out that EDIP "requires that military equipment be designed in Europe, but allows 35% of its value to come from non-European technologies" (Le Journal du Dimanche 2024).

Moreover, the EDIP fund allows up to 35% of a product's value to be derived from non-European technology. As Nicolas Cuoco notes, this endangers the EU's strategic autonomy (Le Journal du Dimanche 2024).

Nevertheless, the initiative points in the right direction. Further proposals include, among others, easier access to bank financing for the European defense industry—for example, by involving the European Investment Bank in military goods, not just dual-use technologies (Pugnet 2025). In addition, Enrico Letta, in his report "More Than Just a Market" (Vie Publique, 2024), advocates for a genuine common defense market with its own regulation. A reform of the Stability Pact—which Letta had already called for in 2021—could also facilitate investment (Letta 2021).

Alongside Franco-German cooperation, the partnership with Poland is gaining new significance—against the backdrop of a war on the EU's border. As the country holding the EU Council presidency (January–June 2025), Poland is placing security at the center. It is a key player in the European security architecture—not least as part of the Weimar Triangle with France and Germany. These three countries represent 190 million of the EU's 450 million citizens and 63% of European defense spending. Poland aims to become Europe's strongest land force in 2025, with 4.7% of GDP. As a NATO member, the war in Ukraine has been a strategic turning point. In the event of an escalation, Poland would be directly affected. Accordingly, the country—like the Baltic states—has integrated the military into civil society. Since the beginning of the war, the foreign ministers and heads of state of the Weimar Triangle have met regularly—especially to coordinate support for Ukraine. This cooperation strengthens the legitimacy of the trilateral format and shows: European integration is increasingly taking place through pragmatic coalitions of action.

4.3 European Cooperation—More Necessary Than Ever

The war in Ukraine, the re-election of Donald Trump, and the sometimes contradictory signals from the US make Franco-German and European cooperation more urgent than ever. The fragmentation of the European defense market—for example, with 20 different fighter jet models or 17 helicopter types—no longer meets the security challenges of our time. Instead, Europe needs a common industrial and technological defense base that takes both short- and long-term goals into account.

The debates following the 2025 Bundestag elections and recent proposals by Ursula von der Leyen to accelerate the European armament process point to a growing awareness of the need to defend the EU. Now, words must be followed by action. To "rearm" Europe, funding alone is not enough—there must be a common setting of priorities, based on the military requirements of hybrid warfare. This demands massive investment in both conventional and new technologies.

France's Defense Minister Sébastien Lecornu put it aptly: "We can be defeated without being occupied. The political debate is necessary: What are we prepared to invest in our defense—not only militarily, but also in the cybersecurity of our hospitals, companies, newsrooms, and municipalities?" This debate must take place both at the Franco-German and European levels. France and Germany—strengthened by their history of reconciliation up to joint action and despite numerous obstacles and differing approaches—can and must drive the European dynamic forward, not for a Europe of defense, but for the defense of Europe.

References

https://www.assemblee-nationale.fr/dyn/16/organes/europe-international/apfa/groupes_travail/politique-etrangere-securite. 18.03.2025.

Barotte, N. (2025, 3. März). *Défense aérienne, renseignement, missiles ... Ces lacunes des armées européennes pour prendre le relais des États-Unis en Ukraine*. Le Figaro. https://www.lefigaro.fr/international/defense-aerienne-renseignement-missiles-ces-lacunes-des-armees-europeennes-pour-prendre-le-relais-des-etats-unis-en-ukraine-20250303. 18.03.2025.

Burkhard, Thierry (2021): Gagner la guerre avant la guerre, vision stratégique du Chef d'état-major des armées https://www.defense.gouv.fr/ema/chef-detat-major-armees/vision-strategique-du-chef-detat-major-armees-fresgb) 30.05.2025.

Rede Annalena Baerbock (2022): https://germania.diplo.de/ru-de/baerbock-ukraine-2513404. 30.05.2025.

Rede Macron an die Nation vom 2. März 2022: https://www.elysee.fr/front/pdf/elysee-module-19386-fr.pdf 30.05.2025.

Assemblée nationale. (2025). *Groupe de travail sur la politique étrangère et de sécurité*.

Commission européenne (2024). *Une nouvelle stratégie pour l'industrie européenne de la défense pour préparer l'Union à toute éventualité en la dotant d'une industrie européenne de la défense réactive et résiliente* (JOIN/2024/10 final). https://eur-lex.europa.eu/legal-content/FR/TXT/?uri=celex%3A52024JC0010. 18.03.2025.

Deschaux-Dutard, D. (2024, 22. Februar). L'impact de la guerre en Ukraine sur la coopération militaire franco-allemande. The Conversation. https://theconversation.com/limpact-de-la-guerre-en-ukraine-sur-la-cooperation-militaire-franco-allemande-223671. 18.03.2025.

Élysée. (2017). *Initiative pour l'Europe—Discours d'Emmanuel Macron pour une Europe souveraine, unie, démocratique*. https://www.elysee.fr/emmanuel-macron/2017/09/26/initiative-pour-leurope-discours-demmanuel-macron-pour-une-europe-souveraine-unie-democratique. 18.03.2025.

Élysée. (2023,). *Conférence de presse à l'issue du Conseil des ministres franco-allemand*. https://www.elysee.fr/emmanuel-macron/2023/01/22/conference-de-presse-a-lissue-du-conseil-des-ministres-franco-allemand. 18.03.2025.

France Info. (2024, 2. Juni). *Étoiles de David, mains rouges, cercueils: comment les sphères prorusses tentent de déstabiliser la France.* https://www.francetvinfo.fr/monde/russie/etoiles-de-david-mains-rouges-cercueils-comment-les-spheres-prorusses-tentent-de-destabiliser-la-france_6590391.html. 18.03.2025.

Gaudiaut, T. (2024). *La France est devenue le deuxième exportateur d'armes dans le monde.* Statista. https://fr.statista.com/infographie/4207/plus-grands-pays-exportateurs-armes-dans-le-monde/. 18.03.2025.

Kaim, M., & Kempin, R. (2024). Die Neuvermessung der amerikanisch-europäischen Sicherheitsbeziehungen—Von Zeitenwende zu Zeitenwende (SWP-Studie 15). *Stiftung Wissenschaft und Politik (SWP).*

Le Journal du Dimanche. (2024, 11. Dezember). *Armement : la souveraineté française sacrifiée au nom de l'Europe ?* https://www.lejdd.fr/sommaire/apres-paris-son-plan-choc-152766. 18.03.2025.

Letta, E. (2021, 20. Oktober). *Enrico Letta : Après le pacte de stabilité, vive le pacte de soutenabilité !* L'Express. https://www.lexpress.fr/monde/europe/enrico-letta-apres-le-pacte-de-stabilite-vive-le-pacte-de-soutenabilite_2160535.html. 18.03.2025.

Marchand, P. (2020). *Atlas géopolitique de la Russie.* Autrement.

Le Grand Continent unter der Leitung von Guiliano Da Empoli (2024). Portrait d'un monde cassé—L'Europe dans l'année des grandes élections »

Ministère des Armées. (2025). *Entretien entre Sébastien Lecornu, ministre des Armées, et Boris Pistorius, ministre fédéral de la Défense d'Allemagne.* https://www.defense.gouv.fr/sites/default/files/ministere-armees/Communiqu%C3%A9_Entretien%20S%C3%A9bastien%20Lecornu%2C%20ministre%20des%20Arm%C3%A9es%20et%20Boris%20Pistorius%2C%20ministre%20f%C3%A9d%C3%A9ral%20de%20la%20D%C3%A9fense%20d%27Allemagne_0.pdf. 18.03.2025.

Pugnet, A. (2025). La Banque européenne d'investissement va investir 2 milliards d'euros dans la défense en 2025. *Euractiv.* https://www.euractiv.fr/section/defense/news/la-banque-europeenne-dinvestissement-va-investir-2-milliards-deuros-dans-la-defense-en-2025/. 18.03.2025.

République Française. (2023). *Décret n° 2023-36 du 27 janvier 2023 portant publication du traité entre la République française et la République fédérale d'Allemagne sur la coopération et l'intégration franco-allemandes, signé à Aix-la-Chapelle le 22 janvier 2019. https://www.legifrance.gouv.fr/jorf/id/JORFTEXT000046131452* 18.03.2025.

Roger-Lacan, B. (2023, 14. Juli). „ Je ne vois pas pourquoi nous nous autoflagellons „, une conversation avec le général Bertrand-Louis Pflimlin. *Le Grand Continent.* https://legrandcontinent.eu/fr/2023/07/14/je-ne-vois-pas-pourquoi-nous-nous-autoflagellons-une-conversation-avec-le-general-bertrand-louis-pfimlin/. 18.03.2025.

Pressemitteilung THALES GROUP (2021). https://www.thalesgroup.com/fr/group/journaliste/press_release/rheinmetall-et-thales-assureront-fourniture-services-dentrainement 30.05.2025

Hubert Védrine, ministre des affaires étrangères—Interview mit dem Handelsblatt 2001 über die Beziehungen der EU mit den USA und der Frankreichs mit den USA. https://www.vie-publique.fr/discours/175709-entretien-de-m-hubert-vedrine-ministre-des-affaires-etrangeres-avec-l 30.05.2025.

Pressemitteilung SIPRI (2024. 11. März). https://www.sipri.org/sites/default/files/AT%20Press%20Release%20FRE.pdf 30.05.2025.

Schnitzler, G., & Arnold, S. (2024). Relancer les instances de coopération franco-allemandes en matière de défense : 8 propositions pour une architecture de coopération bilatérale plus efficace dans le domaine de la défense (Observatoire de l'Allemagne), *Institut de relations internationales et strategiques (IRIS).*

Tenenbaum, É., & Péria-Peigné, L. (2023). Zeitenwende : la Bundeswehr face au changement d'ère (Études de l'IFRI, No. 116). *Institut français des relations internationales (IFRI).*

Vaïsse, M. (2009). La France et l'OTAN: une histoire. *Politique étrangère, 74*(4), 861–872.

Vie Publique. (2024, 26. April). *Compétitivité de l'UE : un marché unique européen à renforcer.* https://www.vie-publique.fr/en-bref/293901-marche-unique-europeen-les-preconisations-du-rapport-letta#:~:text=Un%20rapport%20pr%C3%A9sent%C3%A9%20au%20Conseil,et%20des%20personnes%20en%20Europe. 18.03.2025.

Vincent, E. (2023, 4. März). Le projet de bouclier antimissile lancé par Berlin fâche toujours Paris. *Le Monde.* https://www.lemonde.fr/international/article/2023/03/04/le-projet-de-bouclier-anti-missile-lance-par-berlin-fache-paris_6164094_3210.html. 18.03.2025.

Interview Le Point mit Lecornu, Sébastien (2025). https://www.lepoint.fr/monde/sebastien-lecornu-nous-devons-armer-l-ukraine-sur-le-long-terme-05-03-2025-2583988_24.php 30.05.2025.

Sabine Thillaye A member of the Assemblée nationale, born in Germany and naturalized as a French citizen, she has represented the fifth constituency of Indre-et-Loire since 2017. She was re-elected in 2022 and 2024. From 2017 to 2022, she served as chair of the Committee on European Affairs. She is currently Vice President of the Committee on National Defense and the Armed Forces in the French National Assembly, as well as chair of the Franco-German Friendship Group. Before her political career, she managed a communications and signage agency operating in both France and Germany. Her work focuses on European affairs, Franco-German relations, and issues related to defense and the armed forces.

A Shared Vision for Europe: Airbus as a Showcase of European Agency

Guillaume Faury

Europe stands today at a turning point. Geopolitical tensions, tectonic shifts in the world order, and technological disruptions are forcing us to confront fundamental questions about our future: Can we, as Europe, guarantee our own security, prosperity, and technological sovereignty? Or do we risk losing significance—politically, economically, militarily, and technologically?

The answer to these questions depends crucially on whether Europe now has the will and the ability to act decisively together. And on whether we succeed in merging national interests into a shared European vision—even if that means that, at times, national ambitions must take a back seat to the common European cause.

Airbus is proof that this is indeed possible, and above all, that it is sensible and valuable to pool our strengths in Europe. The creation of Airbus was by no means a given. It was the result of wise and bold industrial policy decisions—and of a clear strategic will. Specifically, this meant that the four Airbus founding states—Germany, France, the United Kingdom, and Spain—were willing to combine their national ambitions in favor of a European project. Together, over the years and decades, we have developed the ability to design and build the best aircraft in the world; far better and more competitively than any country could have done alone. Through its success in both civil and military aerospace, Airbus has become a symbol of Europe's strength through cooperation, of technological excellence through the pooling of capabilities—and of our continent's ability to act when it aligns itself toward a common goal.

This fundamental attitude—strategic, bold, cooperative—is needed today more than ever. For we are confronted with challenges that fundamentally call into question our

G. Faury (✉)
Airbus, Toulouse, France

S. Weeser (ed.), *The Heart Chambers of Europe: Franco-German Impulses for the EU's Security Order*, https://doi.org/10.1007/978-3-658-51096-1_8

previous certainties in security policy and economics, that show us how quickly reality can change—and how dangerous it is not to be prepared for it.

Europe must finally learn to prioritize realism over wishful thinking. This includes building our defense capabilities on our own. It means strengthening a sovereign, competitive industry. And it means developing and applying the strategic key technologies of the future in Europe.

Airbus can and will contribute to this—in three central areas: aviation, space, and the digitalization of civil and military applications.

In aviation, we are currently operating from a position of strength. To secure this, we are investing in new technologies: in lower-emission flying, in digitalization, and in the next generation of modern aircraft and helicopters. The global competition is not sleeping. Those who want to be at the top tomorrow must act today.

Europe has the know-how, the industrial foundation, and the talent—we must activate them decisively. For me, this also means that we must not let up on the issue of sustainability. Lower-emission flying is not only an essential contribution to climate protection, but also a key prerequisite for the competitiveness of European industry. In aviation, it has always been necessary to think of economics and ecology together. That is why at Airbus we will continue to focus intensively on developing new technologies to make flying more sustainable in the future. Hydrogen will play an important role. It is not just about the technology, but also about the infrastructure. That is why this is a joint task for politics and industry as well as science and research.

The importance of space for our security, communication, and defense is indisputable. Strategic investments such as secure launch systems—Ariane 6, for example—and an independent European satellite constellation are not nice-to-haves, but strategic necessities. Airbus is capable, together with partners, of realizing these systems—efficiently, securely, and entirely European. Nevertheless, we are currently facing considerable challenges in the space sector. Here, too, it is becoming increasingly clear that national solo efforts and structures are too fragmented, expensive, and inefficient. Instead, as was successfully done in civil aviation many years ago, European consolidation is needed. Plans for this are currently being reviewed, and we must work together to consistently realize this vision. Here, too, fundamental support from policymakers is required; as well as, at times, the willingness to set aside a purely national perspective in favor of a distinctly European one. For here as well: Only as Europe will we succeed in space and be able to compete with our global industrial rivals —from which the European nation-states will ultimately benefit, and indeed much more than would be possible through national solo efforts.

Defense! We must make up for the strategic and investment shortfalls of past decades in the shortest possible time. I can imagine no greater sense of urgency. This is not just about higher budgets. It is about a fundamentally new way of thinking: European procurement logic instead of national solo efforts, technology-driven innovation instead of piecemeal solutions, strategic autonomy instead of dependence, a European vision of freedom against totalitarian system shifts. This requires smart European coordination among the nation-states. The European Union can play an important role in providing key financial incentives to accelerate and make defense production in Europe more efficient.

Our joint defense projects have the potential to set standards across national borders as an important anchor point and catalyst for deeper European cooperation in defense. Airbus is part of a shared European vision for the defense of the future. And as a distinctly European company with strong roots in Germany, France, Spain, and the United Kingdom, we are ideally positioned to take on an industrial leadership role. As a company with Europe in its DNA, we can be part of the solution—as an industrial enabler and as a bridge between technology and strategic needs.

We have a responsibility to shape a functioning ecosystem in which large corporations, medium-sized companies, start-ups, research institutions, and policymakers work together in partnership—not against each other. And we need a political framework, both nationally and at the European level, that coordinates and actively promotes this collaboration.

Technologies play an important role in this. The war in Ukraine has dramatically shown us: Artificial intelligence is a game changer for military decision-making processes, situational awareness, response times, and precision. Without leading software and AI expertise, there will be no European security architecture. That is why we must invest specifically in research, development, and implementation—and also have the courage to question old taboos. Modern battlefields require mass, flexibility, and networking. Autonomous or highly automated systems are the key to this. The interaction between humans and machines—in the air, on land, and at sea—must be consistently further developed. The war in Ukraine makes clear how dependent a country is without its own infrastructure in space. Satellite communication, reconnaissance, navigation—all of this is now militarily indispensable. Europe needs joint flagship projects to ensure sovereignty in these areas.

The challenges we face in Europe are as immense as they are diverse. We all have a responsibility to overcome them. No country in Europe will succeed alone. But together, of that I have no doubt, we can and will position ourselves successfully.

Airbus is a European project—born out of the will to cooperate. Our success shows that Europe can cooperate and overcome national thinking. Now is such a moment again. Europe must no longer allow itself to be paralyzed by hesitation and nationalism. We must redefine our ambitions—politically, industrially, technologically, and militarily. Time is of the essence. Europe's future is being decided now. Let us shape it—decisively, united, and with clear vision.

Guillaume Faury has been Chief Executive Officer of Airbus SE since 2019. Previously, he headed the commercial aircraft division, Airbus Commercial Aircraft, and held various leadership positions in the aerospace industry, including at Airbus Helicopters and the French automotive group Groupe PSA. As a trained aerospace engineer and certified test pilot, he has extensive experience in both civil and military aviation. A particular focus of his work is the sustainable transformation of the aviation industry and the strengthening of European technological and innovation leadership.

Part V

Perspectives for the Future: Strengthening European Defense Capabilities through Joint Projects

Make European Defense Great Again

André Loesekrug-Pietri

> *"(Much) more money is crucial—but that alone will NOT protect Europeans if we do not act much more strategically and efficiently, and make speed and scale in Europe our top priority. We must prepare for the conflicts of tomorrow, and this will only be possible through consistent strategic foresight and technological leadership."*

This "Briefing for Decision Makers" is a 32-point plan & a call to action with 4 priorities:

A. End illusions—Recognize the weaknesses of European defense in order to make the right decisions → 11 concrete proposals
B. 99% of discussions revolve around the percentage of defense spending. We must FIRST massively reduce complexity and bureaucracy BEFORE the (necessary) increase in budgets takes place → 11 concrete proposals
C. RADICAL reforms—Industry must become the engine of rearmament, economic strength, and technological leadership, with procurement as a strategic tool. Speed must be central → 10 concrete proposals
D. SHAPE the future through technological leaps—A shift of 10% in R&D funding is necessary to avoid another decade of strategic surprise. JEDI, the precursor to a European ARPA, is ready & an integral part of the solution → 14 technology priorities

A. Loesekrug-Pietri (✉)
JEDI, Paris, France

S. Weeser (ed.), *The Heart Chambers of Europe: Franco-German Impulses for the EU's Security Order*, https://doi.org/10.1007/978-3-658-51096-1_9

1 Not the First Time Europe has Tried to Become a Player in Defense

The European Defense Union failed in 1954 because De Gaulle rejected the creation of an integrated European army under a US supreme commander, which would have jeopardized the development of a French nuclear deterrent—as well as due to a diminished sense of urgency after Stalin's death in 1953 and the end of the Korean War that same year. After the fall of the Berlin Wall, European countries' defense budgets shrank massively in the 1990s and 2000s from 3–4% to 1–2% of GDP—in the illusion of a "peace dividend," which led to thousands of tanks, fighter jets, frigates, and garrisons being decommissioned. The growing tensions after September 11 and especially Afghanistan, the Islamic State in Iraq and Syria (ISIS), and finally the annexation of Crimea in 2014 served as a (small) wake-up call. In 2022, the European Union published its "Strategic Compass"—a step forward that raised great expectations, but did not define a clear level of ambition for defense … and nothing has been heard of it since.

2 The Current Plans: The Good and the Bad

The re-election of Donald Trump—though predictable—did not prompt the EU states to take any proactive action, and the continent remained the "continent of strategic surprises." The new Commission, although it appointed an extremely competent Defense Commissioner, acted as before—with the promise of a "White Paper on Defense" within the first 100 days.

Significant steps were taken in February by the then German chancellor candidate—and now Federal Chancellor—Friedrich Merz, a committed Atlanticist, who changed his mind and warned against sole dependence on US protection. Another important announcement came from the President of the EU Commission, who proposed to exclude defense spending from the 3% deficit rule (exception clause)—at the Munich Security Conference, where the speech by Vice President JD Vance shocked the audience.

But what was truly decisive were the accelerated, direct talks between the US and Russia about Ukraine—without European involvement—as well as the escalation in the Oval Office and the public humiliation of President Zelensky. All of this set off alarm bells in Europe.

The sense of urgency has now reached all European heads of government. There is now a clear awareness that the US may no longer provide a security guarantee for Europe—and that Europe urgently needs to step in for Ukraine, as the US has stopped its arms deliveries.

Ahead of the special summit on March 6, the EU Commission proposed a "ReArm Europe" plan, including the reallocation of unused Covid-19 funds (or the issuance of up to €150 billion in bonds) as well as the use of a "fiscal leeway" of up to €650 billion with the help of the aforementioned exception clause.

A positive signal was also the London summit, at which the United Kingdom and major EU states once again clearly reaffirmed their support for Ukraine—in stark contrast to Brexit. Another bright spot is Poland, which is expected to spend 4.7% of its GDP on defense in 2024—2.5 times the level before the Ukraine war. This shows that significantly higher investments in defense are already possible today—even without prior adjustments to the EU framework.

On the negative side, the strategic content of many discussions remains superficial—the focus is more on "How much?" rather than "For what purpose?". Spending more is necessary, but by no means sufficient—as evidenced by the fact that European countries (EU+UK+Norway) spend about 46% of the US defense budget, but are estimated to achieve only about 10% of US capabilities—in terms of operational forces, transport, intelligence, or space. There is hardly any discussion about simplifying procurement processes or innovation frameworks, let alone a radical renewal of the industrial base for mass production. Europe's military objectives regarding Ukraine remain unclear. Despite numerous papers on joint defense strategy, the exact roadmap for a European defense is at best wavering—between "EU defense strategy," "European pillar of NATO," and most recently even "defense with US withdrawal from NATO."

3 What is Missing—4 Priorities and a 32-Point Plan for a Strong European Defense

3.1 Priority A—To Make the Right Decisions, Europeans Must Stop Deluding Themselves About the Current Situation

11 Proposals

- Despite its economic strength, Europe is not a global military power.
- Weapons procurement remains inefficient.
- Nuclear deterrence alone is insufficient.

1. Today, Europe is not a global defense actor—despite being the largest economic area and having a massive interest in global order. Talks about Ukraine are taking place in Riyadh without European participation. Europe is the largest financial contributor, but its influence in the Middle East conflict is virtually zero. Despite enormous trade interests and the need to secure straits such as Bab el-Mandeb (against the Houthis), Malacca, or the Taiwan Strait, Europe cannot do so without the support of the US Navy. Without US arms deliveries, Ukraine will lose the war. Europe's influence in Africa is waning, and its military presence in the Middle East and Indo-Pacific would be practically non-existent without a few French bases.

2. We are 500 million people, but we lack the dynamism of the US, the nationalism of China or Russia, or the resilience and disregard for human life seen in Russia. Simply comparing population numbers says nothing about a society's defense capability. Europe does not know how to leverage its size.
3. The efficiency of European defense spending is low: with less than half the US defense budget, Europeans on average operate five times as many different weapons systems (jets, frigates, tanks, artillery), leading to high costs, inefficiencies, interoperability problems, and thus reduced operational readiness.
4. Three years after the start of the war in Ukraine, most European countries have not significantly increased their defense budgets—with exceptions such as Germany (from 1.3% in 2021 to 2% in 2024) and Poland (from 2.2% to 4.7%). However, these percentages reflect very different realities: for example, France includes its nuclear deterrent, Italy accounts for defense in the Ministry of Economic Affairs, and Germany's share for salaries is comparatively high.
5. Three years after the war began, Europe has not switched to a war economy. The industrial base has grown by only about 10% per year since 2022. Reasons: procurement processes have not become significantly faster or simpler, defense ministries expect industry to take the initiative, while industry waits for orders. Production remains complex and customized, unsuitable for mass and attrition. Programs like Act in Support of Ammunition Production (ASAP), which was supposed to deliver 1 million rounds of ammunition by March 2024, fell far short of the target—only 520,000 rounds were delivered. Hardly anyone talks about it, and even fewer are addressing the root causes (Kington 2024).
6. As a result, European countries are not operationally ready: Germany will not reach its goal of providing 230,000 shells (enough for one month of high-intensity warfare) until 2031 (Defence Industry Europe 2023).
7. The separation of military and civilian technologies is increasingly theoretical and incorrect, as almost all technologies are dual-use—from Starlink to batteries, from drones to AI. Artificial dividing lines, such as in investment classifications or industrial segmentation, should be removed to avoid unnecessary barriers.
8. Nuclear deterrence is crucial—and there is discussion about a possible extension of the French-British nuclear umbrella to other European states . But it must not be misunderstood as a panacea—a wonderful wall that can protect us from all aggression. Ukraine's incursion into Russian territory did not trigger a nuclear response—this shows that deterrence must also be provided by conventional forces. Both must be considered in sync to credibly represent escalation ladders.
9. Citizens—with the exception of countries bordering Ukraine or Russia—feel no sense of urgency. There are doubts about the ability to unite the country in the event of open conflict. According to a 2024 Gallup poll, only 32% of EU citizens are willing to defend their country in an emergency.
10. European intelligence remains heavily dependent on the US, as the misjudgment of Russian capabilities in early 2022 showed. This weakness makes it all the more

urgent to gain better insights into China, whose situation has become even more opaque since the quasi-lockdown year of 2020.

11. Many joint defense programs were designed before the war in Ukraine. They are technically outdated, too expensive, or unsuitable for modern battlefields. Example: The Eurodrone is hardly used in combat due to its enormous unit cost (over €100 million)—by comparison, a Bayraktar TB2 costs €3–5 million, an Iranian Shahed about $35,000—both would no longer be operational today, as they are easily jammed or attacked (Stein 2022; Hollenbeck et al. 2025). MGCS and FCAS are crucial, but urgently need to be updated.

3.2 Priority B—99% of Discussions Revolve Around the Percentage of GDP. Of Course, A Higher Budget is Crucial, BUT Before We Allocate More Financial Resources, Take on More Debt, or Dismantle Our Social Model, We Can Achieve Massive Gains by Radically Reducing Complexity & Changing Processes

11 Proposals

- Streamline procurement and transfer processes.
- Establish strategic foresight to anticipate threats.
- Simplify recruitment to attract top technological talent.

1. Public money should primarily be used for public procurement with clear performance objectives, not for subsidies. The state should not act as an investor: public procurement should drive innovation, foster new players and competition, and accelerate the scaling of promising and sovereign solutions—before private investors step in. This requires procurement agencies with deep technological understanding and real authority to take risks—but this only works with political backing in legal terms, otherwise it remains wishful thinking.
2. Once public procurement has reduced the risk for new players, systems, or technologies, private savings can be mobilized much more easily. Europe has one of the world's largest savings reserves (as emphasized in the Draghi report). One should resist seemingly generous calls to channel even more public funds into start-ups—often these conceal private profit interests.
3. Europe has become the continent of strategic surprises. In view of accelerated times and overlapping crises ("polycrisis"), it is crucial to think ahead—to avoid once again experiencing costly catch-up strategies (as in the digital sector) or entering into new dependencies, consciously or unconsciously. Strategic foresight helps to prioritize issues correctly and to develop a common vision among European partners at an early stage. This foresight tool should be designed for the medium to long term (5–10 years) and updated several times a year. It prevents typical mistakes such as

prematurely committing to supposed "winners"—e.g., in technologies like AI-based language models (LLMs) or certain defense contractors—and prevents one-sided vendor lock-in.

4. Europeans—a term that needs better definition—should not launch joint programs without first defining common threats and strategic objectives. From this, the required capabilities can be derived, which are either necessary for independent decisions or only make sense at scale. Currently, projects start directly with industrial initiatives, which quickly sink into bureaucracy, complexity, and waste. The proposed approach ensures participation and coherence. Without it, an insoluble tension arises between jobs, strategic goals, and sovereignty issues. The EU Court of Auditors recently found that the Commission did not adequately assess needs in Action Plan 2.0 (for military mobility)—making reliable financial planning impossible.
5. Inefficient transfer processes—especially to Ukraine—lead to significant delays. For example, Poland requires several permits for military transfers. Simplifying these procedures is necessary to ensure rapid and effective support—and thus make all defense cooperation more efficient.
6. A system of uncoordinated export controls hinders the development of joint defense programs and undermines the—so far illusory—potential for European scaling. Strategic foresight and effective parliamentary cooperation could help here—beyond existing formats such as the Debré-Schmidt Agreement.
7. Simplified HR processes are needed to attract urgently needed top talent—for example in cyber, AI, quantum, or maintenance (MRO). Salaries will be hard to match with the private sector, but a fast and unbureaucratic process would greatly expand the applicant pool. A significant operational reserve could identify personnel early, increase numbers, secure competencies, and harness the growing engagement of many citizens. Success factor: a modern, AI-supported, extremely agile personnel management system. France's current goal of recruiting 100,000 reservists will hardly be achievable with today's administrative processes—a radical fresh start is needed. Civic engagement for one's own country must be reimagined.
8. R&D instruments (research & development) currently hinder innovation and tax money efficiency due to excessive bureaucracy. They focus more on picking winners, mandatory consortia, and geographic returns, rather than excellence, impact, and performance. This affects both civilian and military instruments. As a result, the best projects often do not even apply—quality suffers. Faster, earlier, and more agile funding would significantly increase concrete impact.
9. Public funding should not aim for a single entry point, but rather foster an ecosystem of publicly and privately structured public-good initiatives. The Defence Innovation Accelerator for the North Atlantic (DIANA), the NATO Innovation Fund (NIF), the European Defence Fund (EDF), or the Joint European Disruptive Initiative (JEDI) bring different approaches—they should be supported and encouraged to collaborate in pursuit of a common strategic goal.

10. Beyond the tragic aspect of the war in Ukraine, it is essential to learn from the knowledge gained there: weapons effectiveness, C2 structures (Command and Control), tactical lessons, integration of industry into war operations, scaling (especially with drones), protection of critical infrastructure. It must also be clear: after the war, Ukraine will be a significant player in the European defense industry. This feedback must be rapidly integrated into our defense planning and industry.
11. A permanent mapping of dependencies in three areas is crucial: know-how (personnel), technologies, supply chains (including critical materials).

3.3 Priority C—Radical Reforms: Industry Must Become the Engine of Rearmament, Economic Strength, and Technological Leadership. Procurement and Speed Must be Used as Strategic Tools

10 Proposals

- Redefine defense planning based on strategic requirements, not industrial preferences.
- Establish a European Security Council with key partners.
- Differentiate procurement speeds: 6 years for highly developed systems, 6 months for mass production, 6 weeks for consumables.

1. Procurement directorates are the favorite bogeyman of the armed forces, and most are indeed extremely bureaucratic. An example is the German procurement office (BAAINBw), where the average procurement cycle is always measured in years (Bosen 2022). It should be seriously considered to build entirely new organizations, rather than investing enormous amounts of time, energy, and money in restructuring them.
2. One way to achieve a common vision according to Priority B could be the establishment of an agile "European Security Council"—in which this common vision, both regarding threats and required capabilities, would be regularly discussed. It would consist of "willing countries" (and not be imposed from above), with selected EU members, but also the United Kingdom, Norway, NATO, or even Switzerland as observers—at the level of their chiefs of staff and heads of their procurement directorates. This council should be highly technology-oriented to include multi-domain operations.
3. A complete restart of current defense programs conceived before the Ukraine conflict—such as the Eurodrone—is necessary. Future program developments like MGCS and FCAS must fully incorporate lessons learned from the war in Ukraine and other current conflicts. Immediately stopping a program would send a very strong signal that "the party is over" and demonstrate a willingness to make bold decisions—similar to the "Last Supper" in the US in 1993. New players should be

given the chance to prove their competitiveness through targeted and challenging programs—as happened in the US with the development of Anduril or Saronic Technologies, which could not have emerged from traditional defense contractors.

4. Non-recurring costs of contracts should be assumed much earlier in the process—in exchange for full compatibility of their weapons systems with future developments as well as technological openness, to avoid vendor lock-in and high maintenance costs.
5. No European program should be launched if, under the same name, different requirements and multiple versions exist, leading to massive cost inflation, complexity, and maintenance nightmares (A400M, NH90 and its … 23 versions …).
6. The procurement process cannot follow the same cycle for all systems—and creating "exceptions" only adds more patchwork and complexity. Radically different cycles for the three types of weapons systems could be a solution: *exquisite* (the highly developed, large systems), *attritable* (those we need in large quantities for a long conflict), and *expendable* (consumable systems). There could even be a maximum time set: a maximum of 6 years for the first category, a maximum of 6 months for the second, a maximum of 6 weeks for the third. These categories must be regularly reviewed to remain aligned with strategic requirements and technological developments.
7. When it comes to radical innovation, governments and the EU should delegate part of R&D funding to external, disruptive innovation agencies that are not subject to the constraints of public funding, in order to achieve the necessary boldness and agility. As for a European DARPA—as has been announced by many leaders over the past 10 years—instead of reinventing the wheel, existing initiatives should be supported and expanded (such as JEDI or others).
8. Integrating the concept of comprehensive societal defense is crucial. This includes societal resilience, industrial capabilities, resistance to coercion, cognitive and informational warfare, as well as economic and technological sovereignty. A comprehensive strategy ensures preparedness in all areas.
9. Actors with an "operating system" approach who also master the industrial aspect should be supported, as this combination enables agility, resilience, and future versatility. This must be supported by a radically different R&D organization, supply chain, and industrial base—often through stronger vertical integration to increase speed and reduce complexity.
10. Adopting a war economy approach could radically transform the European industrial landscape—with a focus on rapid scaling and mass production. Tripling or quadrupling output is essential, while today we are only at a fraction of that, with the risk of being overtaken by our adversaries. New players with strong scaling expertise should be involved—not to replace the current industry, but to significantly emulate it—for example, from the automotive or software sectors.

3.4 Priority D—Shaping the Agenda & Creating Strategic Advantage Through Technological Leaps

14 Technology Priorities

Instead of listing capabilities (anti-missile systems, drones, AI & software, transport, space communication …), which are well known and where the discussion often remains superficial, we have focused on technological building blocks with the greatest potential for disruption and breakthrough innovation, as well as the greatest strategic impact. Of course, this list is not exhaustive.

Overview

1. Disinformation & cognitive warfare
2. Future of GPS/positioning systems
3. Underwater warfare, including detection and communication
4. Energy storage/autonomy
5. Drone swarms
6. Manufacturing/rapidly scalable factories at the intersection of robotics, sensors, AI
7. Heterogeneous data fusion, C2, confidential computing
8. Decentralized/on the edge Command & Control (C2)
9. Future of cloud computing
10. Miniaturized antennas for space ubiquity
11. Future operating systems
12. Next-generation semiconductors
13. AI-driven cyber capabilities, portable quantum (computers)
14. Future AI models

Background Information: About the Joint European Disruptive Initiative

The Joint European Disruptive Initiative (JEDI) is the European initiative for advanced research projects (ARPA). JEDI develops and funds moonshot R&D programs to push the boundaries of science and innovation—with a radically new methodology based on mission-driven research, speed, uncompromising excellence, interdisciplinarity, and bold risk-taking. JEDI's goal is to ensure that Europe maintains a leading role in the current phase of technological and scientific acceleration. Driven by over 6,500 technology and science experts from academia, industry, and deeptech start-ups in 29 countries, JEDI is fully independent and funded by dedicated foundations, companies, individuals, and public institutions. JEDI expects member states and the EU to turn their often-expressed desire for a European ARPA into concrete action—not through yet another bureaucratic construct, but by allocating 1–10% of their research budgets to bold, agile, and independent initiatives like JEDI. The aim is to debureaucratize research funding and give Europe the best possible chance to remain technologically leading.

References

Bosen, R. (2022, 8. Juni). *Germany's military upgrade hobbled by bureaucracy.* Homeland Security News Wire. https://www.homelandsecuritynewswire.com/dr20220608-germanys-military-upgrade-hobbled-by-bureaucracy. Zugegriffen: 28.03.2025.

Defence Industry Europe. (2023, 19. Juni). *Der Spiegel: German stocks of artillery ammunition depleted.* https://defence-industry.eu/der-spiegel-german-stocks-of-artillery-ammunition-depleted/ Zugegriffen: 28.03.2025.

Hollenbeck, N., Altaf, M. H., Avila, F., Ramirez, J., Sharma, A., & Jensen, B. (2025, 19. Februar). *Calculating the Cost-Effectiveness of Russia's Drone Strikes.* Center for Strategic and International Studies. https://www.csis.org/analysis/calculating-cost-effectiveness-russias-drone-strikes. Zugegriffen: 28.03.2025.

Kington, T. (2024, 15. März). *EU sprinkles $560 million over defense firms to grow ammunition output.* Defense News. https://www.defensenews.com/global/europe/2024/03/15/eu-sprinkles-560-million-over-defense-firms-to-grow-ammunition-output/. 28.03.2025.

Stein, A. (2022, 27. Juli). *The TB2: The value of a cheap and „good enough" drone.* Atlantic Council. https://www.atlanticcouncil.org/content-series/airpower-after-ukraine/the-tb2-the-value-of-a-cheap-and-good-enough-drone/. 28.03.2025.

André Loesekrug-Pietri is Chairman and Scientific Director of the Joint European Disruptive Initiative (JEDI), the European Initiative for Breakthrough Innovation (European ARPA), present in 30 European countries. Previously, he held leadership positions in private equity, industry, as a founder, and most recently as chief advisor to the French Minister of Defense, responsible for European defense policy and technology. The Franco-German was one of the first to advocate for technological leadership and sovereignty in Europe, aiming to bring the continent on par with the USA and China in the development of new technologies. He is a member of the Innovation Board of the Munich Security Conference, the advisory board of the Saarland Transformation Fund, and is a reserve colonel in the French Air Force.

Strategic Autonomy—A Fundamental Principle of European Policy Orientation

Joachim Bitterlich

> "All the reservations or obstacles, misunderstandings or divergences—arising from our very different traditions and political systems—should not prevent us from engaging in a profound debate on decisively strengthening the EU's capacity to act, efficiency, and 'strategic autonomy,' so that our political, economic, and social model can survive and play a genuine role on the world stage."

1 Necessity for Greater Capacity to Act and Independence

"Strategic autonomy"—is it a panacea to solve our problems of political, economic, scientific, technological, or military dependencies all at once? Or is it the magic word that enables us to focus on what is essential—a new European political objective?

"Strategic autonomy" or, in other words, "European sovereignty"—these terms have increasingly found their way into our French, German, or European political terminology in recent years.

Should Europe expand its "sovereignty," advocate for "strategic autonomy" in order to emancipate itself, particularly in defense matters, from the United States, but also to better protect its economy and sensitive sectors against global competitors or rivals—or is this merely an illusion in a globalized, interdependent world?

Josep Borrell, the most recent High Representative of the EU, noted in a remarkable blog post, "Why European strategic autonomy matters" (HR/VP Blog 2020), that

J. Bitterlich (✉)
Paris, France

S. Weeser (ed.), *The Heart Chambers of Europe: Franco-German Impulses for the EU's Security Order*, https://doi.org/10.1007/978-3-658-51096-1_10

the foundations of strategic autonomy have been firmly anchored in European policy in recent years.

Yet the EU often uses these two terms without concretely explaining what they mean in the relevant areas. This leads to misunderstandings, divergences, and traditional national reflexes, as well as considerable mistrust among Europeans.

When Germans hear the term "strategic autonomy," their first suspicion is of hidden French protectionism aimed at supporting French companies or distancing from the USA.

Are we once again facing a sometimes typical European "unity in dissent" between Brussels and the member states, or is this simply one of the typical European transitional phases toward new and adapted political objectives?

And this is happening in an existential phase of European integration, which French President Emmanuel Macron has even described as a "mortal danger." It must be acknowledged that Europe has still not managed to truly emerge from a deep internal and external crisis and to agree on the cornerstones of its self-assertion and its future.

In view of the increasing and accelerating global crises—especially the war against Ukraine led by Russia, renewed fighting in the Middle East, the trade war between the USA and China, or uncertainty about future US policy—everyone agrees that Europe must take on greater responsibility, that greater weight on the international stage is necessary, and that it must better protect its political interests—all of which is easier said than done!

2 Significance of "Strategic Autonomy" in Core Areas of European Policy

What do the terms "strategic autonomy" and/or "European sovereignty" really mean? Could this imply "autarky" for Europe? Does it mean reducing dependence on other competitors and rivals?

And to what extent is dependence on competitors from non-EU countries acceptable? Could a different standard be tolerated for allies compared to rivals? Are Canada or Norway exceptions?

Or does it, in truth, simply depend on the specific area and specific products we are talking about!

The French President, as well as other European politicians, seem to want to use these terms in a political sense, close to concepts such as "independence," "autonomy," or "capacity to act," hence the two most frequently used buzzwords in the debate: "strategic autonomy" and "European sovereignty."

The Germans also use these terms, though often with their reflexively more legalistic, even constitutional, approach. Members of the Bundestag do not hide their concern; they fear the judges of the Federal Constitutional Court, who are already very cautious toward

Europe and will critically analyze any new integration within the framework of Article 23 of the Basic Law with regard to the potential relinquishment of national sovereignty.

Take, for example, the term "autonomy" in security and defense matters. When a French person utters it, many Germans think that France is trying to detach Europe from the United States. In my opinion, this is unjustified. Yet the negative perception remains!

"Strategic autonomy" may perhaps be easier to explain in the area of "internal security and migration," especially regarding Schengen.

In reality, despite the development of coordinated policies in certain areas, the EU member states have for years no longer been able to exercise genuine national or European control in the areas of migration, asylum, cross-border crime, or terrorism. In truth, they have long since lost their national sovereignty.

However, they can only regain their sovereignty through more intensive cooperation with other states—hence the need to strengthen permanent European cooperation.

The fact that our European interior and justice ministers have not achieved the necessary cooperation in these sensitive areas in the nearly forty years since the founding of Schengen, as Helmut Kohl rightly demanded in the early 1990s, is part of the current situation. The possible solutions have been on the table for years. Due to a lack of insight into reality, politics in France and Germany, but also in other countries, has decisively lost the trust of citizens; the consequences have become more than evident in voting behavior.

This judgment applies not only to the area of internal security and migration. In other areas as well, closer coordination of policies and a common positioning are not only appropriate but in the vital interest of the EU and its member states.

"Strategic autonomy" appears to be of particular importance, especially for securing future key technologies, for energy policy, and for sensitive sectors such as pharmaceuticals, telecommunications, and defense.

This objective apparently meets with approval and even underscores the necessity in the economic sphere to reduce the dependence and vulnerability of the European economy, especially with regard to China or the USA.

Initial steps have been taken under the leadership or with the support of the European Commission, with the concrete direction differing depending on the area concerned—yet it is still far from a genuine strategy!

Examples include the EU law on critical raw materials or lithium, which is needed for batteries and for which diversification of sources is progressing slowly.

Or medicines during the COVID crisis: Europeans were suddenly appalled by their excessive dependence on pharmaceuticals manufactured in India or China; hence efforts were made to relocate the production of sensitive medicines back to Europe or to diversify production.

Another particular example is energy policy. Even with regard to nuclear energy, Europeans are far from achieving "strategic autonomy." France, for example, still obtains uranium for fuel rods—unchanged and despite Russia's aggression against Ukraine—

primarily from Russia, and Europeans seem only now to be slowly rediscovering their ally Canada as a supplier.

But it is about much more: Is it not long overdue to recall the earliest days of European integration, the common foundations for coal and steel—and today, it is about a core of no less importance for any European policy. It is about energy policy!

Is it not high time to align our—unfortunately very different—national energy policies toward CO_2 neutrality and, to secure our supply, to weigh our imports from third countries more carefully and to create a genuine common European electricity grid?

An energy union with a grid in which electricity flows can be redirected to other member states "in the second" as needed, also to more harmoniously integrate energy from renewable sources such as wind and solar. We know of initial approaches, for example at the French-Spanish border, to enable the exchange of electricity as needed, generated from nuclear power or wind—a model for other border regions in Europe as well!

"Strategic autonomy" is, by its nature, closely linked to the conditions of international trade. The extraterritorial effect of US trade and legal measures regularly causes deep irritation in Europe. When will the EU have similar means? Likewise, the question arises: How can Chinese or American companies buy sensitive technology firms in Europe, but not vice versa?

The EU's top priority should therefore be not to protect sensitive industries through unilateral protectionism, but above all initially by ensuring reciprocity in trade measures vis-à-vis the United States and China before taking unilateral steps—quotas and tariffs are still better than trade wars!

"Strategic autonomy" is particularly important with regard to sensitive goods and the risks of international "supply chains" and the "just-in-time" principle, buzzwords of today's globalized world.

The accident of a giant container ship in the Suez Canal in March 2021, or the Houthi attacks on ships in the Red Sea, or more recently, attempts to sabotage undersea cables in the Baltic Sea between the Scandinavian countries, the Baltics, Poland, and Germany, have underscored the importance and sensitivity of international connections and supply chains for our economies. Do not forget that 60% of German imports arrive by sea!

This vulnerability does not only affect supply chains. Shouldn't diversification of sources be the primary goal to avoid or at least reduce potential problems?

For several years, we have observed a growing debate about how trade and investment can not only defend and assert European interests and values against international competitors, but ultimately also achieve the ability to defend these interests on an equal footing.

Europeans often do not seem to feel secure or satisfied with policy. Think of the debates about the treatment of the Uyghurs in western China or working conditions in low-wage countries in connection with the controversial recent EU directive on supply chains—highly sensitive issues in which the German federal government has so far hardly been able to convince.

Special attention should finally be paid to questions of monetary and economic coordination, which are of extreme political sensitivity. What is the future of our European common financial and monetary area? We have successfully created the euro, but have still not implemented the necessary complete financial system!

Does the Franco-German initiative of 18 May 2020, which ultimately enabled the European recovery plan amounting to €750 billion, called "Next Generation EU," adopted at the end of 2020 and financed by loans, represent a first step toward a new concept of joint debt?

Given Germany's particular sensitivity in financial matters, the topic remains highly politically sensitive! But even here, the EU essentially needs "strategic autonomy" in order to be able to defend the interests of the European economy at the international level.

The report that Enrico Letta presented to the European Council in April 2024 points to new paths to be taken and integrates the urgent challenges facing the EU, even beyond the completion of a genuine European financial market. (Letta 2024) It is the logbook for the future European Commission and Council for the next five years!

A particular area in which "strategic autonomy" appears more necessary than ever is disruptive research and innovation.

In core areas of future technologies, for example to master climate change, secure communication, space technology, to name just a few examples, the EU has in recent decades become increasingly dependent on the USA and China.

We Europeans were once leaders in many areas; today, we are lagging behind. In a small multidisciplinary circle, we therefore founded the "Joint European Disruptive Initiative"—J.E.D.I.—in Paris a few years ago, with the aim of shaking up politics and science and fundamentally changing procedures such as risk-taking.

The basic idea was and is to use a method with which the Americans, over 60 years ago, jump-started their disruptive cutting-edge research. They founded the Defense Advanced Research Projects Agency—DARPA for short—to develop technologies of the future, even when success was by no means assured. In simple terms, they consciously took risks and put themselves at the forefront of the technological movement.

European politicians such as Emmanuel Macron or Angela Merkel seemed to view these ideas favorably. However, in Paris, Berlin, and Brussels, in the relevant ministries and organizations, we ran up against walls: fear of losing control of their budgets and their funding increases. We have not given up, however; at some point, the knot must also be untied for Europeans—the clock is ticking!

3 "Strategic Autonomy" in Security and Defense Policy

The most complex and challenging area remains security and defense policy. In this field, there continue to be significant differences between European nations, including with regard to nuclear defense.

3.1 Franco-German Efforts at Reconciliation

Four years ago, an indirect debate between the French President and then German Defense Minister Annegret Kramp-Karrenbauer triggered a veritable crisis of confidence.

Her provocative statement was clear: "The illusion of European strategic autonomy must come to an end. Europeans will not be able to replace the decisive role of the United States as guarantor of their security" (Politico 2020).

Emmanuel Macron's response in his interview with 'Le Grand Continent' was no less pointed. He emphasized his fundamental lack of understanding of the German minister's position and added that her view was a "misunderstanding of history." (Le Grand Continent 2020)

The German minister's detailed reply did not make its way into the French media. They did not consider it necessary to reproduce the nine (!) pages of her speech at the Bundeswehr University (BMVg 2020).

Paris did not seem to understand the core of the thinking of the majority of Germans, which in part fundamentally differs from the French doctrine. For Germans, it was particularly clumsy of their French neighbor to ignite the political debate publicly by launching a frontal attack on NATO and calling it "brain dead" (The Economist 2019).

That was indeed far over the top, a polemical and provocative statement, but Paris should have understood that NATO and the United States have been and remain the guarantors of Germany's territorial integrity and freedom for over 70 years.

Emmanuel Macron's words even seemed to call into question France's place within NATO. The question arose as to France's true objective. A break with the United States? Certainly not. A realignment of the balance of power in the medium term, rather yes!

Isn't it fundamentally about the EU becoming a genuine European pillar, partially or fully autonomous within NATO? This debate is by no means new, but it has become urgent in Europe.

I have always advocated a 'European caucus' and a European pillar within NATO, a perspective that our American friends have in truth never liked. Even for some of our European partners, this idea is a red flag!

It is little known, even among the interested public, that France and Germany already developed a 'joint security and defense concept' in December 1996, which included a joint agenda for gradual rapprochement and a common definition for key areas, including the most sensitive issue—the nuclear question.

Strangely, this text could today—almost three decades later—form the basis for bilateral or even European discussions. It states: "Collective defense is based on a combination of conventional and nuclear forces adapted to the new strategic landscape. The supreme guarantee of the security of the Allies is provided by the strategic nuclear forces of the Alliance, in particular those of the United States; the independent nuclear forces of the United Kingdom and France, which play their own deterrent role, also contribute to deterrence and the overall security of the Allies. Our countries are prepared to enter into a dialogue on the role of nuclear deterrence in the context of European defense policy" (Bundesregierung 1996).

3.2 Key Points of European Defense

In light of the Russian invasion of Ukraine in February 2022 and possible developments on the US side, the time finally seems ripe to seriously discuss this pillar and a European defense—separable from NATO, but not 'separate'—an idea on which Paris and Berlin unfortunately still do not agree.

Germany, which for too long neglected its defense with a mistaken notion of peace in Europe, was on a "pacifist trip," now seems to be slowly getting back on track with the "Zeitenwende," even if this turnaround is far from sustainable.

The Bundeswehr is today only limitedly capable of alliance and defense. It is obvious that today's Germany finds it difficult, not only in nuclear matters but also in security policy, to adapt to the fundamentals of its partners, including France.

These are a series of fundamental questions that require a genuine debate—within political parties, in parliaments, and ultimately with the aim of achieving at least a minimal societal consensus!

How can this real deadlock be broken? It would be impossible—and unwise—to do so without a thorough debate. In parallel, a work plan should be developed, an intensive agenda for the next five years.

It is not about the right approach, whether federal 'communitarian' or intergovernmental; it is rather about effectiveness! Otherwise, we risk losing all influence on questions vital to us.

This is obviously a controversial topic. Even if one leaves aside the debate with the United States, it is urgently necessary for Europeans to recognize the need to strengthen their defense efforts.

At its core, it will be about building a genuine partnership within Europe—as an expression of taking responsibility and a certain autonomy vis-à-vis the United States. In my view, this will mean a guideline of "3% of GDP!"

It is essential to launch a genuine European program aimed at effective and coordinated spending and, above all, at bringing our cultures closer together.

One of the first steps should be—starting with a core group of member states—a frank assessment of the state of European armies. This naturally also includes the unvarnished status of European equipment and armaments in all essential areas.

Years ago, the European Defence Agency adopted this goal; today, it seems to have been forgotten. Nor is it replaced by the Commission's efforts to present the network of medium-sized defense companies in Europe to governments and the public. Anyone who looks behind the scenes will find that there is much more and better in Europe than many think.

The aim cannot be to exclude the Americans from the European market—purchases in the USA, primarily of equipment that does not exist in Europe, are part of burden sharing with the other side of the Atlantic.

Among the fundamental questions that need to be resolved quickly is certainly the organization of the relevant procurements. Germany would have to summon the political courage to reorganize this area swiftly—my model would be the French Direction générale de l'armement, or DGA for short, which appears far more effective than its German counterpart. The procedures would have to be set up more clearly, more tightly, and more pragmatically.

One of the "bad" examples of recent years was the procurement of the new assault rifle for the Bundeswehr, which had to fail in an almost pitiful manner, admittedly without consequences—while the French DGA, "of all things," quickly completed the procurement of a new assault rifle from Germany.

The so-called "25 million procurement procedures" in Germany should very quickly become a thing of the past. They may have proved rewarding for local MPs and companies in their respective constituencies, but they never became an efficient procurement model; the risks simply went in the wrong direction.

Ultimately, it is about laying the foundations today for a European defense market, which cannot be a copy of the EU internal market, but must be based on the real necessities in this area and be under the control of the member states.

We have lost thirty years in this fundamental area. In 1993 (!), we were negotiating with the then French political leadership about the "exchange" of a whole series of essential armaments for equipping our armies.

The background at the time was the discreet French request to gain time and reduce costs in order to jointly design and manufacture the future combat aircraft for the European air forces by France, Germany, and the United Kingdom. Paris asked us to postpone the Eurofighter decision by two years to bring Dassault—which was at the beginning of the Rafale's development—on board for the joint project.

In return, until the new joint combat aircraft was ready, a French ECR squadron was to be equipped with the (German-British) Tornado and a German squadron with the (French) Mirage 2000. The French First Army was to be equipped with the Leopard 2, the German army with the most modern new French artillery. And the list was slowly getting longer at the time… An unprecedented exchange of armaments! The Chancellor and Defense Minister, as well as the French President, agreed, but the project failed at the time due to the French cohabitation (Bitterlich 2021a, b).

And where do we stand today? Why have we not managed to systematically expand the European defense sector and entrust it with supplying our armies?

The two core Franco-German defense projects agreed since 2017, FCAS as the future combat aircraft system and MGCS as the tank system of the future, are making only hesitant progress, burdened by mistrust in Paris and Berlin—ultimately only thanks to the commitment of the two defense ministers—and it remains uncertain whether they will actually be realized. Mutual mistrust, national reflexes such as reluctance to entrust the respective project to a clear lead nation, are to blame. At present, it seems clear that neither country wants to be responsible for failure—but even here, there is still no willingness to draw clear consequences from the failures of the past thirty years.

Would it not be time today to recall the objective of 1993, to build the future aircraft under the leadership of the French and British and to further develop the German Leopard as the standard tank? This probably sounds too simple!

The future European combat aircraft is also burdened by the required coexistence with the American F35, which has also found increasing supporters and buyers in Europe. The key question here, as elsewhere, remains the creation of the necessary interoperability between the American type and a European model.

The other essential elements of a genuine European pillar in NATO are well known: more joint training, information, formation of joint units in certain areas, and not least a coordinated export policy of the European arms-exporting countries.

With regard to joint structures and units, there are indeed some initial positive examples, such as the German-Dutch Corps, the Alliance's AWACS reconnaissance aircraft. But we should think further—I am thinking, for example, of the minesweepers for the Baltic and North Seas, an example more relevant than ever. Why do we not fully entrust this task to the Dutch and/or a Scandinavian neighbor?

Consensus on export policy remains a sensitive issue in the EU. The most recent Franco-German agreement on export controls of 23 October 2019, which was extended to Spain in 2021, represents an enormous step forward. There have been numerous initiatives in this regard, and progress has been made, but it has nevertheless remained limited and, above all, fragile.

This agreement should form the basis, to which the other European countries with a defense industry should accede. I expressly warn against the attempt to make this an EU directive at the outset—the good foundation would be talked to death far too quickly, both in the Council and in Parliament.

The European Defence Agency should play a central role in this European security and defense policy under the chairmanship of a defense minister.

The EU's "Strategic Compass" is certainly not a panacea for launching a genuine European defense, but it should serve as a necessary political signal for substantial medium- to long-term development.

Based on this assessment and its implementation, we could gradually develop a "European preference" and "strategic autonomy."

However, one fundamental question must be answered from the outset: Who commands European defense capabilities—keyword: "Command and Control"? It can hardly be SHAPE; a European headquarters should form the nucleus of a European command structure. Is it not obvious to build this command structure on the general staff of the Eurocorps in Strasbourg?

3.3 Strategic Autonomy in Foreign and Development Policy

The need for profound reforms applies equally to foreign policy. I consider it essential to redesign it—and above all its actual degree of cooperation—in order to make progress toward Europe's strategic autonomy: by focusing on our vital interests and clear political priorities, by changing methods and working practices (Rapport Schuman 2020).

Instead of blaming either Brussels or the capitals, the aim should be to pool resources in the most effective way. This could also mean entrusting a member state, a group, or the Commission with the leadership of certain topics or projects.

This should also include reflection on decision-making and rapid response methods, including consideration of a European Security Council to steer foreign policy. It would be illusory to rely on qualified majority decisions—it would seem more realistic to me to tie the classic "Luxembourg Compromise" to a "no" from at least two or preferably three member states.

And we should not forget the fundamental revision of development policy: a common policy or at least coordinated policies that first listen to the other side before implementing their own ideas. This applies especially to Africa.

A fresh start, a break with the habits of a largely ineffective international presence through daily statements, is necessary: it is never too late to do the right thing—but the redesign of foreign and security policy is urgent.

4 "Strategic Autonomy" as a Core Element in Achieving European Capacity to Act

Sovereignty is one of the fundamental, constitutive principles of the state. Using this term to emphasize the necessity of a European policy carries the risk of further fueling the debate that, for several years now, has been driven by a number of governments and parties seeking to "regain" their national sovereignty. "Take back control" was not only the slogan of the Brexit supporters, but also of other nationalist and/or populist forces on the continent.

For me, it is about efficiency and control. The term "strategic autonomy," defined according to the relevant area, seems more appropriate to me to express the intended content and objectives, whether in the field of economics or security.

We should add the element of "solidarity" to this concept, the expression of living together within a community: we help those who find themselves in a difficult situation. In this sense, solidarity is not mandated; it develops, it is practiced, and it presupposes increasing mutual trust.

In this sense, "sovereignty and solidarity" are the two fundamental elements that address different situations or spheres of life within a community in which individuals are much more dependent on each other than they perceive. And these elements are complementary.

European integration has, from the very beginning, been an expression of growing solidarity among states. One of the strongest signals of this was the creation of the European Structural Funds.

For this reason, my first thought at the start of the Covid crisis and the urgent need for higher defense spending was to expand the Structural Funds by creating two new funds: one for defense and one for post-Covid recovery.

At the same time, a reform of these funds was necessary to allow for more flexible application. In addition, a certain percentage of the annual investments of the European Investment Bank and comparable national institutions should be earmarked for defense, for climate change, including energy, and for future technologies, as these are the main topics of a necessary profound transformation of key policies.

These approaches and methods are certainly less revolutionary than the Franco-German initiative of May 18, 2020, but they are less complex to manage—they could, together with private investments, form a substantial part of the necessary additional funding.

All the reservations or obstacles, misunderstandings or divergences—arising from our very different traditions and political systems—should not prevent us from engaging in a profound debate on the crucial strengthening of the EU's capacity to act, efficiency, and "strategic autonomy," so that our political, economic, and social model can survive and play a genuine role on the world stage.

In the past two decades, we have sought solutions and reconciliations between our nations, particularly through compromises and pragmatic approaches that often sidestepped the questions at the heart of our divergences. Moreover, observers of the European scene have sometimes had the impression that things simply cannot be straightforward; they must be complicated!

Today, due to internal and international constraints and developments, we find ourselves in a phase of European construction in which the survival of our European political, economic, and social model depends on a clearer definition of our compass and our goals—and on openly stating what we want to achieve together at the European level.

References

HR/VP Blog (2020, 3. Dezember). https://www.eeas.europa.eu/eeas/why-european-strategic-autonomy-matters_en

Bericht an den Europäischen Rat, (2024, April). Enrico Letta. *„Much more than a market"*.

Politico Opinion (2020, 6. November): Annegret Kramp-Karrenbauer. „Europe still needs America".

Le Grand Continent (2020, 16. November). https://legrandcontinent.eu/de/2020/11/16/die-macron-doktrin-ein-gespraech-mit-dem-franzoesischen-staatspraesidenten/

Bundesministerium der Verteidigung (2020, 17. November). https://www.bmvg.de/resource/blob/4483202/a62307ebef4572c1cffa40eb91093417/20201117-dl-grundsatzrede-unibwhh-data.pdf

The Economist (2019, 7. November). https://www.economist.com/europe/2019/11/07/emmanuel-macron-warns-europe-nato-is-becoming-brain-dead

Bundesregierung (1996, 9. Dezember). https://www.bundesregierung.de/breg-de/service/newsletter-und-abos/bulletin/gemeinsames-deutsch-franzoesisches-sicherheits-und-verteidigungskonzept-gebilligt-bei-der-16-sitzung-des-deutsch-franzoesischen-verteidigungs-und-sicherheitsrates-am-9-dezember-1996-in-nuernberg-804480

Bitterlich, Joachim (2021a, Stuttgart). „Grenzgänger: Deutsche Interessen und Verantwortung in und für Europa – Erinnerungen eines Zeitzeugen". Seite 135/136.

Bitterlich, Joachima (2021b, Paris). „Europe souveraine et solidaire – une conception prometteuse ?" Seiten 95–106.

Rapport Schuman sur l'Europe (2020, März). „Die Gemeinsame Aussen- und Sicherheitspolitik der EU, einschl. der Entwicklungspolitik, neu denken. Seite 123–130.

Joachim Bitterlich Ambassador (ret.), is a former advisor on European, foreign, and security policy to Chancellor Helmut Kohl and an honorary professor at ESCP Paris. Previously, he held various senior positions in the Foreign Service, with a particular focus on European integration and transatlantic relations. The lawyer and long-serving foreign policy expert is regarded as a recognized authority on German-French relations and the European security architecture.

Part VI

Euro-Atlantic Security Order, Weimar Triangle & Cyber Warfare

Generational Change in Security Policy in Germany and France

Jacob Ross and Nicolas Téterchen

1 Introduction

In the coming years, Germany and France will foreseeably have to overcome a dual challenge: First, the Russian invasion of Ukraine has finally buried the European peace order. Even after a ceasefire in Ukraine, Russia will continue to threaten European security, especially the EU and NATO partner states in Northern and Eastern Europe. In addition, the foreign and defense policy planning of the governments in Berlin and Paris is further complicated by the looming reduction or end of US security guarantees on the European continent.

Germany and France are dependent on each other, and the rest of the continent is counting on the two historic leading powers to live up to their responsibility. After three mixed years, marked by the poor personal relationship between Chancellor Scholz and President Macron, time is now running out. For decades, the political will for rapprochement and deepening of integration, including on defense issues, has been affirmed. However, several attempts have failed. This is also because the strategic orientations of the two states continue to differ fundamentally.

In the coming years, a new opportunity is emerging for two reasons: First, the urgency of the situation in Ukraine and the rest of Europe makes decisive action more likely than in the past. Second, and this is the focus of the following text, the Russian invasion of Ukraine has triggered developments that are likely to reduce the differences in the strategic cultures of Germany and France. At the same time, a new generation is moving into political decision-making positions. What unites them must be fostered, what divides them must be explained.

J. Ross (✉) · N. Téterchen
DGAP, Berlin/Paris, France

S. Weeser (ed.), *The Heart Chambers of Europe: Franco-German Impulses for the EU's Security Order*, https://doi.org/10.1007/978-3-658-51096-1_11

2 Strategic Cultures in Transition

The fundamental characteristics of national strategic cultures are not static. They vary between social groups and evolve over time. Pivotal events in national politics and international relations, both real and imagined, shape new practices in a state's strategic culture (Johnston 1995). While in peacetime, the culture of the previous generation of political decision-makers is usually continued, external shocks, crises, and wars can lead to abrupt breaks. The result is often an unconscious change in the analytical framework of the affected decision-makers. This can be understood as a challenge to the previous strategic culture by one or more competing subcultures (Johnston 1995).

The following text takes up this idea and applies it comparatively to the debates in Germany and France that have followed Russia's full-scale invasion of Ukraine in February 2022. The hypothesis of several competing strategic subcultures is transferred to Franco-German cooperation in defense policy. The argument is based on statements by selected decision-makers and is therefore necessarily anecdotal. The authors hope that this contribution will sharpen the focus on factors that have been neglected in expert circles and public discussions on Franco-German relations in recent years.

3 Turning Point and Generational Change

Franco-German cooperation is currently shaped by the interplay of two processes of change: First, a deterioration in security on the European continent. Second, a generational change that is leading to shifts in the perception of international politics. The following chapter raises the question of whether these trends are interacting, leading to a challenge to the prevailing national strategic culture, and affecting the bilateral relationship. In both Germany and France, subcultures are emerging and are gradually being carried into political leadership positions. There, they encounter resistance from the dominant strategic culture, which is represented by decision-makers from the Baby Boomer and Generation X cohorts, the current establishment.

4 Initial Situation in Europe

February 24, 2022 accelerated a development that had long been apparent and now has significant consequences for both Germany and France (Kauffmann 2023). The desire for peaceful conflict resolution, which has underpinned the European integration process since the 1950s and was only made possible by the reconciliation between Germany and France after the end of World War II, has, since the Russian invasion of Ukraine, come up against the reality of a brutal war of aggression that has been waged on European soil for several years. As an external shock, the Russian invasion of Ukraine initially hit the European states symmetrically—although the very different reactions between Lisbon and Warsaw served as a fresh reminder to European decision-makers of the enduring importance of geography.

A closer look at the initial reactions in Berlin and Paris, and with some historical distance, reveals significant differences. These can be explained by differences in the strategic cultures of the two countries. The former German Foreign Minister, Annalena Baerbock, stood in February 2022 as a representative of the archetypal reaction of political Berlin: After an urgently convened crisis meeting of the federal cabinet, she said that Germany had "woken up in a different world" (Baerbock 2022). For Baerbock, who grew up and was politically socialized in the late 1990s and early 2000s in the belief in the triumph of liberal, Western democracies, the attack was a brutal break with the certainties of her generation.

In Paris, the immediate shock over the Russian invasion was comparable to that in Germany. The French armed forces would also have been "caught off guard" by a similar attack—even if, unlike the Germans, the French military leadership would never have admitted this publicly (Mais 2022). In a televised address at midday on February 24, in which President Emmanuel Macron addressed the French public, he acknowledged the shock. However, the president added that France had foreseen the Russian attack and "together with our allies" had done everything to prevent the war. Now "it is here, we are ready." Whether Paris had actually foreseen the war is highly questionable. For the present text, however, this question is secondary. What is decisive is that French policy demonstrably considered the Russian attack possible and had factored it into its planning.

Macron, born in 1977, began increasing France's defense budget immediately after his election in 2017. He pushed to be prepared for a world once again shaped by geopolitical rivalries and wars. In the National Assembly, reports were written on the return of high-intensity combat, which were linked to the question of whether the armed forces were ready for comparable scenarios (Assemblée Nationale 2022). More importantly: After the initial shock, Russia's attack on Ukraine was quickly seen in Paris as proof that a historical era had definitively come to a close. French politicians, including those of Baerbock's generation, had understood the liberal hegemony of the 1990s as the exception—not the rule.

This crucial difference is occasionally expressed openly by French politicians, also with reference to Germany. For example, in January 2025, when the French Minister of State for European Affairs, Benjamin Haddad, born in 1985, called on European allies to read more "Kissinger and Machiavelli" again, instead of "Kant and Fukuyama" (Haddad 2025). He said "European partners"—but the main addressee was Berlin, as is easy to read between the lines.

5 Attempts at Rapprochement

Before delving deeper into why the reactions to the Russian invasion of Ukraine were so different in Germany and France, the strategic cultures of both countries must be fundamentally outlined. The focus is on the national approach to military force. In both Germany and France, there is a clearly dominant strategic culture that produces recognizable patterns of decision-making. The most important aspect of strategic culture in Germany is the self-image as a "civilian power" (Kirste and Maull 1996) and the military restraint that goes with it (Barbin and Konopka 2023). This has repeatedly manifested itself in political and public debates about Bundeswehr deployments since the end of the Cold War and can be summed up in the conviction derived from the crimes of National Socialism: "Never again war!"[1]

Despite this guiding principle, German politicians have repeatedly sent soldiers on foreign missions in recent decades. These were usually not allowed to be called wars (Maurer and Rink 2012). In fact, however, they were war missions. Without exception, they were shaped by a second central conviction of Germany's strategic culture: "Never again alone!" The desire for the most coordinated action possible with allies, which was expressed, for example, in the Afghanistan mission in the phrase "in together, out together" (Federal Foreign Office 2012), shaped the missions just as much as the emphasis on the underlying idealistic goals. The Bundeswehr's armed foreign deployments always had to correspond to these goals of German foreign policy. The exception proves the rule: In 2010, the recently deceased former Federal President Horst Köhler was forced to resign after linking the Afghanistan mission to the economic interests of the Federal Republic (Köhler 2010).

A comparable episode would be completely unthinkable in France. There, since World War II and even beyond the end of the Cold War, the priority has been set entirely differently. The core of foreign and defense policy remained the goal, also based on the historical experience of the "strange defeat" (Marc Bloch) in World War II, of being nationally sovereign and globally capable of action. For decades, France waged a "world war" (Goya 2023) in its former colonial territories, the most recent battles of which many observers saw in the Sahel interventions from 2013 onwards.[2]

The decisive point is: The German "civilian power" is and has been confronted by a French state that defines itself largely by its autonomous capacity for action and its willingness to use military force.

It is no secret that these differences make foreign and security policy cooperation more difficult. For decades, governments have sought to bring the strategic cultures of Germany and France closer together. The Elysée Treaty of 1963, for example, aimed at

---

[1] And, associated with it: Never again Auschwitz!

[2] Other significant differences in strategic culture, which derive from France's sovereign nuclear armament since 1966, are secondary for this text and are not discussed here.

doctrinal alignment of the armies, for instance through personnel exchange programs. Against the backdrop of a new US doctrine and the looming reduction of the US presence in Europe, the 1980s were marked by a second wave of Franco-German integration and institutional innovations (Gerbet 2016). Since Emmanuel Macron took office in 2017, a third phase has followed, driven by speeches and summit declarations, culminating in the Aachen Treaty in 2019, after the shock of Brexit and Donald Trump's first success. The treaty states: "The two states undertake to further strengthen cooperation between their armed forces in order to create a common culture [...] (Federal Foreign Office 2019)."

Despite numerous announcements and renewed treaty commitments, the rapprochement of the strategic cultures of Germany and France has not made significant progress since 2017. The reasons have been hotly debated in recent years. Instead of retracing these debates here, we focus on the rapprochement that is now opening up as a result of the double shock of the Russian attack on Ukraine and the foreseeable US withdrawal from Europe.

6 Changes in Germany and France

The Russian attack on Ukraine has led to a questioning of previous defense policy certainties in both France and Germany. France, whose foreign policy coordinates traditionally followed a north-south axis, from the European "metropolis" into the postcolonial space of Africa and the Levant to the French overseas territories in the Indo-Pacific, has begun to shift its focus towards Eastern Europe under Emmanuel Macron. The "pivot to Europe" entails a renewed focus on the requirements of high-intensity combat with technologically equal opponents. Above all, however, it revolves around greater integration with NATO allies. The transatlantic alliance, which Macron had described as "brain dead" as recently as 2019 (The Economist 2019), is therefore becoming an increasingly important factor, also for French planning.

President Macron made the pivot public in May 2023 at the Globsec Conference in Bratislava. He had declared NATO brain dead in 2019, but "today I could say that Vladimir Putin has woken it up with the worst of all electric shocks" (Macron 2023).[3] Macron's announcements are accompanied by the willingness of a new generation of French soldiers, diplomats, and officials who are much more open to rapprochement with NATO and integration into transatlantic strategies than their predecessors.[4] From Berlin's perspective, the French pivot to Europe is an opportunity. During the Cold War,

[3] "In December 2019, I made a harsh statement about NATO and at the time, I remember, pointed to the divisions within NATO between Turkey and several other powers, referring to it as brain dead. Today I could say that Vladimir Putin has woken it up with the worst of all electric shocks."

[4] Cf. background discussions.

the Franco-German relationship was marked by significant differences. The French Sonderweg (special path) taken by de Gaulle (thanks to sovereign nuclear armament and withdrawal from NATO's military command in 1966) distanced France from West Germany. The shift of France's defense policy axis from north-south to west-east now brings it closer to the German one, which, despite deployments in Afghanistan and the Sahel states, has actually always remained committed to the latter over the past twenty years.

The shock of the Russian attack has therefore triggered major movements in both countries. Although these point in different directions, they make a compromise more likely. For Berlin, the return to national and alliance defense and the self-image of the Bundeswehr as the backbone of conventional deterrence in Europe is a confirmation of its traditional identity, which developed from 1955 in NATO and through concepts such as forward defense. Germany's position as the leading power in Central Europe, emphasized by Chancellor Scholz in his keynote speech in Prague in August 2022, corresponds to the old self-image of West Germany and, to a limited extent, also that of reunified Germany. Germany sees itself as an advocate of a multilateral and rules-based world order, which made its return to the concert of international relations after 1945 possible in the first place. The Federal Republic is the hub between the USA, Western and Eastern Europe—logistically as well as geopolitically.

7 Different Frames of Reference and Worldviews

German millennials did not experience the original turning point of the fall of the Berlin Wall. Their predecessor generations—Baby Boomers and Generation X—were shaped in the 1990s by heated debates about German credos such as "Never again war!" and "Never again alone!"—for example, when it came to German interventions in the former Yugoslavia. The millennial generation, on the other hand, was significantly influenced by the 20-year global "war on terror." Baby Boomers and Generation X experienced the end of the Cold War and the development of a country that had been shaped by occupying powers into a sovereign republic that was urged by its allies to become more engaged. Millennials, by contrast, grew up during Angela Merkel's 16-year chancellorship, a period of remarkable stability in Europe.

This stability is part of the explanation for why German millennials seem to have difficulty finding their bearings in a world now shaped by the return of geopolitics. Their worldview is characterized by a foreign policy idealism that is often summed up in Francis Fukuyama's thesis of the "end of history." The French journalist Sylvie Kauffmann, in her book "Les Aveuglés," which analyzes German and French Russia policy, quotes the top diplomat Thomas Bagger, who observes that no other country "has interpreted Francis Fukuyama's 1989 thesis of the 'end of history' as simplistically as Germany" (Kauffmann 2023, p. 199).

The foreign policy discourse of the past three years has focused on values rather than interests. Foreign Minister Baerbock has recently tried to reconcile the two. Values and interests are "not opposites" (Baerbock 2021). However, a generational conflict has become apparent in the Foreign Office between supporters of an idealistic worldview and diplomats of previous generations who, thanks to their experience in the Cold War, have remained familiar with the categories of power politics.[5]

A similar generational change is evident in France. However, the conflict between an idealistic and a realistic worldview is articulated in a completely different way. The debates revolve around the question of what role France can still play in the world in the future. Decolonization and debates about nuclear deterrence have shaped the Baby Boomers since the 1960s. Macron's term in office so far offers several examples of generational conflicts that have arisen with younger generations: In 2017, he declared in his "Speech to African Youth" that he wanted to break definitively with the legacy of Françafrique (Macron 2017a). The failure of the reboot of Franco-African relations since then shows how strong the forces of resistance and conservatism remain in French politics and administration. Millennial decision-makers also face the task of adapting their armed forces, which are accustomed to counterinsurgency and counterterrorism, in the coming years so that they can meet France's leadership ambitions in national and alliance defense in Europe (Burkhard 2023).

8 Current Generation-Specific Dynamics

A second trend is emerging alongside the changing framework of international politics, affecting the politicians of both countries: the increasing rise of millennials to positions of power in foreign and defense policy in Germany and France. The generational change brings with it, in addition to national conflicts, the risk of growing misunderstanding between the two countries. Maurice Gourdault-Montagne, former French ambassador to Berlin, illustrates this with an anecdote from 2019: After Annegret Kramp-Karrenbauer, then Minister of Defense and CDU chairwoman, had proposed "Europeanizing" France's seat on the UN Security Council, he, as Secretary General of the French Foreign Ministry, officially conveyed the government's incomprehension to the German ambassador. Gourdault-Montagne fears that the turning point will further alienate Germany from France. Berlin is acting unilaterally and risks once again taking a historical Sonderweg (special path).

[5] Dispute over the removal of the Bismarck portrait as an anecdotal example, background discussions with German diplomats.

9 National Trends (Germany)

The German think tanker Dr. Ulrike Franke wrote a widely discussed essay in 2021: In her "Reflections of a Millennial on the 'New German Problem' after 30 Years of Peace" (Franke 2021), she pointed out that the unprecedented stability of German domestic politics had shaped the outlook of German millennials with an almost blind faith in the conflict-avoiding effect of economic interdependence. Her generation, Franke argues, finds it difficult to take a realistic view of world politics. Strategic thinking is "not easy for younger German foreign policy decision-makers. It is alien to them" (Franke 2021). Other experts in German defense policy have agreed with Franke's observations for years, such as political science professor Carlo Masala, who notes that "German foreign policy [...] is shaped by idealism" (Hufnagel 2022).

Many observers consider this idealistic orientation to be a challenge in light of the turning point brought about by Russia's war of aggression against Ukraine. Professor Roland Czada, another German political scientist, advocates a turn in German foreign and security policy towards more "realism." Putin's assault on Ukraine, he argues, has confirmed the assumptions of the "realist school of foreign policy," while at the same time refuting the assumptions "of the 'idealistic' school of normative institutionalism, which dominates in Germany," associated with the "ideal of a values-based international legal order" (Czada 2022, p. 16). Nowhere is this struggle more evident than in Baerbock's party: The German Greens, with their roots in the peace movement, have recently often been the loudest in calling for expanded arms deliveries to Ukraine, leading to significant conflicts within the party (Wiedemeyer 2024).

In fact, Germany's "idealistic turn" was increasingly questioned during the federal election campaign. Friedrich Merz, born in 1955, caused a stir at the end of January with his speech on Germany's foreign policy priorities, which he delivered at the invitation of the Körber Foundation in Berlin (Körber-Stiftung 2025). The CDU chancellor candidate repeatedly called for a more realistic German view of the world and announced that, in the event of an election victory, he would once again place interests at the center of German foreign, defense, and development policy.

The foreign deployments of recent years have also led to controversial debates within the German armed forces about the role of values in German defense policy. Many soldiers of the so-called "deployment generation"[6] expressed the feeling that the ideals on which the armed forces as an institution and the soldiers as individuals had largely based their identity since the founding of the Bundeswehr had been put to the test in the fighting in Afghanistan. Marcel Bohnert, a lieutenant colonel in the Bundeswehr, notes in his reflections on the principle of Innere Führung (leadership development and civic education) about his first encounter with battle-hardened soldiers in Afghanistan in 2010: "I

[6] That is, above all, those soldiers who, in Afghanistan, for the first time since 1945, were involved in heavy combat and had to mourn wounded and dead comrades.

had the feeling that they really had nothing to do with the model of the citizen in uniform that Innere Führung prescribes" (Bohnert 2017). Dr. Thomas Wanninger, reserve lieutenant colonel, writes in his critique of Innere Führung in 2023: "Above all, younger officers from the deployment generation have been fundamentally questioning Innere Führung for years. They say an army must above all function in combat" (Wanninger 2023).

The critical engagement with the concept of Innere Führung is rooted in the growing temporal distance of today's soldiers from the debates of the Bundeswehr's founding phase and the gap that has arisen between theoretical ideals and operational realities. In the context of multinational cooperation, German debates are also of great importance to international partners. In cooperation between the Bundeswehr and the Netherlands or France, it is repeatedly noted that the German "Innere Führung" and the concept of the "citizen in uniform" correspond to a similarly liberal attitude in relation to the Netherlands, but in dealings with French soldiers, they encounter a "strongly pronounced hierarchy" and a "patriarchal leadership style" (Klein 1997). Conflicts arising from these differences, as well as generational conflicts within national cultures, must be taken into account in view of the foreseeable intensification of bi- and multilateral cooperation in Europe.

10 National Trends (France)

French policy is currently preoccupied with the already mentioned shift in the geographical orientation of French foreign and defense policy. The traditional north-south orientation, which focused on the overseas territories and African partners with whom France maintained bilateral security agreements, for example in the fight against international terrorism, is playing an increasingly smaller role. A series of coups has forced Paris to give up most of these partnerships and bases in Francophone Africa. Dominique de Villepin, former French foreign minister, attributes the failures of French diplomacy to a "deep ignorance of the new African realities" (France Info 2023).

Given the growing threat to EU and NATO partners in Eastern Europe from Russia, the question of whether France's global leadership ambitions—in the Indo-Pacific and in Europe—are realistic is also becoming more urgent. "The French army still prefers Tahiti to Warsaw," writes journalist Jean-Dominique Merchet about the trade-offs that force the armed forces to divide resources between the European continent and the presence around its own territories in the Indo-Pacific (Merchet 2024).

However, the shift in geographical focus is not just a matter of distributional struggles between branches of the armed forces.[7] Recent deployments have shown how

[7] For obvious reasons, the French army is pushing for a concentration of resources on the European presence, while the navy in particular emphasizes the importance of global presence.

deeply the expeditionary identity of the armed forces is rooted. The Sahel missions Serval and Barkhane were seen by many soldiers as extremely fulfilling. Many of them say they regret the declining prospects for deployments in African states and find missions on their own national territory (such as Opération Sentinelle, initiated after the Charlie Hebdo attack) far less motivating. Surveys show that the "desire to see the world" (voir du pays) is among the most common reasons French soldiers cite for finding their deployments meaningful. In the past, half of those surveyed saw this as a reason for their commitment (Saintot 2009). Whether missions as part of NATO's Enhanced Forward Presence (eFP) in Romania or the Baltics are as attractive as deployments in Francophone Africa or the Levant is doubted by many experienced military personnel.[8]

The geographical reorientation of French foreign and defense policy is accompanied by a structural transformation in the armed forces: Since decolonization, the French army has focused on counterinsurgency, counterterrorism, stabilizing partner states, and training partner forces. Far from French territory, soldiers were deployed to confront threats in asymmetric conflicts. Today, in the context of the Russian attack on Ukraine, operational scenarios and requirements are shifting completely. The fact that light infantry has so far held a central position in the French army is a major challenge—also in comparison with Germany (Müller 2025).

In recent months, senior officers have publicly expressed doubts as to whether the French armed forces can cope with this transformation. Former officer Guillaume Ancel, for example, criticizes that conservatism in the army's officer training is standing in the way of the necessary modernization and a generational change. At the army officer school in Saint-Cyr, he was in the same class as the current Chief of the General Staff, Thierry Burkhard. Ancel reports that his instructors, who still had first-hand experience of Cold War maneuvers, did not pass on their knowledge. Instead, even in the 1990s, the successor units of the so-called Coloniale—the light marine infantry and the Foreign Legion—were highly regarded. The top graduates therefore chose these units, while artillery and drone defense, for example, were neglected (Ancel 2024).

11 Conclusions

In France and Germany, numerous conflicts can be observed in foreign and defense policy that pertain to strategic culture and can only be outlined here in broad strokes. These conflicts, which involve the questioning of old identities and challenge the certainties of previous generations, will be of great significance in the coming years against the backdrop of the ongoing Russian threat to European security. For the Franco-German relationship, it is crucial that corresponding changes are communicated to the partner and understood there.

[8] Background discussion.

The armed forces enjoy very high levels of trust in both France and Germany: 81% of French people state that they trust the military—only medical personnel receive higher ratings (Ministère des Armées 2024). The younger generation stands out in particular: "Antimilitarism has disappeared from the consciousness of young generations," writes sociologist Anne Murxel (2024). In Germany, the Bundeswehr also enjoys high levels of trust: 85% express a correspondingly favorable opinion in surveys, which is the second-highest value after the police (Graf 2024, p. 49). However, compared to France, the correlation with age is reversed: younger people are the age group with the least trust in the military. (Graf 2024, p. 50)

Similar trends are evident regarding the willingness to take up arms oneself. In France, the proportion of respondents willing to join the military in the event of defense decreases with age, while young people express the greatest willingness: 61% of 18- to 21-year-olds are (definitely or possibly) willing to volunteer in the event of war (Murxel 2024, p. 73). According to this survey, 51% of this group would even volunteer if a deployment in Ukraine were under discussion (Murxel 2024, p. 75). In Germany, by contrast, there has been a steady decline in the attractiveness of the Bundeswehr among young people since 2018, a drop of 20 percentage points in six years (Graf 2024, p. 64). The differences between the neighboring countries are certainly attributable to differences in national identity: young Germans tend to define themselves more by abstract democratic principles than by traditional patriotism. Jürgen Habermas coined the concept of constitutional patriotism, which would likely be put to a severe test in the case of national defense (Habermas 1998).

In both countries, the reintroduction of conscription is currently being discussed in light of the challenges in defense policy. It was suspended in France as early as 1996, and in Germany from 2011. The prospects of returning to such a system should be discussed at the Franco-German and European levels. In recent years, France has already experimented with the so-called Service National Universel (SNU), which was, however, recently discontinued (Ross and Téterchen 2024). The debates have in common that they often concern more than just defense capability. In addition to increasing societal resilience, a strengthening of social cohesion is also expected, which seems to have been waning in recent years.

Against the backdrop of US threats to reduce security guarantees in Europe, the idea of European sovereignty is experiencing a renaissance. In order to bring it to life in the coming years, a profound understanding of the partner's way of thinking and acting is essential. Particular focus must be placed on the shifts that Russia's attack on Ukraine has triggered among younger generations.

References

Ancel, Guillaum (2024). Saint Cyr, à l'école de la Grande Muette. Flammarion.

Assemblée nationale (2022). Rapport d'information, n° 5054 en conclusion des travaux d'une mission d'information sur la préparation à la haute intensité. https://www.assemblee-nationale.fr/dyn/15/rapports/cion_def/l15b5054_rapport-information Zugegriffen: 2. Juni 2025.

Auswärtiges Amt (2012). There is no military solution for Afghanistan. https://www.auswaertiges-amt.de/en/newsroom/news/120317-bm-maerkischeallgemeine-249300. Zugegriffen: 2. Juni 2025.

Auswärtiges Amt (2019). Vertrag zwischen der Bundesrepublik Deutschland und der Französischen Republik über die deutsch-französische Zusammenarbeit. https://www.auswaertiges-amt.de/resource/blob/2178596/7b304525053dde3440395ecef44548d3/190118-download-aachenervertrag-data.pdf. Zugegriffen: 3. Juni 2025.

Baerbock, A. (2021). Werte und Interessen sind kein Gegensatz. Auswärtiges Amt. https://www.auswaertiges-amt.de/de/newsroom/2502928-2502928. Zugegriffen: 11.03.2025.

Baerbock, Annalena (2022). Rede von Außenministerin Annalena Baerbock im Deutschen Bundestag zum Sondervermögen. Auswärtiges Amt. https://www.auswaertiges-amt.de/de/newsroom/sondervermoegen-2535176. Zugegriffen: 10. März 2025.

Barbin, J., & Konopka, T. (2023). Militärische Zurückhaltung oder militärisches Engagement? Entstehung und Entwicklung der strategischen Kultur der Bundesrepublik Deutschland bis 1990 im Lichte von Archivquellen. SIRIUS – Zeitschrift für Strategische Analysen, 7(4), 327–353. https://doi.org/10.1515/sirius-2023-4002.

Bohnert, Marcel (2017). Innere Führung auf dem Prüfstand: Lehren aus dem Afghanistan-Einsatz der Bundeswehr. BoD – Books on Demand.

Burkhard, T. (2023). Pour une transformation efficiente de nos armées. Ministère des Armées. https://www.defense.gouv.fr/ema/actualites/transformation-efficiente-nos-armees. Zugegriffen: 2. Juni 2025.

Czada, Roland (2022). Realismus im Aufwind? Außen- und Sicherheitspolitik in der „Zeitenwende". Leviathan, 50(2), 216–238.

France Info. (2023). Retrait des forces françaises en Afrique : pour Dominique de Villepin, la France fonctionne 'très à l'ancienne' et méconnait profondément les 'nouvelles réalités africaines'. https://www.francetvinfo.fr/monde/afrique/niger/retrait-des-forces-francaises-en-afrique-pour-dominique-de-villepin-la-france-fonctionne-tres-a-l-ancienne-et-meconnait-profondement-les-nouvelles-realites-africaines_6055772.html. Zugegriffen: 11. März 2025.

Franke, U. (2021). Betrachtungen einer Millennial über das ‚Neue Deutsche Problem' nach 30 Jahren Frieden. SIRIUS – Zeitschrift Für Strategische Analysen, 5(3), 272277.

Gerbet, P. (2016). Festigung des „deutsch-französischen Duos" (1982-1989). CVCE. https://www.cvce.eu/de/education/unit-content/-/unit/c3c5e6c5-1241-471d-9e3a-dc6e7202ca16/3dc44edece1b-4dde-851d-aa6c2426ae2f. Zugegriffen: 2. Juni 2025.

Goya, Michel (2023). La guerre mondiale de la France. De 1961 à nos jours. Texto.

Graf, Timo (2024). Zwischen Kriegsangst und Kriegstauglichkeit: Sicherheits- und verteidigungspolitisches Meinungsbild in der Bundesrepublik Deutschland 2024. Forschungsbericht 137 (Zentrum für Militärgeschichte und Sozialwissenschaften der Bundeswehr).

Habermas, Jürgen (1998). Die postnationale Konstellation: Politische Essays. Suhrkamp.

Haddad, Benjamin (2025). https://www.vie-publique.fr/discours/296910-entretien-benjamin-haddad-10012025-le-figaro-ue-etats-unis (2025).

Hufnagel, Margit (2022, 28. Februar). Sicherheitsexperte Masala: „Die deutsche Außenpolitik war von Idealismus geprägt". Augsburger Allgemeine. https://www.augsburger-allgemeine.de/politik/interview-sicherheitsexperte-masala-die-deutsche-aussenpolitik-war-von-idealismus-gepraegt-id61912176.html. Zugegriffen: 11. März 2025.

Johnston, Alastair Iain (1995). Cultural Realism: Strategic Culture and Grand Strategy in Chinese History. Princeton University Press.

Kauffmann, Sylvie (2023). Les aveuglés : Comment Berlin et Paris ont laissé la voie libre à la Russie. Stock.

Kirste, K., & Maull, H. (1996). Zivilmacht und Rollentheorie. Zeitschrift für Internationale Beziehungen, 3(2), 283–312.

Klein, Paul (1997). Das Ende der Nationalarmee? SOWI-Arbeitspapier, 101.

Köhler, Horst (2010). Köhler: Mehr Respekt für deutsche Soldaten in Afghanistan. Interview durchgeführt von Christopher Ricke. Deutschlandfunk Kultur. https://www.deutschlandfunkkultur.de/koehler-mehr-respekt-fuer-deutsche-soldaten-in-afghanistan-100.html. Zugegriffen: 2. Juni 2025.

Körber-Stiftung. (2025). Friedrich Merz zu außen- und europapolitischen Prioritäten für Deutschland. https://koerber-stiftung.de/mediathek/friedrich-merz-zu-aussen-und-europapolitischen-prioritaeten-fuer-deutschland/. Zugegriffen: 11. März 2025.

Macron, E. (2023). Sommet Globsec à Bratislava. Élysée. https://www.elysee.fr/emmanuel-macron/2023/06/01/sommet-globsec-a-bratislava. Zugegriffen: 10. März 2025.

Macron, E. (2017a). Discours d'Emmanuel Macron à l'université de Ouagadougou. Élysée. https://www.elysee.fr/emmanuel-macron/2017/11/28/discours-demmanuel-macron-a-luniversite-de-ouagadougou. Zugegriffen: 11. März 2025.

Mais, Alfons (2022). Du wachst morgens auf und stellst fest: Es herrscht Krieg in Europa. https://de.linkedin.com/posts/alfons-mais-46744b99_du-wachst-morgens-auf-und-stellst-fest-es-activity-6902486582067044353-RZky. Zugegriffen: 10. März 2025.

Maurer, J. & Rink, M. (Hg.) (2012). Einsatz ohne Krieg?: Die Bundeswehr nach 1990 zwischen politischem Auftrag und militärischer Wirklichkeit. Militärgeschichte, Sozialwissenschaften, Zeitzeugen. Brill | V&R.

Merchet, Jean-Dominique (2024). Sommes-nous prêts pour la guerre? L'illusion de la puissance française. Robert Laffont.

Ministère des Armées (2024). EcoDef Conjoncture n °248 ‚Opinion des Européens sur la défense au printemps 2024', juillet 2024. https://www.defense.gouv.fr/ssm/ecodef-conjoncture-n-deg248-opinion-europeens-defense-au-printemps-2024-juillet-2024. Zugegriffen: 11. März 2024.

Müller, Björn (2025). 1870 reloaded. Reservistenverband. https://www.reservistenverband.de/magazin-loyal/frankreich-heer/. Zugegriffen: 11. März 2025.

Muxel, Anne (2024). Les jeunes et la guerre: représentations et dispositions à l'engagement. Étude 116 (Institut de recherche stratégique de l'école militaire).

Ross, J. & Téterchen, N. (2024). Frankreichs Armee: Rückzugsort einer verunsicherten Nation. Reservistenverband. https://www.reservistenverband.de/magazin-loyal/frankreich-snu/. Zugegriffen: 11. März 2025.

Saintot, Jean (2009). Militaires français en Opex et populations locales. Les Champs de Mars, 20(1), 35–55. https://doi.org/10.3917/lcdm1.020.0035.

The Economist. (2019, 07. November). Emmanuel Macron warns Europe: NATO is becoming brain-dead. https://www.economist.com/europe/2019/11/07/emmanuel-macron-warns-europe-nato-is-becoming-brain-dead. Zugegriffen: 11. März 2025.

Wanninger, Thomas (2023). Kritik der Inneren Führung: Eine Konzeption der Wehrhaftigkeit in der Demokratie. Miles-Verlag.

Wiedemeyer, Patricia (2024). Die Grünen für den Frieden? Wie sich die Partei wandelt. ZDFheute. https://www.zdf.de/nachrichten/politik/deutschland/gruene-waffen-ruestung-partei-wandel-krieg-100.html. Zugegriffen: 11. März 2025.

Jacob Ross is a Research Fellow at the German Council on Foreign Relations (DGAP), Berlin, focusing on French foreign and security policy as well as Franco-German relations. Previously, he worked at the NATO Parliamentary Assembly in Brussels, the French National Assembly, and the French Ministry of Foreign Affairs.

Nicolas Téterchen is a research assistant in the France Program at DGAP and is pursuing a doctorate on German strategic culture at CY Cergy Paris University. Previously, he worked at the Franco-German Chamber of Commerce and Industry in Paris.

His particular interest lies in Franco-German defense cooperation as a key to a more sovereign Europe.

A "Nuclear Aachen"? The Time is Now

Eckhard Lübkemeier

> *"A true community of destiny cannot exclude nuclear capabilities. A 'nuclear Aachen' would only be logical. To this end, both sides should make it clear that the Force de frappe is also among the military means with which they would support each other."*

Germany is not a nuclear power and should not become one. Legal obligations under the Two Plus Four Treaty and the Nuclear Non-Proliferation Treaty would ultimately not stand in the way of this. For they were entered into under the premise that others would protect us. Since Germany cannot be secure without nuclear protection, it would have to reconsider its renunciation of nuclear weapons should its allies no longer be willing to provide this protection. This would be in line with the Two Plus Four Treaty, in which the four former occupying powers transferred full internal and external sovereignty to united Germany.

But it should not come to that. A revocation of Germany's renunciation of nuclear weapons could trigger a proliferation cascade: states in Europe and Asia might seek salvation in national nuclear armament if, like Germany, they could no longer rely on their American protector. Such an increase in nuclear powers could intensify or activate global and regional rivalries. But even if it did not come to that: whether and how a nuclear-armed Germany would be compatible with European integration would remain an open question.

For 75 years, the United States has provided nuclear protection for Germany—initially for its western part, and since reunification for all of Germany. Our country has not only survived, but thrived as a result. However, it should no longer rely on this secu-

E. Lübkemeier (✉)
SWP, Berlin, Germany

S. Weeser (ed.), *The Heart Chambers of Europe: Franco-German Impulses for the EU's Security Order*, https://doi.org/10.1007/978-3-658-51096-1_12

rity being available in the future at all, or at bearable cost. At least not as the sole safeguard.

Germany needs nuclear reinsurance, for which only France is a candidate. European nuclear forces that could be controlled and deployed by a collective body or in rotation among member states are not to be expected. For that, the European Union of nation-states would have to become an entity with a federal-like constitution. Perhaps that will happen, but it would require a shared European identity that is at least no longer subordinate to national identities. This is (still) a chimera. The United Kingdom is the second European nuclear power. But Germany's interconnection and ties with the UK, not just since Brexit, are far less than those with France.

Nuclear reinsurance by France presupposes that there are national interests on both sides that are so vital that any government would find it hard to ignore them. Albert Einstein is said to have remarked that the difference between genius and stupidity is that genius has its limits. History confirms that nationalistically understood interests can lead to folly. But it also shows that one can learn from it. The German-French reconciliation and its linkage with the European integration process stand as proof of this.

To take these achievements for granted is to put them at risk. That could also happen to Germany and France. Much is at stake: Germany and France are not everything, but without them, Europe cannot function. Ensuring a "sovereign and strong European Union" (Federal Foreign Office 2019)—the mandate set in their "Treaty of Aachen" of January 22, 2019—has not yet been fulfilled. Debating who is to blame is a futile question. Clearly, there has been a lack of will and understanding on both sides.

And this despite the fact that there has been no shortage of circumstances and developments demanding German-French cooperation in and for Europe. The times are rough: Russia is showing itself to be a willing aggressor at a time when Western cohesion is under strain—on the one hand by a polarized and protectionist America whose strategic priority must be the containment of China, on the European side by years of free-riding on defense and declining competitiveness. Democracy and the rule of law are under pressure on both sides of the Atlantic, also because globalization has left too many behind. There has been no decisive success in limiting global warming, nor in reducing the number of migrants fleeing war and hardship. Instead of a rules-based order, rivalries and willingness to use force prevail, while the will to cooperate and compromise has diminished.

If the EU did not already exist in this environment, the core national interests of Germany and France would demand its creation. For the most important currency for asserting oneself in the international arena is power. Those who have more of it and use it more skillfully have a better chance of shaping their environment according to their interests and values. In this sense: power makes one (more) sovereign. Taken alone, Germany and France are larger middle powers; they only become global heavyweights when they and their neighbors act as a European collective power. Ergo: Europe makes one (more) sovereign.

However, only those who can defend themselves are fully sovereign. The United States can do so; Europe, on the other hand, depends on American protection. The Russian attack on Ukraine is strong evidence: Europe alone could not have enabled Ukraine to defend itself. Yet Europe has the financial, personnel, and technological resources to defend itself. What is lacking is the political will to take its fate into its own hands in this area as well.

1 Berlin and Paris Must Lead by Example

Perhaps Europe will never achieve self-defense. But one thing is certain: if Germany and France do not lead by example, it will never happen. In the partially supranationalized EU, no one can exercise hegemony, not even a German-French duo. Leadership must not only be practiced but also accepted. A German-French leadership for a European self-defense union requires Berlin and Paris to convince their EU partners.

There are three starting points for this. First, NATO: the goal is not to replace it, but to strengthen it with a European pillar that, like the USA, could defend itself and relieve the USA. The second is Europe: Berlin and Paris would have to prove themselves as reliable and willing partners for a "united, efficient, sovereign, and strong European Union" (Treaty of Aachen). The third starting point is the bilateral relationship. Leading by example means that Germany and France deepen their bilateral integration and cooperation. The benchmark for this is set in the Treaty of Aachen, in which they commit to "act jointly whenever possible" in foreign and European policy, to create a "German-French economic area with common rules," and to establish "a common area of freedom and opportunity as well as a common cultural and media area" (Federal Foreign Office 2019).

Accordingly, closer defense policy cooperation should be embedded in a NATO, EU, and bilateral framework. The intertwining of German-French security could go so far that the Force de frappe becomes nuclear reinsurance for Germany. This, too, is envisaged in the Treaty of Aachen. In Article 4, Germany and France declare themselves "convinced that their security interests are inseparably linked" and state: "They shall provide each other with all assistance and support within their power in the event of an armed attack on their territories; this includes military means" (Federal Foreign Office 2019). All that would be needed to make this mutual assistance obligation explicitly a French nuclear security guarantee for Germany would be to specify that France's nuclear capabilities are included among the military means.

But that alone would not suffice. A nuclear security guarantee involves three parties: the provider, the recipient, and the potential aggressor whom it is meant to deter. For it to be effective, it must be credible: the recipient must trust it, and the aggressor must not be able to rule out that the provider will fulfill its promise.

This triangular relationship of provider-recipient-aggressor is where extended (nuclear) deterrence takes place. In NATO (Strategic Concept 2022), it has been and continues to be provided by the United States: "The strategic nuclear forces of the Alliance, particularly those of the United States, are the supreme guarantee of the security of the

Alliance." (Federal Foreign Office 2022). The fact that it is called *extended* deterrence marks the distinction from original deterrence.

Extended deterrence is intended to protect allies; original deterrence is reserved for self-protection, that is, the American nation. This implies a hierarchy: the survival of one's own country must take precedence for any US president over the fate of others. Therefore, it is misleading to speak of a nuclear guarantee by the United States for its NATO allies: Hawaii, which is about as far from the American mainland as Europe is from the US East Coast, is part of the "United States of America" and under original deterrence. Since this takes precedence over extended deterrence, the United States cannot offer its NATO partners a nuclear *guarantee*.

This is the background to the recurring debates about whether and how credible a security commitment can be for friend and foe if its fulfillment could endanger the survival of the American nation. Nevertheless, extended deterrence has worked. NATO history suggests there are two reasons for this. First, the risk calculation of the potential aggressor: as long as the Soviet Union and then Russia could not rule out that the United States would stand by its nuclear promise, any attack on an American ally carried the risk of escalation to their own destruction.

The second factor is the strategic value the United States attaches to a Europe allied with it. This value includes Europe's importance for America's global power status vis-à-vis China and Russia, its role as an economic and (world) political partner, systemic affinity through democracy, as well as centuries-old ties through history and human relationships. This strategic value, together with the risk calculation it influences for the party to be deterred, forms the foundation of the effectiveness of extended deterrence.

2 Force De Frappe for Germany

It would be no different in the case of France. Bringing Germany under the umbrella of the Force de frappe would have to be a core national interest of both countries. So far, it has not been. Not on the German side, because only the United States was able and willing to provide the indispensable protection for Germany and Europe, not only through its nuclear but also its enormous conventional military capabilities.

Added to this was the raison d'être of the Force de frappe. France has nuclear weapons to underscore its international claim to power and status as a permanent member of the UN Security Council. But above all, it has them because it does not want to depend on a nuclear security guarantee from the United States. Consequently, the Force de frappe is considered a guarantor of national sovereignty and security. French presidents have repeatedly stated that France's vital interests extend beyond French territory, and NATO communiqués routinely include this formula: "The independent strategic nuclear forces of the United Kingdom and France play a distinct deterrent role and make a significant contribution to the overall security of the Alliance" (Federal Academy for Security Policy [BAKS] 2021).

However, unlike Washington, neither London nor Paris has ever explicitly extended the protective effect of their nuclear weapons to allies. This would have raised two questions. First, whether they could do so at all, since they possess nuclear weapons precisely because they distrust the reliable protective effect of nuclear security guarantees. Second, it would have provoked the question of whether the American security guarantee might not be as reliable as claimed. All parties involved—the USA and its NATO allies, including the nuclear powers France and the UK—had no interest in undermining the credibility of extended deterrence by the USA.

That is no longer the case. As early as 1963, just 14 years after NATO was founded, a study by three research institutes from France, the UK, and the Federal Republic of Germany stated: "But the day may come when it is no longer seriously believed that an American president would threaten the destruction of his own cities to protect some distant outpost; and then a Western Europe that still relied for its existential protection on the strategic backing of the United States could find itself in grave danger—unless by then it had developed its own large nuclear arsenal or more effective means of local defense" (Buchan and Windsor 1963, p. 8).

Perhaps that day will never come. But the possibility that it could come not at some distant point, but soon, can no longer be dismissed as a Cassandra call. For the security of Germany and its European partners is now under pressure both from within and from without.

On the one hand, in the internal relationship between the USA and its European NATO allies: the reliability of the American security commitment is crumbling, and the costs and risks of Europe's dependence on American protection are rising. If NATO did not already exist: would Washington today enter into an alliance that, as a nuclear leading and protecting power, would expose the USA to existential risk?

The question is hypothetical, but no longer far-fetched. To justify it by pointing to the re-elected President Trump is not wrong, but it falls short. The good news is: Europe retains its strategic value for the USA even under a President Trump. The worrying news has two facets. The current one is that Trump may not ignore this value, but will sharply increase the price for continued US protection by demanding that Europeans massively rearm and buy US arms, impose tariffs, and require participation in the containment of China. But even if Europe were to accept this because it cannot defend itself: even then, there would be no guarantee that an erratic President Trump would honor the NATO treaty's security commitment.

3 America's Strategic Reorientation

Trump will be history in 2028. But probably not Trumpism, and certainly not the strategic reorientation of the USA. US politics remains highly polarized, demographic change with a growing share of the population without European roots will continue. Even if

Europe retains global strategic value: the strategic priority of the USA under any president will be the relationship with China and its containment.

This structural aspect of the transatlantic relationship is all the more worrying because the external threat has increased. Even after the end of the war in Ukraine or the Putin regime—regaining trust in Russia to organize common security with Moscow will, if possible at all, take a long time. Germany and Europe must prepare for the containment of a Russia whose claim to world power status is based largely on its military and nuclear potential.

Europe would therefore do well to be able to defend itself. Especially since only then can it be fully sovereign: "Ensuring external security, being able to defend oneself, is the prerequisite and innermost core of any state's sovereignty" (Schäuble and Lamers 1994). This is not possible without nuclear backing, and it cannot be achieved through original deterrence: as long as Europe remains a union of nation-states, there will be no collective control over nuclear weapons or their delegation to rotating member states.

What remains is extended deterrence by France and the UK. At first glance, this conclusion leads to a dead end. Extended deterrence cannot offer a nuclear guarantee; original deterrence's priority of self-protection stands in the way of that. So how can European nuclear powers provide a substitute for the US security commitment?

The key to the answer lies in what makes extended deterrence effective: the strategic value the protected party has for the protector. Within Europe, that is, in the relationship between France and the UK as protectors and their continental partners as protected, this value is much greater than it can be in the transatlantic relationship. It starts with geography: unlike France and the UK, the USA has no European neighbors. The Atlantic Ocean does not make the USA invulnerable, but it does make it far less susceptible to wars in Europe—at least as long as they remain below the threshold of strategic nuclear weapon use.

The second reason is the intra-European interdependence of peace and security, prosperity, and global self-assertion. No European nation-state can realize these core national interests on its own—except at a prohibitive price. This also applies to London after Brexit, but even more so to Paris, whose EU integration with its European neighbors extends to the monetary union.

A third factor comes into play. Europe's economic and political integration, the creation of a European peace community in which war has become unthinkable—these achievements were not made possible solely by converging national interests. They indicate that, alongside national identities, there is a "Europeanness": the bond of a shared space of history, culture, and values. Not only in a positive sense, but also shaped by wars and enmities whose devastation compels coexistence.

Taken together, these three factors (geography, interests, connectedness) favor European self-defense with national nuclear means. They do not eliminate the difference between original and extended deterrence: even for a French president, national interests come first. But the fate of the French nation is more closely linked to that of its European neighbors than is the case between the USA and its European allies. This increases the willingness to fulfill a nuclear security commitment.

4 Intertwined Security

This applies especially to the German-French relationship. If Germany is not secure, neither can France be; France benefits from German economic strength and purchasing power as well as from being part of a monetary union in which Germany is a key pillar.

As obvious as this is, it is not necessarily compelling. At least not for the *Rassemblement National* under the leadership of Marine Le Pen. The party insists, in contrast to President Macron, that the Force de frappe serves exclusively to protect France. It may well do so if it wins the presidential elections in 2027. But it could also be difficult for it to ignore the interests of its own country. The flip side of the benefits both Germany and France derive from a harmonious and profitable partnership is the considerable harm that could befall France from a rift with economically and technologically superior Germany. Even the stability of the monetary union could be at risk, and if France were to deny its eastern neighbor nuclear protection when the USA became unreliable as a protector, Germany could reconsider its renunciation of nuclear weapons.

It is up to today's political leaders in Berlin and Paris to prevent it from coming to that. In a world in turbulent conflict, where power matters, only European collective power provides a degree of self-assertion that no European state could achieve on its own. Germany and France are European heavyweights, but they can only create this collective power in concert with other member states and EU institutions such as the Commission and Parliament.

To achieve this, Germany and France must pull together and lead by example. The challenge is to keep both in balance: to further develop bilateral cooperation without appearing as a duo with hegemonic ambitions. Those who lead cannot always please everyone. But Berlin and Paris can rightly claim that Europe can only thrive with a German-French axis.

Accordingly, the first two articles of the Treaty of Aachen are devoted to cooperation in "European affairs." The mutual assistance obligation "in the event of an armed attack" (Federal Foreign Office 2019), enshrined in Article 4, underlines this: if Germany and France see themselves as a community of destiny, it is easier for them to find common ground in European policy as well.

A true community of destiny cannot exclude nuclear capabilities. A "nuclear Aachen" would be only logical. To this end, both sides should clarify that the Force de frappe is also among the military means with which they would assist each other. They could underpin such an assurance with concrete steps such as a nuclear consultative group within the framework of the German-French Defense and Security Council, German liaison officers with the French nuclear forces, and the temporary or permanent stationing of French nuclear weapons and their delivery systems on German soil.

In this way, France could provide its western neighbor and closest partner with nuclear reinsurance: as the nucleus of a European self-defense union, as part of a European NATO pillar, and structured so that operational control remains with the French president and Germany remains a non-nuclear-weapon state. For "could" to become "would," it will require political leadership in Berlin and Paris that advocates for and promotes this among their populations. The time is now.

5 Epilogue

Some readers may think after reading: "All well and good, but why should what is desirable become reality this time?" The pessimism is justified. I have been asking myself for years what it will actually take for upheavals such as autocratization and polarization, which are accompanied by increasing willingness to use force up to and including Russia's invasion of Ukraine, together with ruptures such as transatlantic alienation, to lead to a European awakening. Donald Trump did not stage a coup to become president; this time he even received the most votes nationwide. He by no means represents all of America, but he is not an accident either. If NATO did not exist, with him it would either not exist at all or only as an offer that we Europeans could not refuse, but really should. For us to afford that without jeopardizing our security, Europe must finally begin to stand on its own feet in defense policy as well. That will only happen if Berlin and Paris want it and drive it forward together with willing partners. Anyone looking for a litmus test for the foreign, security, and European policy of the new federal government under Chancellor Merz—Voilà, here it is.

References

Auswärtiges Amt. (2019, 22. Januar). *Vertrag zwischen der Bundesrepublik Deutschland und der Französischen Republik über die deutsch-französische Zusammenarbeit und Integration* (Aachener Vertrag). https://www.auswaertiges-amt.de/resource/blob/2178596/7b304525053dde3440395ecef44548d3/190118-download-aachenervertrag-data.pdf 30.05.2025.

Auswärtiges Amt. (2022, 29. Juni). *Strategisches Konzept der NATO 2022*. Deutsche Vertretung bei der NATO. https://nato.diplo.de/nato-de/01-natostatements/2539668-2539668 30.05.2025.

Buchan, A., & Windsor, P. (1963). *Arms and stability in Europe: A British-French-German enquiry*. A Report by Alastair Buchan and Philip Windsor. The Institute for Strategic Studies. London.

Bundesakademie für Sicherheitspolitik (BAKS). (2021). *Deutschland und die nukleare Teilhabe der NATO* (Arbeitspapier Sicherheitspolitik Nr. 7/2021). https://www.baks.bund.de/sites/baks010/files/arbeitspapier_sicherheitspolitik_2021_7.pdf 30.05.2025

Schäuble, W., Lamers, K. (1994, 1. September), *Europa einen neuen Impuls geben*, https://www.bundesstiftung-helmut-kohl.de/aktuelles/schlaglichter/detail/vor-30-jahren-europa-einen-neuen-impuls-geben-das-schaeuble-lamers-papier (2025).

Dr. Eckhard Lübkemeier Ambassador (ret.), is a visiting scholar at the German Institute for International and Security Affairs (SWP) in Berlin. He has served, among other roles, as ambassador to Ireland and the United Arab Emirates, as well as for many years in senior positions at the Federal Foreign Office and the Federal Chancellery. He holds a doctorate on "Extended Nuclear Deterrence" and has published numerous studies and opinion pieces (including in FAZ and SZ) on issues of European integration and security, transatlantic relations, and Germany's role.

Navigating the Storm: Europe in the Age of Global Uncertainty

Christian Badia

> *"The era of lasting security is over, and a new reality full of challenges and uncertainties is dawning. Geopolitical tensions, rapid technological change, social upheavals, and the withdrawal of traditional partners confront Europe with immense tasks. European resilience and stability can only be strengthened through increased cooperation, innovative capacity, and adaptability among the member states."*

1 Challenges for NATO, Europe, and the European Union

We live in a world characterized by unprecedented complexity, interconnectedness, and dynamism. Rapid technological developments, profound geopolitical changes, the erosion of the rules-based international order, and novel challenges—especially in cyberspace and outer space—mark the dawn of a new era. This epoch threatens to be dominated by instability and an omnipresent risk of conflict, spanning the entire spectrum from terrorism and organized crime to interstate confrontations between nuclear powers. Borders are losing their significance. Attacks in the cyber and space domains are already part of daily reality. Mechanisms of influence such as propaganda and disinformation, amplified by technologies like artificial intelligence, have led to a battle for interpretive authority and thus for our convictions. A fundamental change from earlier times is that we no longer face just one or another threat, conflict, or crisis, but all of them simultaneously in an unprecedented concurrence. Lack of communication and the

C. Badia (✉)
Five Star Strategy and Defence GmbH, Siegburg, Germany

S. Weeser (ed.), *The Heart Chambers of Europe: Franco-German Impulses for the EU's Security Order*, https://doi.org/10.1007/978-3-658-51096-1_13

silence of "red phones" create a climate of uncertainty and foster misunderstandings. The resulting misjudgments could have devastating consequences.

For Europe, this means a profound transformation. The era of lasting security is over, and a new reality full of challenges and uncertainties is emerging. Geopolitical tensions, rapid technological change, societal upheavals, and the withdrawal of traditional partners present Europe with immense tasks. European resilience and stability can only be strengthened through enhanced cooperation, innovative capacity, and adaptability among the member states.

In addition to global challenges and the need for European unity, Europe must also adjust to a changed role of the USA. It is becoming apparent that the reliability of the United States of America for European security and defense must be questioned. Whether security guarantees and agreements still count is becoming increasingly uncertain. The strategic reorientation of the USA toward the Indo-Pacific was, however, already initiated under President Obama (Manyin et al. 2012 Summary). The strategic goal of forming a necessary counterweight to the strategic challenger China is therefore neither new nor surprising. The associated withdrawal of troops and capabilities from Europe, especially those that are difficult to redeploy, is understandable. The previous US doctrine of being able to operate simultaneously in two theaters of war is no longer tenable in the face of a potential peer conflict. In this context, President Trump's demands for a significantly greater European commitment to the security of its own continent are also neither surprising nor new. At most, these demands served as a wake-up call during his first term from 2017–2021. The question that must be asked is whether the wake-up call was heeded at the time and appropriate measures were initiated, or whether in 2021 the "snooze" button was pressed instead. Recent events, news, and statements from the White House clearly highlight the urgent need for action. The common value foundation of Europe and the USA has been deeply shaken. Ukraine, a European state at war with an overwhelming aggressor, is being abandoned, and the necessity of a European alternative to the US nuclear umbrella is being publicly discussed.

Russia's brutal war of aggression against Ukraine has now entered its fourth year, with no end in sight. The current negotiations between Russia and the USA offer little chance of a sustainable agreement between the parties to the conflict. Particularly problematic is that Ukraine has so far been excluded from these talks. This increases the risk of a dictated peace, which at least one side will find difficult to accept and thus does not represent a lasting solution. There therefore remains an urgent need to provide comprehensive support to Ukraine. At the same time, European states must intensify their efforts to rearm. Russia has already fully converted its economy to a war footing and, at least for now, appears able to maintain it successfully. Meanwhile, European states face challenges such as the need to rebuild their military capabilities, limited resources, and bureaucratic hurdles.

For Europe and NATO, it must be clear that Russia will remain a serious threat for the foreseeable future. However, due to its technological disadvantages compared to the West, Russia will continue to focus on actions below the threshold of open armed conflict. This means that Russia will increasingly rely on attacks in the cyber and information domains, operations in space, electronic warfare measures, and covert special operations. Disruption of critical infrastructure, such as undersea cables and energy infrastructure, will increase.

In addition to Russia, the growing cooperation among autocratic states also poses a challenge to European security. The new axis of autocrats, consisting of Russia, China, North Korea, and Iran, supports each other in their struggle against the West and the rules-based international order through interest-driven collaboration. This cooperation spans various areas: from trade and diplomacy to joint military exercises, technology transfer, and proliferation in sensitive fields such as aerospace, cyber, and electronic warfare.

A normalization of relations with Russia is therefore unthinkable in the near future. China, as a strategic rival, will continue to distance itself from the West, and the future of the values-based partnership with the USA is uncertain. Europe must therefore reposition itself in all areas: from the economy and energy to innovation and defense.

The following article addresses the question of how, in particular, the European pillar of NATO, but also NATO as a whole, must respond to the changed security environment, how the EU-NATO partnership should develop, and what role the Franco-German partnership plays in this. In particular, it examines the tasks facing Germany as a European leading nation.

2 NATO in Transition

At the NATO summit in Washington, D.C. in summer 2024, the 32 NATO member states reaffirmed the following three core tasks of the alliance (NATO 2024):

- Deterrence and defense
- Crisis prevention and management
- Cooperative security through partnership

The heads of state and government of the NATO member states also decided on a comprehensive security approach, the need for a capable defense industry, and the strengthening of whole-of-government resilience. The 35 partner nations of NATO were identified as an essential component of credible deterrence and defense. These commitments remain fully valid and underscore the importance of NATO as a key pillar of European security, even in light of potential changes in transatlantic relations.

Over the past three decades, troop numbers and capabilities in Europe, especially after the end of the Cold War, have declined significantly and no longer correspond to the current security situation. Although the European part of NATO, with 2 million soldiers and defense spending of 476 billion USD, is clearly superior to Russia with 1.3 million soldiers and 129 billion USD, historical examples show that numbers alone do not guarantee deterrence (Luzin 2025; NATO 2024; Statista 2024, 2025). The question, therefore, is how credible deterrence can be achieved. According to deterrence theory, peace and stability are ensured when a potential aggressor is convinced that the costs and risks of an attack outweigh any possible gains. This conviction arises from four factors: credible and ready military capabilities, the determination to use these capabilities, clear communication of this determination, and consistency.

For NATO, this means that the alliance must be able to achieve credible effects in all five domains—land, air, sea, cyberspace, and space. To achieve this credible effect, not only defensive but explicitly offensive capabilities are of crucial importance. As in earlier times, when defense was conducted not only with the shield but also with the spear, the ability to attack is an integral part of credible deterrence. Only the ability to penetrate deep into enemy territory and inflict significant costs on the adversary creates the necessary dilemma that deters a potential attacker from launching an assault.

A key aspect of effective deterrence is to signal unambiguously to the adversary that one is capable of repelling potential attacks and effectively limiting and managing the resulting damage. This requires not only strong military capabilities but, above all, a high level of whole-of-government resilience. This encompasses a holistic approach that, in addition to military capabilities, includes the protection of critical infrastructure, cybersecurity, economic stability, social cohesion, and active measures to detect and neutralize disinformation campaigns. Only by strengthening resilience in all areas can a state credibly convey that it can withstand crises and attacks and maintain its functionality.

NATO defense planning is based on political guidelines and geographic defense plans to derive requirements for capabilities and force structures for credible deterrence and effective defense. These requirements are detailed in "Minimum Capability Requirements" (MCR) and handed over to member states as concrete capability targets. The current planning cycle reveals a significant increase in capability needs compared to the previous cycle four years ago. In addition, there is a need to address a historic deficit resulting from years of underfunding in the member states. This cumulative additional requirement, the so-called "double delta," poses an enormous challenge and requires substantial additional investments in financial resources, personnel, and industrial production. To master this mammoth task and provide the necessary capabilities on time, innovative approaches, the use of new technologies, and close integration with the security and defense industry are required. NATO must significantly increase its responsiveness and adaptability. Speed in identifying technological advantages through new technologies, their rapid introduction, and effective application are decisive for victory or defeat. New technologies should not be overhyped as "gamechangers." However, in combination with ubiquitous networking and the exponentially growing flood of information, they are fundamentally and sustainably changing the character of warfare. To use these new technologies effectively, close cooperation between ministries, procurement organizations, and the security and defense industry is necessary. The current lack of coordination means that industry avoids risk and does not invest in the necessary capacity expansion (Bressa et al. 2024, p. 4). Long-term investments are essential to be able to respond flexibly to challenges and adjust capacities as needed.

An adequate response to today's challenges requires an integrated approach more than ever, synchronizing all instruments of state action—diplomatic, political, economic, financial, and military. At the same time, a networked view of all military dimensions and domains is necessary to fully understand threats and make decisions more quickly. The importance of such a whole-of-government approach is greater today than ever before. NATO is addressing this insight with the concept of Multi-Domain Operations (MDO):

> "Multi-Domain Operation means the orchestration of military activities across all military domains and the simultaneous synchronization with non-military activities to enable the alliance to achieve the necessary effects at the right time and in the right place" (NATO ACT 2025).

Digital transformation, the availability of new technologies, and a corresponding mindset at the decision-making level are fundamental prerequisites for the effective implementation of MDO. Without MDO, it will not be possible in the future to achieve information and decision dominance, which would be tantamount to losing engagement and escalation dominance. To remain the most successful military alliance of the modern era, this scenario must be prevented at all costs.

3 The European NATO Pillar

To achieve the necessary transformation of NATO under the new political framework conditions described, and at the required speed, a strong and sovereign European pillar within the alliance is needed more than ever. Thirty of the 32 NATO member states are located in Europe, of which 23 are also members of the European Union. Three other EU states maintain close partnership relations with NATO through the Partnership for Peace program. In total, 26 of the 27 EU states are NATO members or at least have very close ties with NATO. The need for close coordination and intensive cooperation between the EU and NATO is therefore obvious. However, coordinating national strategies in the field of defense is often difficult in practice. This is evident not only at the NATO and EU level but also at the regional and bilateral level. For example, there are more than 80 different individual agreements at the bi-national or multinational level in the field of defense within Europe. The lack of coordination of these agreements quickly leads to duplication of capabilities or, even more seriously, to capability gaps (Bressa et al. 2024, p. 5).

To address this issue, a clear situational picture is needed first. This situational picture can be developed on the basis of the coordinated annual review process for defense (CARD) of the European Defence Agency (EDA), in a European approach. On this basis, efforts should then be harmonized, in line with the objective of the EU Strategic

Compass to bring more coherence to existing security and defense policy initiatives and to provide new impetus for European cooperation (Federal Academy for Security Policy 2022). The fundamental idea of the European Defence Industry Reinforcement through common Procurement Act (EDIRPA), to avoid duplication and capability gaps and to effectively exploit economies of scale, as well as that of the EDA, are aimed in this direction.

With regard to Europe's strategic autonomy, current procurement practices in the acquisition of armaments must continue to be reviewed and regulated. At present, procurement is not predominantly European, nor is the EU target of jointly procuring 35% of armaments projects being met. In fact, for example, between February 2022 and June 2023, 78% of armaments projects were procured outside the EU, 63% of which came from the USA (Clapp 2024). There are several reasons for this, with the faster availability of systems and the larger and more flexible production capacities compared to the European security and defense industry likely being the main factors. Another factor is a lack of coordination between politics and industry, leading to missing or misunderstood "demand signals." This makes it difficult for industry to expand capacity and respond flexibly to needs without incurring enormous economic risk through the necessary upfront investments. The "European Defence Union" announced by Commission President Ursula von der Leyen at the start of her second term in 2024 could provide a remedy here. The European Defence Union is to be understood as complementary to NATO and is intended to strengthen European security through joint regulations, pooling of resources, and the use of synergy and scale effects. This explicitly includes tools to promote the European security and defense industry and create incentives for joint development and procurement. The "European Defence Industrial Strategy" (EDIS) adopted by the EU in March 2024, as well as the "European Defence Industry Programme" (EDIP), which is currently in the EU legislative process and is intended to translate the EDIS into concrete measures, are important steps in this direction (Koenig 2024, p. 2).

The volatile security environment and strained transatlantic relations are increasing the pressure on European governments and, in particular, defense ministries. Intensive efforts are underway to equip European defense with the necessary capabilities to ensure credible deterrence and defense readiness. Through close coordination with European industry, the triad of innovation, modernization, and consolidation is to be optimally utilized. Above all, in the field of high technology, European developments are to be promoted and capabilities built up that European nations have not previously been able to provide.

A central element in European defense research and development is the European Defence Fund (EDF). The EDF has a multiannual financial framework of €7.3 billion (2021–2027) and is intended to promote cooperation in the development of innovative defense technologies. The EDF supports projects, for example, in the areas of cyber defense, space, artificial intelligence, and advanced sensor technology (European Commission 2025). It is to be seen as complementary to NATO initiatives and institutions such as the NATO Innovation Fund and the Defence Innovation Accelerator for the North Atlantic (DIANA).

It is important, with all the outstanding approaches, initiatives, and projects of the EU, not to focus solely on the NATO-EU overlap. A strategically autonomous European pillar of NATO must necessarily include all European NATO states and partner nations.

4 The Role of the Franco-German Partnership

On the path to a credible European pillar within NATO, Germany and France bear a special responsibility. Their partnership, deeply rooted in the history of European security, has formed its central element for decades. Since the Élysée Treaty of 1963, their cooperation has often been described as the driving force of European integration. It was recognized early on that a close connection is both in their own interest and strengthens the stability and security of the entire continent. This is reaffirmed by numerous joint initiatives and projects, such as the founding of the Eurocorps in 1992.

Today, Germany and France stand for the joint pursuit of Europe's strategic autonomy. This explicitly includes the continued fulfillment of European obligations within the NATO alliance. Through joint European projects such as the Future Combat Air System (FCAS) and the Main Ground Combat System (MGCS), both nations intend to strengthen the European defense industry and reduce technological and industrial dependencies. Germany and France regularly underscore their determination to further deepen this cooperation. Most recently, the defense ministers of both countries reaffirmed their determination to further deepen cooperation in January 2025 (Ross and Téterchen 2025, p. 2).

Despite the central importance of Franco-German cooperation for Europe in NATO, Europe's strategic autonomy, as an independent pillar within NATO, must not be limited to this bilateral level. The driving force for European autonomy must therefore go beyond a binational approach and necessarily include the United Kingdom as well as the other European NATO members.

5 Conclusion

Security is crucial for preserving freedom and prosperity. From a European perspective, this means strengthening NATO as the most successful system of collective security in modern times. In the future as well, a NATO with 32 members, able to act quickly and effectively across all capability categories, is indispensable. To deter potential aggressors and secure the long-term commitment of the USA to NATO, European states must demonstrate through their actions and investments in defense that they are willing to take responsibility for European security. To this end, a strong European pillar must be further developed to ensure the alliance's full deterrence and defense capability.

In defense matters, there must be no more solo efforts in the future. The capability planning of NATO nations must be consistently aligned with NATO targets. Measures by the European Union as well as bi- and multinational agreements and initiatives must supplement these targets and support their achievement. Increased defense spending is necessary to achieve these goals. The NATO summit commitment from Wales in 2014 to spend 2% of each country's gross domestic product (GDP) on defense is no longer sufficient. To resolve the described double delta of NATO capabilities as quickly as possible, future spending of more than 3% of GDP will be necessary. NATO states must commit to this higher spending as soon as possible. An important signal in this direction is the "ReArm Europe" initiative, with which the EU states clearly advocated for increased defense spending at the special summit in March 2025 (European Parliament 2025, p. 2).

Financing is an essential, but not the only, factor in maintaining European deterrence and defense capability. Innovation processes must be revised and an innovation ecosystem created that enables the rapid introduction of new technologies and digital transformation. Only in this way can Europe keep pace with the enormous speed of technological development. The key is future capability for Multi-Domain Operations. In the future, those who are not able to use state-of-the-art technologies across all dimensions and domains to create a comprehensive situational picture, command, achieve effects, and coordinate with other instruments of state power will no longer play a decisive role in conflicts or be able to make sovereign decisions.

To achieve this, risks must be consciously accepted. This applies to both defense ministries and procurement organizations as well as the security and defense industry. Lengthy processes shaped by a desire for security are no longer effective. Planning and procurement must be designed flexibly so that new technologies and approaches can be introduced without bureaucratic delays or lengthy approval procedures. Industry, for its part, must maintain flexible production capacities that enable timely delivery even in the event of a sudden increase in demand. The need to take risks and accept potential negative effects must be communicated transparently and openly by the state to create broad public acceptance.

For this to succeed, the major European nations must lead by example. Leadership roles must not only be proclaimed but also actively assumed. Germany bears a special responsibility in this regard. As the leading economic power in Europe, contributing the second largest share to NATO and the largest to the EU budget, Germany must act as a driver for other EU and NATO states with a clear strategy. The 2023 national security strategy is a starting point for a comprehensive strategy development process. This process must formulate strategic goals based on cross-party consensus and an understanding of national security interests that transcends legislative terms. Given the current situation, it is important to advance this process quickly without neglecting certain principles. Through a continuous and transparent process of thinking, assessment, and action in strategy development, resulting in operational and achievable goals, the overall societal discourse will be promoted and understanding of strategy and defense in society will be strengthened. This will make a significant contribution to increasing whole-of-government resilience.

The implementation of such a strategy requires achievable goals and the provision of necessary resources. In 2024, Germany reached the NATO target of investing 2% of GDP in defense for the first time. However, the regular defense budget will remain frozen at around €50 to €53 billion until 2027. From 2028, when the special fund is exhausted, a funding gap of about €30 billion (Matlé and Tausendfreund 2025, p. 1) threatens according to the current situation. A new federal government must act as quickly as possible to close this gap and enable the increase in defense funding toward 3% of GDP and beyond.

To strengthen the security and defense industry, procurement security, the promotion of innovation through the reduction of bureaucracy, and more joint European armaments and procurement projects are needed. The introduction of a planning and procurement acceleration law following the National Security and Defense Industry Strategy published in December 2024 is the right and necessary step in this direction. It is time to move away from the "more of the same" approach and instead consistently focus on innovation, digitalization, and new technologies so that the Bundeswehr, as well as other European armies, can develop greater combat power even without an unrealistic increase in personnel strength.

In conclusion, it can be stated that nothing less is at stake than the preservation of the transatlantic alliance, which has been a guarantor of European security for over 75 years. The European NATO states, above all Germany, France, and the United Kingdom, are obliged to form a strong European pillar of NATO in order to carry the alliance into the future together with the USA. The strengthening of the European pillar must be at the center of joint efforts to ensure NATO's ability to act and at the same time consolidate European sovereignty. The continued support of Ukraine, which is bravely fighting for the freedom and democracy of Europe, is not only a moral obligation but also a key contribution to European security. Only a strong and united Europe, firmly embedded in the transatlantic alliance, can successfully meet current and future challenges.

References

Bressa, G. M. et al. (2024). Building European defence capabilities for a more uncertain world (European Defense Report). *Boston Consulting Group.*

Clapp, S. (2024). European Defence Industrial Strategy (EPRS Briefing). *European Parliamentary Research Service.*

Bundesakademie für Sicherheitspolitik. (2022). *Der Strategische Kompass: Ein Fahrplan für die Europäische Union als sicherheitspolitische Akteurin.* https://www.baks.bund.de/de/arbeitspapiere/2022/der-strategische-kompass-ein-fahrplan-fuer-die-europaeische-union-als-0. 25.03.2025.

European Commission. (2025). *The European Defence Fund at a glance.* https://defence-industry-space.ec.europa.eu/eu-defence-industry/european-defence-fund-edf-official-webpage-european-commission_en. 25.03.2025.

European Parliament (2025). Outcome of the special European Council meeting of 6 March 2025. https://www.europarl.europa.eu/RegData/etudes/BRIE/2025/765784/EPRS_BRI(2025)765784_EN.pdf. 7.03.2025.

Koenig, N. (2024): From Soft Talk to Hard Power, Ten To-Dos for the European Union (Analysis 3/2024). *Munich Security Conference.*

Luzin, P. (2025, 22. Januar). *Russia's Year of Truth: The Runaway Military Budget.* Center for European Policy Analysis. https://cepa.org/article/russias-year-of-truth-the-runaway-military-budget/. 25.03.2025.

Manyin, M., et al. (2012). Pivot to the Pacific? The Obama Administration's "Rebalancing" Toward Asia.Congessional Research Service.

Matlé, A., & Tausendfreund, R. (2025). Eine Europäisierung der NATO ist unabdingbar – Was Berlin hierfür tun muss (DGAP Memo Nr. 05). *Deutsche Gesellschaft für Auswärtige Politik (DGAP).*

NATO. (2024). *Defence Expenditures of NATO Countries (2014-2024).* https://www.nato.int/nato_static_fl2014/assets/pdf/2024/6/pdf/240617-def-exp-2024-en.pdf. 25.03.2025.

NATO (2024). Washington Summit Declaration. https://www.nato.int/cps/en/natohq/official_texts_227678.htm. 14.03.2025.

NATO ACT (2025). Multi-Domain Operations and Digital Transformation: Enabling Converged Effects in the Modern Battlespace. https://www.act.nato.int/article/mdo-dt-enabling-converging-effects/. 17.05.2025

Ross, J., & Téterchen, N. (2025). Deutsch-französische Verteidigungskooperation: Jetzt oder nie (DGAP Memo Nr. 12). *Deutsche Gesellschaft für Auswärtige Politik (DGAP).*

Statista. (2024). *Armed forces of Russia – statistics & facts.* https://www.statista.com/topics/9957/armed-forces-of-russia/#topicOverview. 25.03. 2025.

Statista. (2025). *Truppenstärke der Streitkräfte der NATO nach Staaten von 1990 bis 2024.* https://de.statista.com/statistik/daten/studie/36914/umfrage/streitkraefte-der-nato/. 25.03.2025.

Christian Badia Retired General, served as Deputy Supreme Allied Commander Transformation of NATO, Norfolk, Virginia, from July 2022 to July 2025. Previously, he was Head of Planning at the Federal Ministry of Defence. The experienced Air Force officer has held various leadership positions, including command of the European Air Transport Command (EATC). His particular focus is on the strategic development of NATO as well as deepening transatlantic and European defense cooperation.

Protecting Critical Infrastructure in Europe: Using Technical Attribution of Cyberattacks Effectively

Annegret Bendiek and Jakob Bund

> *"The era of lasting security is over, and a new reality full of challenges and uncertainties is dawning. Geopolitical tensions, rapid technological change, social upheavals, and the withdrawal of traditional partners confront Europe with immense tasks. European resilience and stability can only be strengthened through increased cooperation, innovative capacity, and adaptability among the member states."*

1 Introduction

Leaking pipelines in the Baltic Sea, severed data cables, and interruptions in satellite communications have raised the question in European capitals of how to respond politically, criminally, and even militarily to suspected attacks on critical infrastructure.[1] In light of incidents affecting Germany and at least six other member states, NATO allies in May 2024 drew attention to the extent of documented Russian efforts to destabilize supporters of Ukraine (NATO 2024). The documented hybrid activities of Moscow range

[1]This chapter is a revised German version of the report "The Attribution Dividend: Protecting Critical Infrastructure from Cyber Attacks," previously published by the German Institute for International and Security Affairs: https://www.swp-berlin.org/publications/products/comments/2024C46_CyberAttacks.pdf.

A. Bendiek (✉) · J. Bund
SWP, Berlin, Germany

S. Weeser (ed.), *The Heart Chambers of Europe: Franco-German Impulses for the EU's Security Order*, https://doi.org/10.1007/978-3-658-51096-1_14

from disinformation campaigns and electronic interference with flight signals, to coercion and assassination attempts against regime critics, and acts of sabotage, including with the help of cyberattacks. To strengthen member states' capabilities in combating hybrid threats, the EU Council agreed at the end of May 2024 to establish EU rapid response teams for the analysis and defense against hybrid threats (Council of the European Union 2024a). However, the effective use of such mechanisms in the EU also depends heavily on a shared technical understanding among member states of how the threat actor operates, what capabilities and how much political or state support it can draw upon. As far as cyber-enabled acts of sabotage are concerned, the tactics, techniques, and procedures of cybercriminals have been tested and refined over many years. The public attribution of such malicious activities demonstrates that, especially in the context of Russia's war against Ukraine, they have had significant implications for the functioning of infrastructure in Ukraine and beyond (Egloff and Smeets 2021). Not least, election systems and power suppliers became targets of Russian cyberattacks after Russia's invasion of Crimea in 2014 (European Repository of Cyber Incidents 2025a, b).

Compared to other types of cyber operations, sabotage actions aimed at destroying data or disrupting operations have been at the center of public attributions. Unlike cyber espionage and influence attempts, the consequences of successful sabotage are often publicly visible. This immediate visibility also increases public pressure to combat such cyberattacks and hold those responsible accountable. Such sabotage attempts are designed to manipulate systems to cause a specific disruptive effect. Concerns in this regard focus, for example, on shutting down substations to interrupt power supply or altering chemicals in water treatment plants to hazardous concentrations. Such physical consequences can make it easier for investigators to identify initial impacts and likely strategic intentions, which can help infer the perpetrators.

Espionage operations, on the other hand, pursue their objectives through cumulative effects. This can be achieved either by the depth of penetration, with individual targets being surveilled over long periods, or by widespread surveillance of entire sectors. This campaign approach requires similarly sustained effort on the attribution side to develop a coherent situational picture from partial observations.

In this context, the attribution of acts of sabotage targeting critical infrastructure is part of a broader political effort to enforce UN-level agreements on responsible behavior in cyberspace. The credibility of the red line drawn by these agreements to protect critical national infrastructure in peacetime depends on whether violations of norms are uncovered and perpetrators are held accountable. Notably, attribution efforts against state-sponsored disruptive actions have expanded to include espionage operations conducted in preparation for such acts of sabotage. Criminal groups that threaten critical infrastructure, especially in the health sector, for extortion purposes have also come into focus. These changes in the threat landscape are reflected in an increase in the attribution of malicious cyber activities.

2 Critical Infrastructure as a Crisis Hotspot

To assess threats to critical infrastructure, a fundamental distinction is necessary. The network environments of many essential service providers, such as power utilities or water treatment plants, are broadly divided into IT and operational technology components. The latter are also known as operational technology, or OT for short. While IT networks are used for administrative tasks such as sending emails or issuing invoices, OT controls the actual operation of industrial facilities. Industrial control systems (ICS) play a central role within OT, managing processes responsible, for example, for water filtration, power distribution, or switching for road and rail traffic control. The vast majority of malware or intrusion techniques affecting critical infrastructure do not reach OT components. However, the increasing interconnection of IT and OT networks means that disruptions to IT devices can have cascading effects.

In the case of the large-scale ransomware attack on Colonial Pipeline, for example, the largest U.S. pipeline operator decided in May 2021 to halt the supply of gas and kerosene, resulting in temporary shortages at gas stations along the East Coast (European Repository of Cyber Incidents 2025c). The Russian ransomware group DarkSide had previously succeeded in encrypting the company's billing system (Cybersecurity and Infrastructure Security Agency 2021). Although only administrative systems were affected by this intrusion, Colonial Pipeline decided on a temporary supply stop as a precaution (Wood 2023). In contrast to such secondary effects of ransomware attacks, malware that directly targets OT remains rare. To date, only nine cases have been publicly tracked (Graham et al. 2024). Even rarer are destructive impacts on OT systems through cyber capabilities (Greenberg 2024). Increasingly, OT systems originally designed to operate in isolated networks are being put online to support remote maintenance. These connections change the risk modeling for critical infrastructure operators, as they can introduce new vulnerabilities. OT components and protocols developed for independent operation in a protected zone (air gap) are not designed for the potential risks associated with greater integration with IT networks, which offer a larger attack surface. In the digital transformation of industry, it is crucial to better secure OT connectivity.

2.1 Russian Efforts to Undermine Support for Ukraine

Russia's use of offensive cyber operations is a central component of its military strategy to undermine international support for Ukraine. However, these attacks are not orchestrated solely by the Kremlin. Various hacktivists with suspected ties to Russian state entities, such as the Cyber Army of Russia Reborn (CARR), operate partly autonomously (European Repository of Cyber Incidents 2025d). When these groups act relatively independently of state authorization, this entails a significant risk of escalation. Repeated warnings from the United Kingdom's Government Communications Headquarters (GCHQ) in 2023 and 2024 point to these risks (National Cyber Security Centre 2023; Keast-Butler 2024).

The capabilities of these threat actors remain limited, as revealed by disclosures in connection with U.S. sanctions imposed on July 19, 2024, against two prominent CARR members (Miller 2024a). Even though these actors do not (yet) possess advanced capabilities, the U.S. government has classified their activities under Executive Order 13694 as a "significant threat to the national security, foreign policy, or economic health and financial stability" (U.S. Department of the Treasury 2024).

This classification is less a judgment of the hackers' technical abilities than a warning about the ongoing difficulties in closing security gaps in threatened critical infrastructure in a timely manner. Both then-National Security Advisor Jake Sullivan and the Environmental Protection Agency (EPA) have called for increased support for local utilities in this context, emphasizing that strengthening resilience must be a key component of the defense strategy (Regan and Sullivan 2024).

2.2 Chinese Preparations for a Geopolitical Contingency

The strategic intentions behind attempts to spy on sensitive networks are difficult to determine by technical means alone. This is especially true for operations that initially seek to establish access, which could also be used for possible acts of sabotage in the future. Signs of such destructive intentions are due to their forward-looking nature, in most circumstances, only hypothetical. In May 2023, for example, U.S. intelligence agencies uncovered a series of deep compromises of several critical infrastructure operators on the U.S. mainland and overseas bases, which they linked to Volt Typhoon (Zettl-Schabath and Hemmelskamp 2024; European Repository of Cyber Incidents 2025e). The group is suspected of being controlled by the Chinese military. Although the uncovered activities focused on the IT environments of organizations in telecommunications, logistics, and energy and water supply, U.S. intelligence agencies assess that they fundamentally differ from other espionage operations attributed to China. This distinction is based on observed efforts to prepare for further penetration into OT areas and to deliberately collect information about the functioning of the affected organizations' industrial control systems.

2.3 Cybercrime as a New National Security Threat

The increase in ransomware attacks on critical infrastructure with low tolerance for disruption, especially in healthcare, represents a new dimension of national security threat posed by criminal actors. For 2023 and 2024, there has been a sharp rise in ransomware attacks on hospitals (Orange Cyberdefense 2024). The healthcare sector is now among the most affected industries. To ensure the provision of healthcare and prevent the illegal dissemination of sensitive medical data, for example, the U.S. pharmaceutical distribution company Cencora agreed to pay a ransomware group $75 million—the highest publicly known sum to date (Manson 2024). Another ransomware attack in June 2024 led to delays in the analysis of blood donations in London, resulting in restrictions on blood transfusions (European Repository of Cyber Incidents 2025f). Such incidents underscore the potentially catastrophic impact of ransomware on essential services, including healthcare. These incidents mark a significant shift in the tactics of these criminal organizations. Ransomware groups had previously been reluctant to target organizations in the healthcare sector, as such serious cyberattacks against healthcare risked immediately attracting the attention of law enforcement authorities.

The threat posed by criminal cyber actors is increasingly being recognized at the highest levels of government. Within its first 100 days, the newly appointed European Commission in December 2024 launched a cybersecurity action plan for the healthcare sector (European Commission 2024). The Polish EU Council Presidency has named the development of cyber defense capabilities as a priority of its political program for the first half of 2025. The EU's cyber-sanctions package of June 2024 already included criminals for the first time, in order to protect critical infrastructure regardless of the success of conventional law enforcement measures (Bund 2024).

3 Why Technical Attribution Pays Off

From a political perspective, the immediate purpose of attribution is to name those responsible for such attacks and deter them from future criminal activities (Eichensehr 2020). As cybersecurity expert Jason Healey points out, the real goal is to gain a better understanding of these malicious activities in order to prevent them more effectively in advance (Healey 2012). Attribution efforts are generally divided into three categories: technical, political, and legal measures (Lin 2016). Forensic investigations initially aim to identify the tools, tactics, techniques, and procedures (TTPs) used in an operation and to trace the systems and networks through which an operation was conducted. In such technical assessments, this information is compared with a series of other compromise attempts to identify known patterns and approaches based on previously known operations. Trends and behavioral patterns of threat actors can indeed change over time. The initial focus is on reconstructing the course of the incident, as these findings in turn allow for targeted countermeasures. Recurring intrusion techniques and access points in networks can be more easily detected. Targeted monitoring for known attack tools can impose operational costs on threat actors by forcing them to adapt their methods to avoid early detection.

The results of this technical investigation can be used for political attribution, in which responsibility is assigned to a state (Rupp and Paulus 2023). This form of attribution allows for a broad spectrum of state responsibility assignment (Healey 2012).

In addition to establishing direct authorship of an operation, such assignments against states can also refer to the support of proxies or to the failure to exercise due diligence in preventing criminal activities originating from their territory (Zettl-Schabath 2023). Public and private communications about the methods of threat actors can influence their cost calculations and deter them from continuing operations, insofar as these depend on secrecy. An important lesson in this regard was the Russian influence attempts ahead of the 2016 U.S. election (Schiff 2025). The delayed response of the U.S. government to the exposure of the Russian government-directed campaign against the then-Democratic presidential candidate allowed the stolen data to be circulated and used to influence her electoral prospects (Department of Homeland Security & Office of the Director of National Intelligence 2016). When, in August 2024, several U.S. media organizations were confronted with internal documents from the Trump campaign, they decided not to report details from the stolen files, suspecting that the files had been obtained by a foreign power. Early warnings from Microsoft and supporting statements from U.S. intelligence agencies, which linked the leak to a state, prevented the attempt at political influence (Watts 2024; Office of the Director of National Intelligence, Federal Bureau of Investigation, & Cybersecurity and Infrastructure Security Agency 2024).

Legal attribution, in addition, aims to hold perpetrators and their supporters accountable in order to enforce international law and compliance with norms for responsible state behavior in the long term—beyond individual cases (Finnemore and Hollis 2020). Proof of violations of international law and illegitimate actions provides an important basis for political responses, which in turn can press for the validity of international law.

While political and legal responses are based on the conclusions of forensic investigations, technical attribution, including by state actors, can be carried out independently of decisions on political assignment of responsibility and the question of legal consequences (Grienberger 2023). In its public response to the compromise of the defense company RUAG, for example, the Swiss government deliberately limited itself to technical attribution and attributed the incident only to the Turla espionage group, without making any further assessment of suspected political sponsors (Egloff and Smeets 2021). Rapid attribution is important in that it allows other potential victims to be informed early about TTPs and to take appropriate countermeasures. This makes technical attribution so relevant, because disseminating knowledge about perpetrators' methods can directly influence their chances of success.

In the current threat environment, political and legal measures have only limited potential to deter states that are at war or preparing for conflict from conducting cyber operations that remain below the threshold of the use of force. This limitation is due, not least, to the fact that the same set of measures is also claimed in response to broader political tensions with the same actors. The same applies to the ability to reduce the financial incentives of criminals who often operate from these states or with state support. Technical attribution, on the other hand, can have a direct impact on the capabilities of such actors, both by supporting a shared knowledge base for attackers' TTPs and by enabling tailored countermeasures.

In the best case, early detection can prevent a cyberattack. In 2022, for example, OT cybersecurity company Dragos, in cooperation with the U.S. government, discovered a toolkit capable of causing physical destruction in electrical systems, oil and gas pipelines, water systems, manufacturing plants, and military control systems (Lee 2024). Because the tool uses the inherent functionalities of the target systems, its use cannot be prevented by a software update as with a software vulnerability. Instead, detecting a possible compromise requires constant vigilance. Given the often sought but rarely achieved resilience of the tool and its broad applicability across a variety of sectors, analysts named it PIPEDREAM. The name also highlights the success of the investigation, as its deployment has so far been thwarted.

Plans to expand early detection capabilities, such as the announcement by the UK's National Cyber Security Centre (NCSC) in August 2024 to expand its Active Cyber Defence (ACD) program, aim to disrupt adversary activities (National Cyber Security Centre 2024). In particular, the NCSC is preparing to expand the ACD portfolio to include deception measures. These considerations include digital tripwires and honeypots designed to deliberately maneuver threat actors into traps, thereby revealing their identities and methods. Providing these services, especially for small and medium-sized enterprises that otherwise lack the necessary resources, can also further increase the visibility of threat activities that support technical attribution.

Such deception measures also have a psychological component. Even the mere suspicion by potential attackers that such measures exist in target networks can have a deterrent effect on the behavior of threat actors—a means of influence that the NCSC is deliberately considering.

4 Maintaining the Attribution Dividend

The Chinese National Computer Virus Emergency Response Center and the 360 Digital Security Group have made efforts in several reports to co-opt analyses by Western cybersecurity firms in order to portray the allegedly state-directed Chinese group Volt Typhoon as a criminal ransomware group (China National Computer Virus Emergency Response Center 2024a, b). Without providing evidence, the Chinese organizations argued that corrections in industry reports were made at the direction of the U.S. government, with the aim of concealing Volt Typhoon's supposed ransomware identity. In doing so, Volt Typhoon's stealth-oriented methods differ markedly from the usual behavior patterns of ransomware groups. Ransomware groups are typically motivated to publicize their activities to put pressure on victims to meet their demands. This difference alone makes the claims put forward by the Chinese side appear dubious. Despite the lack of evidence, Chinese officials have repeatedly cited these reports and attempted to portray the official revelations about Volt Typhoon as a "disinformation campaign" by U.S. intelligence agencies (Ministry of Foreign Affairs of the People's Republic of China 2024a, b).

Despite these efforts to deflect from state responsibility, the political attributions have not led to any noticeable change in behavior. In early August, Sherrod DeGrippo, Director of Threat Intelligence Strategy at Microsoft—who first reported on Volt Typhoon's activities—noted that the group's activities continue unabated (Miller 2024b). DeGrippo pointed to "consistency and persistence" in the attack patterns. The former Chief Security Officer of Yahoo and Facebook, Alex Stamos, further explained that the disclosure of their actions did not sufficiently deter cybercriminals and their sponsors (Miller 2024b).

As Volt Typhoon demonstrates, these effects have a short half-life for well-resourced groups with long-term strategic goals, even when coordinated efforts are made to remove the group from target networks through a targeted technical attribution campaign. While technical attribution does increase costs for threat actors, it is in constant competition with adversaries' efforts to continually change their TTPs. For professional actors who cannot be easily pushed out of the market, these investigative successes only temporarily restrict their room for maneuver. The advantages that defenders gain through technical attribution are therefore part of a larger cycle: (1) With knowledge of exploited vulnerabilities and TTPs, threat actors can be excluded from already compromised networks and their room for maneuver restricted. (2) To regain access or penetrate other targets, new access vectors must first be developed at cost. (3) By developing and applying new penetration techniques, threat actors try to regain their advantage—a knowledge gap that (4) must again be closed through intelligence and attribution efforts.

However, not all parts of the attack infrastructure are equally easy to replace. Takedowns enabled by technical attribution, as in the case of the KV botnet in January 2024, can set attackers back (U.S. Department of Justice 2024a). Volt Typhoon had attempted to conceal its operations using hijacked small office/home office routers from the botnet.

The FBI-led takedown of a second botnet with links to China in September 2024 underscores the success of a consistently pursued technical attribution (U.S. Department of Justice 2024b). Flax Typhoon, the group that controlled the botnet, tries to remain inconspicuous in its operations by minimizing the use of malware and avoiding easily identifiable attack patterns. This approach allowed the group to remain undetected during a multi-year espionage campaign against critical infrastructure targets, including in Taiwan and the U.S. (Sabin 2024). To make the findings about Flax Typhoon known beyond the countries involved in the operation, the U.S., together with its Five Eyes partners, published a notice documenting more than 60 vulnerabilities that Flax Typhoon exploited to expand its botnet. Creating a comprehensive situational picture of these compromises provides insight into the attack infrastructure and can determine the focus of preventive measures. The consistent pursuit of actor groups that enables significant disruption of their infrastructure raises the bar for threat actors' efforts to remain undetected over the long term.

In a new espionage campaign reported in August 2024, targeting U.S. internet service providers and digital services for government and military users, Volt Typhoon was observed exploiting a zero-day vulnerability in Versa Director, a software that enables centralized management and monitoring of network devices (Black Lotus Labs 2024; European Repository of Cyber Incidents 2025g). Such previously unreported software vulnerabilities are a rare resource. Volt Typhoon's use of a zero-day vulnerability makes it clear that the group must resort to costly means to regain access. It also shows their efforts to avoid early detection and technical attribution, with the aim of continuing their operations for as long as possible.

5 The Linkage of EU Sanctions and Attribution

The EU's response to malicious cyber activities has steadily evolved in recent years (Bendiek and Bund 2023). The EU's cyber sanctions regime was officially introduced with Council Regulation (EU) 2019/796 and Council Decision (CFSP) 2019/797 of 17 May 2019 (Council of the European Union 2019a, b). This legal framework established the basis for imposing targeted restrictive measures against individuals, organizations, and entities responsible for cyberattacks that threaten the EU or its Member States. However, it also made a clear distinction between the imposition of sanctions and attribution, that is, the assignment of responsibility to a third state. It is explicitly emphasized that attribution of responsibility is a sovereign political decision that each Member State can make independently on a case-by-case basis, regardless of a sanctions decision.

The first rounds of sanctions under this regime, imposed on 30 July 2020 and 22 October 2020, were the result of careful deliberations (Council of the European Union 2020a, b). These measures were imposed with a significant time lag after the actual cyberattacks. They relied heavily on existing public attribution assessments at the national level as well as reports from partner countries and cybersecurity firms, in order to keep the barriers to information sharing among Member States low. In its first use of the sanctions instruments, the EU made it clear that the imposition of restrictive measures should have a deterrent effect and is to be distinguished from the assignment of responsibility to a state actor.

Over time, the EU's approach to attribution of responsibility in the imposition of cyber sanctions has evolved. This is certainly also due to the growing complexity of the threat landscape. In the Council conclusions of 21 May 2024 on cybersecurity, the threat situation in Europe was cited as the main reason for the review of the 2020 EU Cybersecurity Strategy (Council of the European Union 2024b). The background is an increase in the frequency and severity of cyberattacks, particularly through disruptive actions against critical infrastructures and essential services, using ransomware and wiper malware.

These changes in the threat environment were a direct impetus for the third round of EU sanctions imposed on 24 June 2024 (Council of the European Union 2024c). This most recent round marked a significant shift in the EU's approach, more closely linking attribution with the sanctions process. The EU relied not only on attribution to justify its sanctions, but also as a tool to hold individuals accountable for specific malicious activities. In particular, two individuals were sanctioned by the EU who had not previously been indicted or sanctioned by other countries. However, the Ukrainian security service had already identified them as employees of the Russian domestic intelligence service (FSB). For the first time, the EU thus imposed sanctions on individuals who had not already been publicly indicted by other partner countries. This approach signals a new willingness on the part of the EU to take a leadership role in enforcing red lines in the cyber and information space.

Despite this progress, there are further areas where the EU has room to catch up with partner countries in attribution, coordination, and sanctions procedures. For example, the United Kingdom and the USA have often documented and sanctioned threat actors based on intelligence that was not publicly available at the time, demonstrating a higher degree of agility and coordination in their response. In the Council's press release on the third round of sanctions, the intention was expressed to strengthen cooperation with the United Kingdom and the USA in combating cybercrime and implementing appropriate countermeasures (Council of the European Union 2024d). For such a proactive approach, which seeks to weaken threats through targeted disclosure of attack tools, the EU still lacks the foundation of trust that, for example, the Five Eyes countries have built up over decades of information sharing. External influences, such as the ongoing conflict in Ukraine, are also having an impact on the EU's handling of attribution. For instance, the EU High Representative attributed the cyber-enabled disruption of connections to the KA-SAT satellite network shortly before the Russian invasion of Ukraine in February 2022 to Russian state actors soon after the event (Council of the European Union 2022; European Repository of Cyber Incidents 2022). This comparatively rapid response, in contrast to earlier official statements, reflects a general trend toward faster information sharing about threats and an overall reduction in the time required to attribute cyberattacks.

The 2023 revised implementation of the guidelines for the EU Cyber Diplomacy Toolbox (CDT) underscores the EU's commitment to more effective use of attribution mechanisms. Among other things, the guidelines contain detailed recommendations for the strategic use of attribution in diplomatic communication, while political attribution remains the sovereign decision of the Member States. The guidelines specifically address the strengthening of information sharing in order to enable a coordinated political response at the EU level based on a common situational picture. In addition, the guidelines acknowledge the foundational role of technical attribution in decisions on political countermeasures, but do not go into detail on how technical attribution could become a diplomatic tool in its own right and thereby enhance its deterrent effect.

6 Effectively Using Technical Attribution: Recommendations for the EU

The technical dimension of attribution is still little used by EU institutions due to the limited provision of analytical capabilities by the Member States. In contrast, the EU can significantly strengthen its engagement through strategic partnerships, support for international efforts to ensure accountability, and an explicit focus on the victims of cyberattacks.

6.1 A Victim-Oriented Approach in Cyber Diplomacy

One of the most effective ways the EU can support attribution efforts is by improving the intelligence-gathering capabilities of partner countries. Supporting third countries to enable them to build and enhance their own attribution capacities, which in turn can contribute to the stability of the cyber and information space, is of critical importance. By focusing on developing such partnerships, the EU can build a network of countries capable of conducting credible attribution assessments in a timely manner.

The EU should prioritize coordination with countries that have been victims of cyberattacks, especially in implementing the diplomatic response framework for cyberattacks. The European External Action Service can play a central role in these efforts, for example in consultations with Ukraine. Ukraine's experiences and its ongoing defense efforts offer important insights that can feed into a more victim-oriented approach to cyber diplomacy. At the law enforcement level, steps are already being taken in individual cases to collect knowledge about the behavior of ransomware groups and thereby prevent further compromises. Diplomatic initiatives can systematize this technical exchange between victims and potential targets at the international level. The recent exchange within the framework of the cyber dialogue between the EU and Ukraine signals a shift toward a more victim-oriented approach that recognizes the experiences of frontline states for identifying targeted countermeasures. Such technically guided dialogues not only provide a platform to discuss strategic priorities for promoting local cybersecurity capacities, but also to determine how coordinated disclosures can impair adversary capabilities and thereby improve the defensive posture of the victim.

6.2 Supporting the International Legal Order through Best Practices

In addition to capacity building, the EU also plays a crucial role in developing and disseminating best practices for technical attribution at the global level. A key prerequisite for this is an understanding within the international community, or at least among like-minded states, on clear, coherent, and legally sound standards for the attribution of offenses. Such common standards can also facilitate coordinated reporting of cyberattacks by Member States and their international partners.

Supporting the International Criminal Court (ICC) in its investigations to clarify war crimes in the context of cyberattacks is closely linked to the EU's multilateral efforts to enforce international law. In June 2024, ICC representatives confirmed ongoing investigations into four cyberattacks against Ukraine that are being classified as possible war crimes (Deutsch et al. 2024). The EU can actively support these investigations, in which the application of international humanitarian law in cyberspace plays a role. Moscow's war of aggression against Ukraine is putting international agreements on the application of international humanitarian law to cyber operations to the test. Cyberattacks targeting civilian infrastructure, disrupting essential public services, or otherwise contributing to war crimes challenge the traditional interpretation of international humanitarian law. Here, the EU could support the legal and technical classification of serious cyberattacks in order to ensure the applicability of international humanitarian law to the cyber and information space as well.

References

Bendiek, A., & Bund, J. (2023). *Shifting paradigms in Europe's approach to cyber defence: Ambitions to disrupt malicious cyber activity need to protect norms as well as networks* (SWP Comment 2023/C 48). Stiftung Wissenschaft und Politik. https://www.swp-berlin.org/en/publication/shifting-paradigms-in-europes-approach-to-cyber-defence. 29.04.2025.

Black Lotus Labs. (2024). *Taking the Crossroads: The Versa Director Zero-Day Exploitation.* Lumen Technologies. https://blog.lumen.com/uncovering-the-versa-director-zero-day-exploitation/. 29.04.2025.

Bund, J. (2024). *Bureaucratic initiative redefines German law enforcement cyber operations.* BindingHook. https://bindinghook.com/articles-hooked-on-trends/bureaucratic-initiative-redefines-german-law-enforcement-cyber-operations/. 29.04.2025.

China National Computer Virus Emergency Response Center. (2024a). *A Conspiratorial Swindling Campaign targets with U.S. Congress and Taxpayers conducted by U.S. Intelligence Community.* https://web.archive.org/web/20240710175525/https:/www.cverc.org.cn/head/zhaiyao/futetaifengEN.pdf. 29.04.2025.

China National Computer Virus Emergency Response Center. (2024b). *Volt Typhoon. A secret Disinformation Campaign targeting U.S. Congress and Taxpayers conducted by U.S. Government agencies.* https://web.archive.org/web/20240708120352/https:/www.cverc.org.cn/head/zhaiyao/futetaifengerEN.pdf. 29.04.2025.

Council of the European Union. (2022). *Russian cyber operations against Ukraine: Declaration by the High Representative on behalf of the European Union.* https://www.consilium.europa.eu/en/press/press-releases/2022/05/10/russian-cyber-operations-against-ukraine-declaration-by-the-high-representative-on-behalf-of-the-european-union/. 02.05.2025.

Council of the European Union. (2024a). *Hybrid threats: Council paves the way for deploying Hybrid Rapid Response Teams.* https://www.consilium.europa.eu/en/press/press-releases/2024/05/21/hybrid-threats-council-paves-the-way-for-deploying-hybrid-rapid-response-teams/. 29.04.2025.

Council of the European Union. (2024b). *Council Conclusions on the Future of Cybersecurity: implement and protect together* (Document No. ST 10133/2024 INIT). https://data.consilium.europa.eu/doc/document/ST-10133-2024-INIT/en/pdf. 29.04.2025.

Council of the European Union. (2024c). *Council Decision (CFSP) 2024/1779 of 24 June 2024 amending Decision (CFSP) 2019/797 concerning restrictive measures against cyberattacks threatening the Union or its Member States.* Official Journal of the European Union, L 2024/1779, 1–5. https://eur-lex.europa.eu/legal-content/EN/TXT/PDF/?uri=OJ:L_202401779. 29.04.2025.

Council of the European Union. (2024d). *Cyber-attacks: six persons added to EU sanctions list for malicious cyber activities against EU member states and Ukraine.* https://www.consilium.europa.eu/en/press/press-releases/2024/06/24/cyber-attacks-six-persons-added-to-eu-sanctions-list-for-malicious-cyber-activitiescyberattacks-against-eu-member-states-and-ukraine/. 02.05.2025.

Cybersecurity and Infrastructure Security Agency. (2021). *DarkSide Ransomware: Best Practices for Preventing Business Disruption from Ransomware Attacks.* https://www.cisa.gov/news-events/cybersecurity-advisories/aa21-131a. 29.04.2025.

Department of Homeland Security & Office of the Director of National Intelligence. (2016). *Joint statement from the Department of Homeland Security and Office of the Director of National Intelligence on election security.* U.S. Department of Homeland Security. https://www.dhs.gov/archive/news/2016/10/07/joint-statement-department-homeland-security-and-office-director-national. 29.04.2025.

Deutsch, A., van den Berg, S., & Pearson, J. (2024, 14. Juni). *ICC probes cyberattacks in Ukraine as possible war crimes, sources say.* Reuters. https://www.reuters.com/world/europe/icc-probes-cyberattacks-ukraine-possible-war-crimes-sources-2024-06-14/. 02.05.2025.

Egloff, F. J., & Smeets, M. (2021). Publicly attributing cyber attacks: A framework. *Journal of Strategic Studies*, 46(4), 1–32.

Eichensehr, K. E. (2020). The law and politics of cyberattack attribution. *UCLA Law Review, 67*(3), 520–578. https://www.uclalawreview.org/wp-content/uploads/securepdfs/2020/09/Eichensehr-67-3.pdf#page=8. 29.04.2025.

European Commission. (2024). *European action plan on the cybersecurity of hospitals and healthcare providers.* https://digital-strategy.ec.europa.eu/en/library/european-action-plan-cybersecurity-hospitals-and-healthcare-providers. 29.04.2025.

European Repository of Cyber Incidents. (2022). *Major Cyber Incident: KA-SAT 9A.* https://eurepoc.eu/publication/major-cyber-incident-ka-sat-9a/. 02.05.2025.

European Repository of Cyber Incidents. (2025a). *Incident details: Attack on Ukrainian Voting System.* https://eurepoc.eu/table-view/?cyber_incident=653. 29.04.2025.

European Repository of Cyber Incidents. (2025b). *Incident details: Ukraine Power Outage 2015.* https://eurepoc.eu/table-view/?cyber_incident=786. 29.04.2025.

European Repository of Cyber Incidents. (2025c). *Incident details: Colonial Pipeline Hack.* https://eurepoc.eu/table-view/?cyber_incident=1417. 29.04.2025.

European Repository of Cyber Incidents. (2025d). *Incident details: The state-sponsored hacktivist group Cyber Army of Russia Reborn disrupted the Tipton West Wastewater Treatment Plant in Indiana, USA.* https://eurepoc.eu/table-view/?cyber_incident=3415. 29.04.2025.

European Repository of Cyber Incidents. (2025e). *Incident details: Chinese state-sponsored hacking group Volt Typhoon gained access to critical infrastructure organisations on Guam and US mainland beginning in mid-2021.* https://eurepoc.eu/table-view/?cyber_incident=2276. 29.04.2025

European Repository of Cyber Incidents. (2025f). *Incident details: Qilin Ransomware Group Targeted Healthcare Provider Synnovis in London With Ransomware Attack On 3 June 2024.* https://eurepoc.eu/table-view/?cyber_incident=3521. 29.04.2025.

European Repository of Cyber Incidents. (2025g). *Incident details: China-linked APT Volt Typhoon exploited a zero-day in Versa Director in June 2024.* https://eurepoc.eu/table-view/?cyber_incident=3737. 29.04.2025.

Finnemore, M., & Hollis, D. B. (2020). Beyond Naming and Shaming: Accusations and International Law in Cybersecurity. *European Journal of International Law,* 31(3), 969–1002.

Graham, M., Ahlers, C., & O'Meara, K. (2024). *Impact of FrostyGoop ICS Malware on Connected OT Systems.* Dragos, Inc. https://hub.dragos.com/hubfs/Reports/Dragos-FrostyGoop-ICS-Malware-Intel-Brief-0724_.pdf. 29.04.2025.

Greenberg, A. (2024). *How a group of Israel-linked hackers has pushed the limits of cyberwar.* WIRED. https://www.wired.com/story/predatory-sparrow-cyberattack-timeline/. 29.04.2025.

Grienberger, R. (2023). *Cyberangreifer benennen, globale Normen stärken: Erfahrungen mit dem Attributionsverfahren der Bundesregierung.* Bundesakademie für Sicherheitspolitik. https://www.baks.bund.de/de/arbeitspapiere/2023/cyberangreifer-benennen-globale-normen-staerken-erfahrungen-mit-dem. 29.04.2025.

Healey, J. (2012). *Beyond Attribution: Seeking National Responsibility for Cyber Attacks.* Atlantic Council. https://www.atlanticcouncil.org/in-depth-research-reports/issue-brief/beyond-attribution-seeking-national-responsibility-in-cyberspace/. 29.04.2025.

Keast-Butler, A. (2024). *CyberUK 2024: GCHQ Director Keynote Speech.* National Cyber Security Centre. https://www.ncsc.gov.uk/speech/cyberuk-2024-gchq-director-keynote-speech. 29.04.2025.

Lee, R. M. (2024, 6. Februar). *Securing operational technology: A deep dive into the water sector.* [Zeugenaussage vor dem Subcommittee on Cybersecurity and Infrastructure Protection, House Committee on Homeland Security, 118th Congress]. https://homeland.house.gov/wp-content/uploads/2024/02/2024-02-06-CIP-HRG-Testimony.pdf. 29.04.2025.

Lin, H. (2016). *Attribution of malicious cyber incidents: From soup to nuts* (Aegis Paper Series No. 1607). Hoover Institution. https://www.hoover.org/sites/default/files/research/docs/lin_webready.pdf. 29.04.2025.

Manson, K. (2024, 18. September). *Gang got $75 million for Cencora hack in largest known ransom.* Bloomberg. https://www.bloomberg.com/news/articles/2024-09-18/gang-got-75-million-for-cencora-hack-in-largest-known-ransom. 29.04.2025.

Miller, M. (2024a). *Sanctioning members of the Cyber Army of Russia Reborn.* U.S. Department of State. https://2021-2025.state.gov/sanctioning-members-of-the-cyber-army-of-russia-reborn. 29.04.2025.

Miller, M. (2024b, 9. August). *Major Chinese hacking group ‚active to this day' despite US efforts to stop them.* Politico. https://www.politico.com/news/2024/08/09/china-hacking-group-cybersecurity-00173454. 29.04.2025.

Ministry of Foreign Affairs of the People's Republic of China. (2024a, 15. April). *Foreign Ministry Spokesperson Lin Jian's Regular Press Conference on April 15, 2024.* https://www.fmprc.gov.cn/eng/xw/fyrbt/lxjzh/202405/t20240530_11347736.html. 29.04.2025.

Ministry of Foreign Affairs of the People's Republic of China. (2024b, 8. Juli). *Foreign Ministry Spokesperson Lin Jian's Regular Press Conference on July 8, 2024.* https://www.fmprc.gov.cn/eng/xw/fyrbt/lxjzh/202407/t20240730_11463255.html. 29.04.2025.

National Cyber Security Centre. (2023). *Heightened threat of state-aligned groups against western critical national infrastructure.* https://www.ncsc.gov.uk/news/heightened-threat-of-state-aligned-groups. 29.04.2025.

National Cyber Security Centre. (2024). *Introducing Active Cyber Defence 2.0.* https://www.ncsc.gov.uk/blog-post/introducing-active-cyber-defence-2. 29.04.2025.

NATO. (2024). *Washington Summit Declaration by NATO Heads of State and Government.* https://www.nato.int/cps/en/natohq/official_texts_225230.htm. 29.04.2025.

Office of the Director of National Intelligence, Federal Bureau of Investigation, & Cybersecurity and Infrastructure Security Agency. (2024). *Joint ODNI, FBI, and CISA statement on Iranian election influence efforts*. https://www.dni.gov/index.php/newsroom/press-releases/press-releases-2024/3981-joint-odni-fbi-and-cisa-statement-on-iranian-election-influence-efforts. 29.04.2025.

Orange Cyberdefense. (2024). *Cy-Xplorer 2024: The report on cyber extortion*. https://www.orangecyberdefense.com/be/resourses/cy-xplorer-2024. 29.04.2025.

Rat der Europäischen Union. (2019a). *Verordnung (EU) 2019/796 des Rates vom 17. Mai 2019 über restriktive Maßnahmen gegen Cyberangriffe, die die Union oder ihre Mitgliedstaaten bedrohen*. Amtsblatt der Europäischen Union, L 129, 1–12. https://eur-lex.europa.eu/legal-content/DE/TXT/PDF/?uri=CELEX%3A32019R0796. 29.04.2025.

Rat der Europäischen Union. (2019b). *Beschluss (GASP) 2019/797 des Rates vom 17. Mai 2019 über restriktive Maßnahmen gegen Cyberangriffe, die die Union oder ihre Mitgliedstaaten bedrohen*. Amtsblatt der Europäischen Union, L 129, 13–19. https://eur-lex.europa.eu/legal-content/DE/TXT/PDF/?uri=CELEX%3A32019D0797. 29.04.2025.

Rat der Europäischen Union. (2020a). *Beschluss (GASP) 2020/1127 des Rates vom 30. Juli 2020 zur Änderung des Beschlusses (GASP) 2019/797 über restriktive Maßnahmen gegen Cyberangriffe, die die Union oder ihre Mitgliedstaaten bedrohen*. Amtsblatt der Europäischen Union, L 246, 12–18. https://eur-lex.europa.eu/legal-content/DE/TXT/PDF/?uri=CELEX%3A32020D1127. 29.04.2025

Rat der Europäischen Union. (2020b). *Durchführungsverordnung (EU) 2020/1536 des Rates vom 22. Oktober 2020 zur Durchführung der Verordnung (EU) 2019/796 über restriktive Maßnahmen gegen Cyberangriffe, die die Union oder ihre Mitgliedstaaten bedrohen*. Amtsblatt der Europäischen Union, L 351, 1–4. https://eur-lex.europa.eu/legal-content/DE/TXT/PDF/?uri=CELEX%3A32020R1536. 29.04.2025.

Regan, M. S., & Sullivan, J. (2024). *Disabling cyberattacks are striking water and wastewater systems throughout the United States*. Environmental Protection Agency. https://www.epa.gov/system/files/documents/2024-03/epa-apnsa-letter-to-governors_03182024.pdf

Rupp, C., & Paulus, A. (2023). *Official Public Political Attribution of Cyber Operations State of Play and Policy Options*. Stiftung Neue Verantwortung. https://www.interface-eu.org/storage/archive/files/official-public-political-attribution-of-cyber-operations.pdf#page=12. 29.04.2025.

Sabin, S. (2024). *Chinese hacking „typhoons" threaten U.S. infrastructure*. Axios. https://www.axios.com/2024/09/20/china-critical-infrastructure-cyberattacks. 29.04.2025.

Schiff, A. [@RepAdamSchiff]. (2025, 18. Februar). *Tweet*. X. https://x.com/RepAdamSchiff/status/1822419022412984537. 29.04.2025.

U.S. Department of Justice, Office of Public Affairs. (2024a). *U.S. Government Disrupts Botnet People's Republic of China Used to Conceal Hacking of Critical Infrastructure*. https://www.justice.gov/archives/opa/pr/us-government-disrupts-botnet-peoples-republic-china-used-conceal-hacking-critica. 29.04.2025.

U.S. Department of Justice, Office of Public Affairs. (2024b). *Court-Authorized Operation Disrupts Worldwide Botnet Used by People's Republic of China State-Sponsored Hackers*. https://www.justice.gov/archives/opa/pr/court-authorized-operation-disrupts-worldwide-botnet-used-peoples-republic-china-state. 29.04.2025.

U.S. Department of the Treasury. (2024). *Treasury sanctions leader and primary member of the Cyber Army of Russia Reborn*. https://home.treasury.gov/news/press-releases/jy2473. 29.04.2025.

Watts, C. (2024). *Iran targeting 2024 US election*. Microsoft. https://blogs.microsoft.com/on-the-issues/2024/08/08/iran-targeting-2024-us-election/. 29.04.2025.

Wood, K. (2023). Cybersecurity Policy Responses to the Colonial Pipeline Ransomware Attack. *Georgetown Environmental Law Review*. https://www.law.georgetown.edu/environmental-law-review/blog/cybersecurity-policy-responses-to-the-colonial-pipeline-ransomware-attack. 29.04.2025.

Zettl-Schabath, K. (2023). *Staatliche Cyberkonflikte: Proxy-Strategien von Autokratien und Demokratien im Vergleich*. transcript Verlag.

Zettl-Schabath, K., & Hemmelskamp, J. (2024). *APT Profile – Volt Typhoon vs. Flax Typhoon: In the eye of the Chinese typhoons*. European Repository of Cyber Incidents. https://eurepoc.eu/publication/apt-profile-volt-typhoon-vs-flax-typhoon/. 29.04.2025.

Dr. Annegret Bendiek is Senior Fellow in the EU/Europe Research Division at the German Institute for International and Security Affairs (SWP) and Co-Head of the research cluster "Cybersecurity and Digital Policy." Her research focuses on digital geopolitics, EU cyber diplomacy, and European cyber defense.

Jakob Bund is a research associate in the same research group and a member of the "Cybersecurity and Digital Policy" cluster. He coordinates threat analysis as part of the "European Repository of Cyber Incidents" (EuRepoC) project.

Franco-German Cooperation as a Pioneer for the Integration of European Armed Forces

Andreas Marlow

Europe faces major challenges due to a dramatically changed security environment and an eroding world order. In particular, Russia's violation of international law with its attack on Ukraine and the skepticism toward the European Union expressed by the United States at the Munich Security Conference 2025 are fueling the debate about Europe's assumption of responsibility for its own security and defense. In this context, the special role of Germany and France is repeatedly emphasized. Both nations are firmly rooted in democratic and liberal values. They are among the driving forces of European integration and have thus laid the foundation for peace and freedom in Europe. At a time when geopolitical challenges and security threats are increasing, the need for close cooperation between the two largest economies in the European Union is becoming ever more apparent. However, Germany and France have different strategic cultures, which affect all areas of defense and the military. There are understandable reasons for this, especially from a historical perspective. While Germany, in view of the experiences of two world wars and the crimes of the Third Reich, often assumes a restrained military role, France pursues a more dynamic and proactive foreign and security policy, in which its own economic interests, its permanent seat on the UN Security Council, and not least its overseas territories play an important role. For France, the overseas territories represent a protective obligation toward its own population. France fulfills this obligation through the constant power projection capability of its armed forces and its nuclear deterrent capability. The security and defense policy instruments of both countries—especially the armed forces—are therefore organized differently, in terms of structure, equipment, and personnel. Traditionally, the Bundeswehr is oriented toward NATO

A. Marlow (✉)
Bundeswehr, Berlin, Germany

S. Weeser (ed.), *The Heart Chambers of Europe: Franco-German Impulses for the EU's Security Order*, https://doi.org/10.1007/978-3-658-51096-1_15

requirements. France, on the other hand, has always emphasized the sovereignty of its armed forces and deploys them outside NATO and the EU as well.

Despite these differences, the reconciliation of the two states after the Second World War created a close bond that now firmly connects both the German and French armies. This is reflected in reciprocal exchange programs for aspiring officers and joint armaments projects, as well as in jointly established units such as the Franco-German Brigade, which in 1989 was the first binational large unit to be established in Central Europe during peacetime. The same applies to the Eurocorps, founded in Strasbourg in 1993, and the joint operation of C-130 transport aircraft in Evreux, France.

Franco-German cooperation strengthens Europe's security integration—within NATO and the EU. This is a matter of existential importance. It is now clear that Putin's ambitions will not end at Ukraine's borders and that Russia is seeking to reconstitute itself as a great power. This is a goal that can only be achieved through confrontation with NATO and will have a profound impact on Europe. Only together with allies can Russia be effectively deterred.

These security policy challenges have prompted both Germany and France to rethink their defense strategies, to strengthen NATO, and *at the same time* to promote a European defense identity. In many respects, both states share the same security challenges and, in the face of these, are compelled to modernize their armies and harmonize Europe's defense efforts.

This idea is not new. As early as 1988, President François Mitterrand and Chancellor Helmut Kohl established the Franco-German Defense and Security Council to harmonize the defense policies of both countries. It has now been revived by politicians and diplomats on both sides, for example through the Aachen Treaty in 2019.

But even today, the deepening of defense and security policy cooperation is underlined by decisions on joint projects. On January 23, 2025, Defense Ministers Boris Pistorius and Sébastien Lecornu reached agreements in Paris on the integration of the Franco-German Brigade into the NATO Force Model and on the armaments project Main Ground Combat System (MGCS).

1 Structures and Dynamics of Franco-German Military Cooperation

The return of imperialism and war to Europe is not the first turning point that Germany and France have had to overcome. For Germany, rearmament after 1955 was a domestic political feat, while France, in the context of decolonization, was challenged and withdrew from US tutelage by temporarily leaving the NATO command structure. The end of the Cold War once again brought about a fundamental change in security policy for both nations. The need to maintain large armies with hundreds of thousands of soldiers disappeared overnight, so that in the following years, European armies shrank drastically and uncoordinatedly between the individual EU member states. Important, often very costly military capabilities almost completely disappeared from the toolbox of foreign and security policy of European states. As a result, dependence on the USA increased significantly. At the same time, for more than two decades, an era of international crisis management began, with numerous missions in Afghanistan, Africa, and the Middle East, in which coordination between France and Germany, and among Europeans in general, lost much of its necessity.

In 1987, shortly before the end of the Cold War, French Prime Minister Jacques Chirac and Chancellor Helmut Kohl decided to establish the Franco-German Brigade. Chirac explained that "the threat to [France's] security begins at the borders of its neighbors" (Rühl 1987). Against this background, the unit was intended to make an additional contribution to the territorial defense of Germany. The founding was—and still is from today's perspective—a stroke of luck for Franco-German army cooperation after the end of the Cold War. For it meant that French units remained in Germany and the interest in cooperation between the two armies remained consistently high.

With the security policy focus shifting to international crisis management, both armies realigned themselves, and the role of the Franco-German Brigade was also renegotiated. However, differing security interests, mutually exclusive areas of interest, and political and strategic divergences often prevented the brigade from being deployed in one of the joint foreign missions. Nevertheless, the brigade has found its character and added value in many multinational operations. Members of the brigade served together first in the Western Balkans, then also in Afghanistan and Mali—not under unified command, but always together in the same operation. The daily work in a binational environment carried out in advance helped German and French soldiers to succeed in all areas of deployment, since missions are now conducted almost exclusively in a multinational context. They learned, and continue to learn, from the experiences of the other nation and acquire intercultural competence, which particularly qualifies brigade members for further tasks in their respective armed forces.

The recent integration of the Franco-German Brigade into the NATO Force Model gives the large unit, for the first time, a clearly defined military objective with a concrete defense mission to which both nations are committed. However, this requires the governments of both countries to allocate resources to restore the brigade's operational capability. Only then can the Franco-German Brigade once again become a signal for a joint European security and defense policy, and above all for the leading role that Germany and France want to assume in it once again.

From this year, the brigade will initially be available to NATO for exercises. Exercises play an important role in establishing operational readiness and improving interoperability within NATO. They are also, so to speak, a currency of deterrence, an important means of demonstrating the capabilities of our armed forces and the will to use them. In the longer term, and after all personnel, structural, and material prerequisites have been met, the brigade will then be ready for rapid deployment on NATO's eastern flank.

The brigade is ultimately to be assigned to the Multinational Corps Northeast, whose area of operations also includes Poland. This opens up, after years of stagnation, an opportunity to revitalize the so-called Weimar Triangle. This forum for promoting Franco-German-Polish cooperation had receded into the background during the national-conservative government in Poland until 2024, but will gain in importance in the future—especially due to Poland's proximity to the Russian aggressor and a potential reduction in the US troop presence in Eastern Europe. The joint mission of German and French soldiers in Poland is a strong signal in this regard.

Germany, Poland, and France also cooperate in the Eurocorps, and just like the Multinational Corps Northeast, it is currently led by a Polish general. The corps, originally founded by Germany and France, now consists of six framework nations—Poland, France, Germany, Belgium, Spain, and Luxembourg—as well as five other associated member nations. As a command staff for both NATO *and* the EU, the Eurocorps possesses a unique duality that reflects the deep integration of Germany and France into both organizations. Neither state relies solely on one pillar for its security policy; rather, NATO and the EU are seen as two necessary and complementary pillars of a resilient and comprehensive security architecture.

Currently, the Eurocorps serves as the tactical headquarters of the EU Battlegroup under German leadership. If necessary, this is supplemented by the forces of the Rapid Deployment Capacity anchored in the Strategic Compass 2020. It thus commands the EU forces that enable rapid military action. Subsequently, the corps will be reintegrated into NATO's command structure, where the corps staff is to be capable of leading operations in so-called non-Article 5 missions by 2027 at the latest. This enables NATO to respond quickly to crises without neglecting deterrence, and at the same time serves as a transmission belt for interoperability between NATO and the EU.

The Franco-German model serves as an example for other important cooperation projects. Multinational large units are now the norm in many armies. The Franco-German Brigade and the Eurocorps paved the way for the German-British Pioneer Bridge Battalion 130 in Minden and the cooperation of the German and Dutch armed forces, whose army brigades are all subordinated to a German division. France also intends to integrate units of the Belgian army into its divisions in the future. Given the rapidly increasing complexity of land forces, the costs of equipping and maintaining independent large units have risen immensely and are disproportionately high for medium-sized states in Europe. Through cooperation with Germany and France, multinational European large units gain significant combat power.

2 Armaments Cooperation as a Strategic Element of European Defense Integration

Historically, much has been achieved in armaments cooperation between France and Germany, for example through the joint use of the C-160 Transall or the joint development of the MILAN anti-tank guided missile and the ROLAND missile system in the early 1970s.

But it is precisely in the field of armaments that the peculiarities of both nations can be both an obstacle and a benefit for both sides. The different perspectives can complement each other and foster a dynamic dialogue on security issues. Both Germany and France have strong and future-oriented defense industries, whose autonomy and continued existence are of strategic importance for national sovereignty. However, the merging of national industrial sectors into bi- and multinational companies, such as Airbus Defence or KNDS, also shows that, in order to maintain the international competitiveness of the European defense industry, cooperation is more necessary than ever.

On the political side, cooperation is strengthened by joint armaments projects. At the EU level, the Permanent Structured Cooperation of the European Union (PESCO) has thus established an important cooperation platform. France and Germany are among the most active EU member states in PESCO. In the land domain, both countries are involved, among other things, in the development of a European standard model for unmanned, ground-based weapon systems. For both armies, the introduction of unmanned weapon systems, both in the air and on the ground, represents an important innovation for success on the battlefield of the future.

In addition to PESCO, binational armaments projects such as the development and procurement of the Main Ground Combat System (MGCS) are also of particular importance. The MGCS advances the main battle tank concept, with the aim of procuring a new and innovative "system of systems" for ground combat for both countries. The project will thus have a tremendous impact on the future way of fighting for both armies. It is therefore not surprising that both armies are following the development with great commitment and by contributing their own ideas. Nevertheless, there is agreement that the project must be future-proof by integrating drones, manned-unmanned teaming, stand-off defensive measures, and the ability to engage targets beyond the line of sight. Implementing these modern capabilities in a ground-based system is a challenge that will best be met with the expertise of the four participating companies, each of which is a world leader in its respective defense sector.

In addition to the MGCS, the European Long-Range Strike Approach (ELSA) project, launched jointly with Italy and Poland, also has the potential to significantly strengthen the military capabilities of Germany and France. Sweden, the Netherlands, and the United Kingdom have now also joined the project. ELSA aims to develop a ground-launched cruise missile with a range of 1,000 to 2,000 km. The goal is to provide an adequate system to counter Russian systems, which can already reach almost all European states today. So far, these ranges within NATO are only achieved with US systems, and the USA is closing this important gap for Europe by stationing intermediate-range missiles in Germany. However, these are means that are not necessarily reliably available to Europe. Establishing the European pillar of NATO independently in this field is therefore above all a strengthening of the entire alliance and in the interest of the USA.

As projects of the land forces, MGCS and ELSA, alongside the air force project Future Combat Air System, are among the most important future projects for both countries. The fact that Germany and France are cooperating closely in this area is an important step toward the standardization and harmonization of European defense equipment.

3 Exchange and Networking: The Importance of Franco-German Officer Programs for Strategic Cooperation

Cooperation projects—both binationally established units and bi- and multinational armaments projects—can only be successful if the people working together have understanding for and trust in each other. This is demonstrated by the aforementioned deployment of exchange and liaison officers at all levels and in all branches of the armed forces, as well as by mutual participation in important advanced training courses for several generations. The decades-long close cooperation between the German and French armies has created a robust network for this purpose. The development of this network was taken to a new level with the introduction of a program for reciprocal officer training.

Since 2007, up to five officer cadets from each nation have been able to begin a five-year training program with the other army each year. The Franco-German officer training program generates a large pool of shared experience, which forms the basis for mutual trust. At the core of these shared experiences is deep insight into the social, cultural, and military structures and mindsets of the respective armed forces. In this way, exchange officers gain an understanding of the strategic culture of the other nation and the resulting particularities. Officers from both nations continue to be notably successful after reciprocal training, and many have subsequently completed advanced training, such as the national general staff course on the German side and the école de guerre of the French armed forces. This elite training also takes place reciprocally and further deepens the already existing individual relationships. Annual networking meetings of former participants in the training program and an alumni organization further strengthen and maintain the network.

In the wake of the agreements to establish the Franco-German Brigade and the joint corps staff, there have been numerous other initiatives. The deployment of liaison and exchange officers has proven particularly valuable. The latter, in particular, serve for years as full-fledged staff officers in the upper command authorities and ministries of the other country. This is unique in European history and, in addition to the work within the framework of military attaché staffs, enables both armies to gain deep insights into the functioning of the other. The result is not only a better understanding of the differences in our thinking and actions; it also makes it possible to introduce German and French positions at a very early stage outside publicly accessible formats and to significantly simplify coordination between the two nations. The network of senior decision-makers in both armed forces that has developed over decades as a result has become a guarantee of good and, above all, efficient cooperation.

4 Summary: The Franco-German Defense Alliance as the Foundation of European Security

From the level of the state, through the organizational perspective of the armed forces, to the importance of the individual for the development of bilateral defense cooperation, a multifaceted picture emerges of the cooperation between Germany and France. It can rightly be described as unique in European military history. Driven by geostrategic developments, security interests, historical experiences, and the peculiarities of national strategic cultures, the cooperation between the two countries has developed dynamically since the end of the Second World War.

It is a key to Europe's security and sovereignty. This applies to security policy cooperation on a large scale as well as to army cooperation on a smaller scale. It is now much more than a symbol and so resilient that constant reaffirmation of mutual friendship has long since ceased to be necessary. The substantial joint projects presented here are proof of this. In light of the existential challenges facing Europe today, there is no alternative to the firm and trusting cooperation between Germany and France, unless we want to lose relevance together. Within the land forces, this self-evident cooperation is a daily lived reality.

When Germany and France pull together, other states will follow. But in the future, even more than before, it will be necessary to leave national egotism behind.

References

Rühl, L. (1987, 29. Dezember). Die deutsch-französische Militärkooperation ist das Kernstück der europäischen Sicherheit. *Die Welt*.

Andreas Marlow, Lieutenant General (ret.) was Commander of the Military Basic Organization in the Army Command and, since 2023, also Deputy Inspector of the Army. Previously, he served, among other roles, as Commanding General of the I. German-Netherlands Corps and Chief of Staff of the NATO Resolute Support Mission in Afghanistan. The experienced officer led the Special Training Command of the EU Training Mission for the Ukrainian Armed Forces from 2022 to 2024. His particular interests include the further development of land forces, multinational cooperation, and strengthening the operational readiness of European armed forces.

Franco-German Impulses for the Security and Defense of the EU

Jean-Pierre Metz

1 Introduction

"France is our closest partner; the United States of America is our most important partner." This sentence, which I often heard from German political leaders during my three years in Berlin as Defense Attaché at the French Embassy, explains Germany's position toward its most important Western allies quite simply and rather clearly. To my knowledge, there is no equivalent phrase on the French side—Paris presumably simply does not feel the need to rank its relationships with Berlin and Washington.

The most interesting aspect of this sentence is that it reveals a great continuity in Germany's stance since the signing of the Élysée Treaty—a continuity that was not called into question by the fall of the Berlin Wall and reunification, nor by the episode of the "Franco-German front against the war" in Iraq in 2003. It certainly explains the majority of decisions Berlin has made on defense and security issues since the founding of the Federal Republic of Germany and the Bundeswehr—protected under the American nuclear umbrella—starting with the addition of the famous NATO preamble during the Bundestag's ratification of the Élysée Treaty.

Nevertheless, between 2017 and 2021, doubts arose in Berlin about the solidity and inalienability of the transatlantic bond, especially during Trump's first presidency—doubts that were expressed, among other occasions, by Chancellor Merkel in one of her speeches at the Munich Security Conference. In parallel, France and Germany launched an ambitious capability package during the same period, comprising five major joint programs and covering military needs that, while not identical, are very similar. The shared vision of a strengthened European sovereignty was a defining feature of this phase.

J.-P. Metz (✉)
Fondation du SMA, Strasbourg, France

S. Weeser (ed.), *The Heart Chambers of Europe: Franco-German Impulses for the EU's Security Order*, https://doi.org/10.1007/978-3-658-51096-1_16

This vision faded with the change of government in Washington. The relief and renewed rapprochement in German-American relations in the defense sector under the Biden administration were spectacular, particularly in the area of military equipment procurement, "sponsored" and driven by the war in Ukraine and the need for rearmament, for which the Bundestag approved a special fund of €100 billion. In some respects, the four years under Biden were a return to "business as usual"—even though the fear of a "Trump II" or another administration with similarly disruptive ideas lingered in some minds. Yet the almost perfect transatlantic alignment on the issue of unconditional support for Ukraine has not enabled any significant progress in security and defense cooperation between France and Germany. Nor has the war in Europe allowed Paris and Berlin to reassert a leadership role in these matters: on the one hand, because of the failure of the Minsk Agreements I and II, which were developed within the Normandy Format (France, Germany, Russia, Ukraine) and for which Paris and Berlin bore responsibility; on the other hand, because the heightened perception of the Russian threat in Central and Eastern Europe revived the division between old and new Europe—a division that the Bush Jr. administration had already exploited and overused at the time of the Iraq war. From a historical perspective, it hardly matters that the intervention in Iraq failed in all its strategic objectives and produced the opposite effects (chaos, instability, Islamist terrorism, etc.). The caution and arguments put forward by the Franco-German duo 22 years ago were not heeded. Their voices are still barely heard today when it comes to considerations of the security architecture in Europe vis-à-vis Russia.

The beginning of Donald Trump's second term reveals numerous ruptures, especially in the area of Europe's collective security. Both in his stance on the conflict in Ukraine and in his vision of what NATO should be, the new American administration seems ready to reconsider everything. The countries most dependent on the transatlantic bond—including Germany—will certainly be forced to radically and profoundly revise their defense policy and investments, unless they are willing to forgo being a credible and capable actor—which is exactly the opposite of Germany's intentions.

All these recent developments invite us to reflect on the reality, stability, and even the usefulness of what is called the Franco-German engine in France. Beyond invocations and calls for a renewed leadership to promote European sovereignty, beyond memories of what Franco-German reconciliation once was and brought to Europe, but also beyond criticism or even rejection of Franco-German cooperation as a model and source of inspiration for a stronger and more autonomous European defense, the question arises as to whether Paris and Berlin can consolidate their partnership and develop a joint security and defense policy in the new geopolitical context—one with which other European countries could identify and to which they could adhere.

At its core, the issue is the choice between a joint "co-responsibility" of France and Germany in the field of European defense, which other countries could join, or the option of a more far-reaching "transfer of sovereignty" in the area of security, to be granted by all member states to the European Union.

Franco-German defense cooperation has an overall solid track record. It is based on three pillars that make this partnership both special and unique.

2 Training: A Remarkable Field of Cooperation

In the field of training, Berlin and Paris have gradually explored all possible areas. A number of exchange programs are quite similar and correspond to what is common between all other NATO and EU allies, and even with other partner countries. This particularly concerns the training of officers of the French and German armed forces, especially at the war college level, even though the number of course participants has been gradually reduced over the past twenty years. The downside of this drastic reduction, justified by financial constraints, is now felt in the French armed forces, which have difficulty finding officers with sufficient German language skills to serve as exchange officers in German staffs or even just as liaison officers. In the French armed forces, German has (once again) become a rare language. The slight increase (two army officers plus one navy or air force officer per year at the Command and Staff College) observed over the past three years will not be able to remedy this deficit quickly. It seems urgently necessary to allow higher participant numbers in order to strengthen future military leaders' understanding of German military culture—a prerequisite for high-quality and trustful cooperation.

In parallel with these training courses, the French and German armed forces have created joint specialist training programs, particularly through the establishment of schools or training centers dedicated to certain jointly developed or procured equipment. This is especially the case with the schools in Le Luc and Fassberg around the Tiger attack helicopter. In addition to the logic of sharing resources, this approach also strengthens the mutual understanding of our armed forces, even if the equipment models or operational methods differ. It is enough to talk to the personnel working in these institutions to grasp the full richness and benefit of these centers—both individually and collectively. In connection with the A400M, instructor exchanges have also been established, helping to strengthen the tactical and technical culture of both instructors and trainees.

Finally, Paris and Berlin have developed a specific and unique program in the area of basic training for young naval and army officers (EFENA programs—French officer cadets in training at the German Naval Academy/EOFIA—officer cadets in basic training in Germany—and their German counterparts). This is a sign of deep trust, as it means entrusting another country with the training of part of its young officers, even though our officer basic training systems are very different. Even if the annual volume remains rather small, it is a significant step forward in promoting interoperability of thinking. It is a concrete contribution to the development of a common strategic culture, as desired by the President of the Republic. With the benefit of hindsight, it is clear that this exchange program delivers very good results.

It therefore seems appropriate to consider expanding this program to other branches of the armed forces (air force) or other specialist areas. This has already been considered, but its implementation faces particular difficulties, such as the recognition of specific competencies. However, if one is looking for a way to increase the significance and reach of the Franco-German connection within our respective armed forces, this possibility deserves special attention.

3 Operational Cooperation: On the Way to a New Dynamic?

The second pillar is operational cooperation. In this area, it is less about interoperability and the ability to operate together—which is ensured in particular by NATO rules and standards as well as by mutual participation of detachments and officers in each other's staffs at various levels—than about Franco-German units or formations.

Within the army, the most telling example is the Franco-German Brigade (DFB). To this day, it is also the only example, since the Eurocorps, originally a Franco-German initiative, was very quickly expanded to include Belgium, Luxembourg, and Spain, and more recently Poland, bringing the number of framework nations to six.

The DFB is the result of strong political will and was established on October 2, 1989—before the fall of the Berlin Wall and at a time when France was not part of NATO's integrated structure. It was stationed exclusively in Germany, and the French regiments that made it up belonged to the French Forces in Germany. Its coherence was based on linguistic interoperability between German and French soldiers as well as shared geographical proximity—some barracks housed both French and German units. Intended as a symbol, it found its place and operational role, especially during the conflicts in the former Yugoslavia.

Geographical and cultural proximity was eliminated during the restructuring of the French armed forces in 2007–2008. In addition, many critics accuse it of not having been deployed as a closed unit in foreign operations for about twenty years. Its deployment in Mali in separate contingents (the French as part of Operation Barkhane, the Germans as part of the EUTM Mali and MINUSMA missions) was revealing—even though this deployment enabled the development of synergies between the forces deployed in Mali. On closer inspection, the Franco-German Brigade seems to suffer from a double handicap: geographical separation (only the headquarters and the command and support battalion in Müllheim are truly Franco-German)—exacerbated by the almost exclusive use of English as the operational language, to the detriment of the partner language—as well as dual subordination (1st Division and 10th Armored Division), which in practice complicates planning and thus operational readiness. For these reasons, the reality of the Franco-German Brigade is often described as the coexistence of two half-brigades.

Recent efforts to breathe new life into this Franco-German project by focusing on its operational readiness within NATO demonstrate the shared will to preserve this unique brigade and open up new operational perspectives for it. However, subordinating it to the command of the Multinational Corps Northeast in Szczecin—whose framework nations are Poland, Germany, and Denmark—means trying something again that was already attempted when the Franco-German Brigade was assigned to the Eurocorps as a reaction brigade. To revitalize the brigade and give new impetus to this special cooperation project, it might be appropriate to seek new approaches—especially to eliminate its double handicap. Relocating brigade units to shared barracks to reestablish Franco-German cohesion and develop a common tactical culture could be a step in this direction.

Ending the dual chain of command by alternating the brigade's subordination between a French and then a German division—for example, on a four-year cycle—would also enable better integration into planning cycles and thus into operations. Such an approach, which would be innovative, requires great mutual trust and the willingness to "give up" a large unit for four years in order to subsequently have a complete large unit (and not permanently just a half-brigade).

In the maritime domain, the Franco-German Naval Force (Force navale franco-allemande, FNFA) is a temporary cooperation structure that can be activated for certain exercises or clearly defined, time-limited missions. As a flexible structure adapted to the environment, it is unfortunately only activated very sporadically, even though it is regularly mentioned in the conclusions of the Franco-German Security and Defense Council (DFSVR/CFADS). Especially in the current security environment, this cooperation model seems particularly suitable—without the accusation that it seeks to weaken or bypass NATO. On the contrary: there is nothing to prevent its use within NATO—in all our maritime approaches and shared areas of interest (Mediterranean, Atlantic, North Sea, Baltic Sea). This format could also play a role in projection missions in the Indian Ocean or the Pacific, as the German Navy is now regularly engaged in these regions—as part of our respective Indo-Pacific strategies.

As for the air forces, Berlin and Paris have established a joint transport squadron based in Évreux. Decided in 2017 and established in 2021, this project demonstrates the strength of the Franco-German connection when there is a shared will. The "Rhin/Rhein" squadron is fully integrated in its organization and operation and reached full operational capability as early as 2024—after a very rapid build-up phase. In this specific case, the aim was to jointly use and operate identical aircraft (the American C-130 J), which both countries acquired only in limited numbers—in order to save costs while developing synergies. In parallel with the build-up phase, intensive work was done to coordinate operational doctrines—a necessary prerequisite for achieving the level of responsiveness required for such a unit. The attitude of the French and German defense ministers on this issue seems to be the most effective and appropriate: "Everything that is not expressly prohibited by national operational rules is permitted for this squadron." Accordingly, the Franco-German transport squadron is able to carry out a wide range of missions—including emergency operations, evacuation missions for nationals, or planned transport tasks for our countries as well as within the EU or NATO.

The entire process of creating this unit—from the decision to establish it to its first missions, through the build-up, construction of infrastructure, financial commitment for equipment procurement, and even the involvement of the city of Évreux to facilitate the arrival of Bundeswehr soldiers and their families—represents a successful example of what Franco-German defense cooperation can produce in terms of a concrete capability.

4 Capability Cooperation: An Ambition Despite the Difficulties

The third pillar is capability cooperation. This is a very sensitive topic, about which much has been said and written—rarely anything positive. It is certainly the area where the unspoken reservations and mistrust between Paris and Berlin are strongest and most numerous.

In the economic sphere, every armaments cooperation provokes criticism and mutual accusations, for example regarding lobbying, suspected or actual protectionism of national companies, or the desire to lead at the expense of the partner's firms. When it comes to cooperation between France and Germany, the two most important countries on the European continent, the question of political dominance is also added.

Accusations of "French arrogance," of our alleged need always to play the role of the "Grande Nation," are countered by complaints about Germany's slowness, its bureaucracy, its inability to make quick decisions—due to parliamentary oversight—and its tendency to buy American in any case.

Finally, the 1990s and 2000s, marked by the so-called peace dividend era, were years of defense budget cuts on both sides of the Rhine—with potential cooperation programs among the first victims.

On a purely military level—and despite decades of matching initial needs (for main battle tanks, infantry fighting vehicles, artillery, deep precision strike capability)—France and Germany have not been able to launch major cooperation programs since the 1970s—with the exception of the "Tiger" attack helicopter. All sorts of arguments have been put forward to justify this lack of cooperation: the Germans swear by tracked vehicles for Central Europe, while the French want wheeled vehicles for their overseas operations, especially in Africa; the difficulty of reaching agreement between the French armaments directorate DGA and its German counterpart, BAAINBw (Federal Office of Bundeswehr Equipment, Information Technology and In-Service Support), which is considered too slow and cumbersome; differences in specifications, even over-specification, which ultimately lead to a joint program splitting into separate programs.

The launch of a major capability package in 2017 reflected the desire to restore a Franco-German rapprochement in defense—through the joint development and procurement of new major equipment. A new start with a new ambition, encompassing important and structuring armaments programs—not only for the French and German armed forces, but for all European armies. Given the time horizon of such armaments programs—from joint definition of requirements, to building the project team and dividing responsibilities and tasks between countries and the various industrial partners, to research and development, manufacturing, and introduction into operational service—a final assessment of this initiative cannot yet be made today.

It should be noted, however, that the two most important and symbolic programs—FCAS (Future Combat Air System) and MGCS (Main Ground Combat System)—are making progress, albeit rarely at the desired pace and not without repeated tensions and crises. However, everything politically possible currently seems to be done to ensure their success. A major difficulty is that both projects are intended as "game changers" and not as mere further developments of the Rafale and Eurofighter fighter jets or the Leopard 2 and Leclerc main battle tanks. The research and development phases for demonstrators are therefore all the more complex and sensitive.

The FCAS program is complicated due to the division of responsibilities and tasks among three state actors (Spain has joined the program) and all the industrial companies involved in the four pillars defined within the program. The aim is to avoid the mistakes made in the A400M program, which led to significant cost overruns and delays. It is also about ensuring the most balanced distribution possible—by combining the "best athlete" principle in each area, guaranteeing fair industrial compensation in line with the responsibilities assumed by each company, and addressing the central issue for each industrial partner: the protection of intellectual property.

As for the MGCS, the difficulties lay above all in the inclusion of a second German industrial group, Rheinmetall, in the project at Berlin's request, which was originally led solely by KNDS—a joint venture between Nexter and Krauss-Maffei Wegmann. The move from two to three industrial partners, one French and two German, disrupted the balance in the division of tasks and responsibilities. This balance could only be restored by including a fourth partner, a French company. Thales joined the project in spring 2024, enabling a genuine dynamic to resume.

Some programs were discontinued for various reasons. In the case of the Mark 3 version of the Tiger helicopter, it was primarily a matter of the Bundeswehr questioning the need. In light of recent conflicts around the world, the German Army's military leaders questioned the sense of investing in a combat capability—the attack helicopter—that appears increasingly vulnerable on an ever more "transparent" battlefield. These considerations, which were already well advanced in 2020 and were also shared with the French military leadership, were reinforced by the first lessons from the war in Ukraine. They led the army to decide against this modernization, while France continued the project with a reduced target size and higher costs. Naturally, Germany's withdrawal from this cooperation project caused incomprehension and some annoyance. Beyond the program itself, this calls into question the two Franco-German training centers in Le Luc and Fassberg sooner than expected.

Cooperation on the MAWS (Maritime Airborne Warfare System) program was also abandoned. Although Berlin and Paris identified an identical need to renew their outdated maritime patrol aircraft at almost the same time, France was forced to continue this important program alone after Germany decided at short notice to purchase off-the-shelf US P-8 aircraft.

On this issue, which is sensitive for France—since it is linked to nuclear deterrence—it seems that the German Ministry of Defense did not seriously consider the capability options offered by France to bridge a temporary capability gap between the early retirement of the P-3 Orion and the possible commissioning of the MAWS (mid-2030s). This incident has reinforced mistrust of Berlin, which is seen as an unreliable partner focused entirely on the rapid implementation of the €100 billion special fund for Bundeswehr rearmament.

The much-noted, unfriendly remarks on both sides about Franco-German armaments projects overshadow the trust built up over years between certain French and German companies, which benefits the armed forces on both sides of the Rhine. In this context, the remarkable cooperation between SAFRAN and MTU can be mentioned.

In addition to the issue of "off-the-shelf" arms purchases, especially from the USA, by the German partner—which runs counter to France's goal of strengthening Europe's strategic autonomy—two other issues complicate armaments cooperation between Paris and Berlin.

First, there is the issue of export rules for military equipment. The rules are not identical on either side of the Rhine. Differences in the assessment of export opportunities for armaments are an obstacle to joint projects as soon as the partner's approval is required before any export to a third country. Aware of this difficulty, which can potentially block many cooperation initiatives, France and Germany signed an agreement on arms export controls in 2019, which was replaced in 2021 by a multilateral agreement involving Spain. Often referred to as the "de minimis agreement"—because of the third part of the agreement—it is, however, the first two parts on intergovernmental cooperation and industrial cooperation to strengthen the integration of the partner states' defense industries that are crucial.

Since its signing, several export cases have been decided positively. With this agreement, which according to French and German officials works well, Paris and Berlin have created an effective tool to address a structural difficulty in jointly developed programs. Incidentally, the issue of exporting jointly developed military goods is not an exclusively Franco-German problem. For several years, London has been seeking a similar agreement with Berlin to create favorable conditions for the development of new German-British projects. Accession to the multilateral agreement is being seriously considered.

The second issue concerns taxonomy. While the French industrial and technological defense sector (BITD) benefits from a rather positive and supportive national environment, this is not the case in Berlin, where defense companies have to exert strong influence within the political class. In a country where arms manufacturers were long equated with the tobacco industry and thus considered harmful, and therefore could not count on the goodwill of the banking sector, issues of image and long-term investment capacity pose significant challenges. However, this has not prevented the development of leading national companies, which—like in other industries—benefit from the "Made in Germany" quality label, nor the recent developments in Germany, which is increasingly seeking to better protect its defense industry and sovereignty—for example, by defining key technologies and by state participation in certain armaments companies.

In recent years, the issue of taxonomy has been instrumentalized in Brussels, particularly by German Green MEPs, with the aim of achieving European regulation. France—among others—rejects this. The latest geopolitical developments, especially in connection with decisions and positions taken by Washington, could serve to dampen these supposedly virtuous efforts—efforts that claim to create a uniform and secure framework within the EU, but in reality are restrictive and dangerous, as they limit the development opportunities of armaments companies.

Beyond all these achievements and the overall rather positive balance, the question arises as to the limits and opportunities available to the Franco-German duo. In other words: can and should Paris and Berlin go further in their defense cooperation—and with what pull effect on other EU or NATO countries?

5 Obstacles to Deepening Defense Cooperation

One of the main obstacles, perceived both within the political classes of Germany and France and in the media on both sides of the Rhine, lies in the persistence of prejudices that systematically fuel mistrust whenever a crisis occurs or even a simple dissonance is perceived. Without listing them all, some recur particularly frequently.

Among the most widespread prejudices about the Bundeswehr is the notion that the German armed forces neither want to fight nor are able to, and that they are incapable of rapid operational deployment. Never mind that the Bundeswehr has proven the opposite—especially in Afghanistan, where it suffered 59 fatalities, and during the emergency evacuation operation in Kabul in August 2021, when no one waited for the Bundestag to convene before deploying troops and resources. Yet prejudices persist, especially when one does not make the effort to understand the other's specific cultures and rules.

Mistrust also arises whenever Paris or Berlin makes an announcement or takes an uncoordinated initiative. In most cases, the respective partner suspects a hidden agenda—implicitly assumed to be less than honorable or at least an attempt always to take the lead. Unilateral statements often fall into this category—from the Sorbonne speech to the ESSI (European Sky Shield Initiative). This is all the more regrettable since France and Germany have equipped themselves with the necessary instruments for better coordination.

Moreover, the Franco-German relationship is by its nature a bilateral one. To believe that it can unfold and find a natural field of application within multilateral or multinational institutions such as the EU and NATO is a mistake. Of course, Paris and Berlin coordinate within these organizations, but without making it an absolute rule and without a special mechanism. There is no Franco-German axis within NATO. Likewise, specific formats such as the E3 (Germany, France, United Kingdom) or the Weimar Triangle do not directly lead to a strengthening of the Franco-German relationship.

Finally, Franco-German reconciliation and understanding are also based on the awareness that France and Germany are the two leading European powers. The idea that this special relationship is based on necessary equality and that both countries must be able to speak to each other on an equal footing—which the German expression "auf Augenhöhe" perfectly expresses—is absolutely fundamental. Any excessive imbalance will call this relationship into question. If one partner becomes too weakened, whether politically, economically, or militarily, the relationship will become more complicated and dependent on the other partner's policy of extending a helping hand. In this respect, France's current financial situation also represents a liability for the Franco-German relationship, which has been clearly recognized by certain political actors in Germany.

6 Opportunities in the Current Geopolitical Context

Despite these limitations and difficulties, Franco-German defense cooperation—provided there is the will in Berlin and Paris—can be deepened and further developed. The two capitals have provided themselves with the means to do so, particularly through the Treaty of Aachen, which complements, expands, and strengthens the Élysée Treaty.

The first starting point is joint strategic reflection. To this day, there is no joint strategic document between France and Germany. Of course, the most important allies are always included in national strategic deliberations. This was the case with the 2013 White Paper in France and its German counterpart in 2016. The same applies to strategic review processes. But several years after the Sorbonne speech, and at a time when the discussion about a possible extension of the French nuclear security guarantee to its main European allies—including, of course, Germany—is resurfacing, it seems quite inconceivable that France and Germany have never begun a joint reflection on their major strategic guidelines.

Naturally, critics will cite all sorts of insurmountable difficulties: very different decision-making cycles, the excessive complexity of such an exercise even at the national level, divergent interests in certain subject areas or world regions. To these difficulties one can also add the issue of unsynchronized political—especially electoral—calendars. These difficulties are understandable. So why not attempt to create a joint synthesis document in the form of key points (Eckpunktepapier) that sets out our major strategic guidelines for the next 15 to 20 years? Such a document could then serve as a basis and reference for further joint deliberations, whether thematic (innovation, artificial intelligence, etc.) or geographic (Mediterranean, Arctic, Indo-Pacific).

Similarly, though on a lower level, the current geopolitical moment calls for a joint Franco-German doctrinal reflection on two dimensions: that of operations outside collective defense under Article 5 of the NATO Treaty, which could be integrated into a coordinated Franco-German approach within the framework of the European Intervention Initiative, and that of the defense of Europe, both within NATO and under Article

42.7 of the Treaty of Lisbon. Such reflection would certainly facilitate the deployment of our Franco-German operational units (DF Brigade, Staffel Rhein, FNFA).

Finally, Russian aggression in Ukraine and the pressure from Washington on its European allies to do more for their defense and the security of their continent have led to numerous considerations regarding military service. France suspended conscription fifteen years earlier than Germany. The arguments in favor of this were identical on both sides of the Rhine—particularly cost reduction (the famous "peace dividends"), inequality in access to service, and the need to have a military instrument tailored to overseas operations.

With the reemergence of a Russian threat in Eastern Europe, the question of the size of our armies is once again arising with great urgency—both for effective deterrence and for the ability to conduct a prolonged war in significantly expanded theaters of operation. The obstacles to a return to conscription are similar in both countries. They are both material (costs, infrastructure, equipment, organization) and psychological (acceptance, equality).

Likewise, Paris and Berlin—seeking to meet the need for "mass"—are considering the development of all forms of voluntary service and a genuine expansion of the reserves. All these considerations, which primarily affect the youth of France and Germany, would deserve a joint approach.

The Franco-German defense relationship is difficult and demanding. But it represents a tremendous opportunity for our countries and for Europe. The reconciliation process between Paris and Berlin is unique and exemplary. It has been carried forward by several generations of political men and women, with a long-term vision and a firm will to permeate the decision-making levels and our societies as a whole.

This process has now certainly reached its end. It is time to initiate a new phase—that of Franco-German co-responsibility for Europe. The security policy challenges facing our continent argue for a deepening of Franco-German defense cooperation—in the spirit and in support of such co-responsibility, which is intended and advocated as a new vision by Paris and Berlin.

General Jean-Pierre Metz is Chairman of the "Service Militaire Adapté" (SMA) Foundation, an organization dedicated to the professional integration of young people from the overseas territories. Previously, he held several high-ranking positions, including Deputy Chief of Staff for "Operations" at Eurocorps and Defense Attaché at the French Embassy in Germany. He also held strategic responsibilities within the French armed forces, with a particular focus on promoting international military cooperation.

Part VII

Conclusion

Final Chapter: Shaping European Security on Our Own Terms: Review, Outlook, and Mission

Sandra Weeser

Europe stands at a turning point in defense policy. Russian aggression, tectonic shifts in the global order, and disruptive technologies have called supposed certainties into question, exposed illusions, and are forcing a strategic reality check. This collection of essays brings together perspectives from politics, industry, the military, and academia. The range of voices in this volume extends from defense policy thought leaders such as General Jean-Pierre Metz, Christian Badia, retired General, and Andreas Marlow, retired Lieutenant General, to strategic drivers such as Dr. Annegret Bendiek and Jakob Bund, Jacob Ross and Nicolas Téterchen, as well as André Loesekrug-Pietri, and (defense) industry leaders such as Armin Papperger, Guillaume Faury, and Dr. Hans C. Atzpodien. Political voices, such as Dr. Marie-Agnes Strack-Zimmermann, Armin Laschet, and Sabine Thillaye, and from diplomacy such as H.E. François Delattre, Dr. Eckhard Lübkemeier, former Ambassador, and Joachim Bitterlich, former Ambassador, also contribute to the overall picture. They express a broad, albeit not contradiction-free, consensus: Europe must take greater responsibility for its own security. This concluding overview aims to consolidate the key findings, identify opportunities and obstacles, and formulate concrete measures—realistic, ambitious, and necessary.

S. Weeser (✉)
Betzdorf, Germany
e-mail: buchprojekt@weeser.com

S. Weeser (ed.), *The Heart Chambers of Europe: Franco-German Impulses for the EU's Security Order*, https://doi.org/10.1007/978-3-658-51096-1_17

1 The Situation: Challenges and Consensus

The essays paint a picture of a Europe in transition—from security policy self-evidence to a new sense of responsibility. In their depth and breadth, the authors describe a strategic vacuum—political, military, industrial, and societal. H.E. François Delattre warns of European weakness amid geopolitical upheaval, Dr. Marie-Agnes Strack-Zimmermann calls for more independence and leadership, Joachim Bitterlich calls for strategic autonomy.

At the same time, a growing consensus is emerging: Europe is vulnerable if it is not able to defend itself—and it remains dependent as long as it relies on external security guarantees. The French initiative for an "Économie de Guerre" is emblematic of this new thinking—even if, as Dr. Hans Christoph Atzpodien shows, the concept of a "resilience economy" resonates more in Germany. The common denominator remains the goal: a robust, responsive, and resilient European security architecture.

2 Europe's Potential: Cooperation Instead of Paralysis

Despite the challenges, the conditions for a European security turnaround are in place. Europe has resources, industry, know-how, and talent—but it still uses them too hesitantly and in too fragmented a manner. Airbus CEO Guillaume Faury exemplifies how European cooperation can lead to global success. Projects such as FCAS, MGCS, or the Eurodrone are more than industrial collaborations—they are real-world laboratories for European capacity to act.

At the same time, these projects are also litmus tests for political coherence. Retired Lieutenant General Andreas Marlow urges the overcoming of structural differences between partner armies. Rheinmetall CEO Armin Papperger emphasizes the need for uniform export rules and a strategic industrial policy. And the perspective of the younger generation, as drawn by Jacob Ross and Nicolas Téterchen, shows: a new strategic culture is emerging—more pragmatic, more willing to integrate, more security-conscious.

3 What Needs to Be Done Now: Measures Between Feasibility and Vision

The global political situation has once again intensified following the Israeli airstrike on Iranian military targets in June 2025. The escalation in the Middle East highlights Europe's vulnerability—militarily, economically, and diplomatically. Security policy inertia in large parts of Europe can no longer be sustained in light of such developments. NATO remains an anchor of collective security, but it needs a strong European foundation. The European pillar within the alliance must become more visible. This means it must become even more capable of action—operationally, technologically, and politically. Retired General Christian Badia emphasizes that Europe's security policy credibility is inextricably linked to its ability to remain coherently embedded in NATO while also retaining independent capacity to act.

Short-term requirements:

- Establishment of a permanent EU defense procurement body (e.g., EU Defence Joint Procurement Board) to pool requirements and enable rapid decision-making.
- Focus on market-available high-impact capabilities: e.g., large-caliber ammunition, mobile air defense, secure communication technologies, and strategic airlift.
- Development of a European cyber competence center for attribution, response, and resilience—as a hub for intelligence, IT security, and responsiveness to hybrid attacks.
- Clear financial planning: Multi-year commitment authorizations beyond 2027, as well as legal simplifications to accelerate procurement and contracting.
- Prioritization of strategic stockpiling and reserves of critical components for high-tech products.

Medium-term goals:

- Establishment of a European Strategic Headquarters for independent coordination of joint EU missions.
- Development of a European stockpiling economy for critical materials—with a focus on energy, raw materials, semiconductors, and defense goods.
- Introduction of a European defense technology talent and training program—to secure the next generation in key technologies and security-relevant industries.
- Reform of EU state aid law and public procurement law in favor of security-industrial cooperation—for example, through exemptions under Article 107 TFEU.
- Joint situational awareness and early warning system for strategic risks—not only military, but also cyber-technological, economic, and societal.

Long-term aspirations (strategically important but politically sensitive):

- Politically embedded European nuclear reassurance—ideally through a French-supported extension within the EU and NATO.
- Establishment of a European defense budget under parliamentary control—to jointly invest in key areas (e.g., AI, hypersonics, space).
- Creation of a European Armaments Agency (embedded in the EU Defense Agency)—with industry-oriented management, strategic direction, and an operational mandate.
- A joint European defense concept that brings together EU strategy, national requirements, and NATO objectives.
- Development of integrated European armed forces under the democratic mandate of the EU Parliament and national parliaments.

4 Obstacles and Opportunities: Shaping Reality Instead of Lamenting

The obstacles are real—national self-interest, insufficient political leadership, complex procurement law, short-sighted budgeting, and a public that is often not mobilized on security policy. Yet it is precisely in these weaknesses that opportunities for change lie.

Strategic communication, as has long been standard in Sweden or Finland, can also contribute to societal resilience in Germany and France. Overall, it is necessary to establish a common European communication, awareness, and a new culture regarding security policy issues and their urgency. Germany and France, as the heart chambers of European security with an already existing media cooperation such as the broadcaster ARTE, should take a stronger lead here and shape both the debate and cultural awareness in Europe. Education, parliamentary debate, political leadership, and clarity in the security industry—all of this can create momentum. Ukraine has demonstrated what determination can achieve. Its ability to defend itself is based on industrial preparation, political will, and international cooperation. Europe can learn from this—and must do so.

5 Conclusion: Europe's Moment of Decision

The 15 essays in this volume are united by a clear appeal: Europe must decide. Between dependence or self-assertion. Between geopolitical marginalization or security-strategic significance. The partnership with the USA remains important—but it can no longer serve as a pretext for European inaction.

Germany and France, as the two heavyweights in the EU—economically and in terms of population—must take the lead. Security and economic policy interests must be clearly articulated. Both countries are aware of the need to increase the defense budget. But other European countries, especially the Baltic and Eastern European states, also see this necessity. That is why, at the NATO summit at the end of June, there was no rejection of the required NATO target of 5%. This means 3.5% for defense and 1.5% for defense-related infrastructure, measured as a share of gross domestic product.

What is lacking is the political will to use them. Europe's defense does not begin with new concepts—but with the implementation of what has already been decided. What is needed is clarity, courage, and speed.

Europe can be anything it wants—but it must not be weak. Now is the moment to prove it.

The manufacturer's authorised representative in the EU is Springer Nature Customer Service Centre GmbH, Europaplatz 3, 69115 Heidelberg, Germany. If you have any concerns regarding our products, please contact ProductSafety@springernature.com

Printed and bound by CPI Group (UK) Ltd, Croydon, CR0 4YY
05/10/2026
02228057-0016